THROUGH THE VALLEY

THROUGH
THE VALLEY
MY CAPTIVITY IN
VIETNAM

WILLIAM REEDER JR.

Naval Institute Press • Annapolis, Maryland

This book has been brought to publication with the generous assistance of
Marguerite and Gerry Lenfest.

Naval Institute Press
291 Wood Road
Annapolis, MD 21402

Library of Congress Cataloging-in-Publication Data
Names: Reeder, William, Jr., author.
Title: Through the valley : my captivity in Vietnam / by William Reeder Jr.
Other titles: My captivity in Vietnam
Description: Annapolis, Maryland : Naval Institute Press, [2016] | Includes
    bibliographical references and index.
Identifiers: LCCN 2015044277| ISBN 9781591145868 (hardcover : alk. paper) |
    ISBN 9781682470596 (mobi)
Subjects: LCSH: Reeder, William, Jr. | Vietnam War, 1961–1975—Prisoners and
    prisons, North Vietnamese. | Prisoners of war—United States—Biography. |
    Prisoners of war—Vietnam—Biography. | United States. Army. Aerial
    Weapons Company, 361st—Biography. | Helicopter pilots—United
    States—Biography. | Helicopter pilots—Vietnam—Biography. | United
    States. Army—Officers—Biography. | Vietnam War, 1961–1975—Aerial
    operations, American. | Vietnam War, 1961–1975—Personal narratives, American.
Classification: LCC DS559.4 .R44 2016 | DDC 959.704/37—dc23 LC record available at http://
    lccn.loc.gov/2015044277

Maps created by Christopher Robinson.

Author Disclaimer: I have written this book more than forty years after my experience as a
prisoner of war in Vietnam. I wrote it because so many encouraged me for so long, and in the
end because once I started, I was driven to get the story told. After all these years, many of my
memories remain crystal clear. Others have been dulled by the passage of time. At every turn,
I endeavored to confirm my recollections by conducting research and checking facts with
other participants whenever possible. Even so, there are surely some errors that remain. For
those I apologize and can only promise that I will accept all criticism in the spirit of correcting
those mistakes in any future editions of this book that might be published.

For Tim and Wayne

To my father and mother, and all who went before
To my children and grandchildren, and all who will come after
To Melanie for bringing me love and joy

Though I walk through the valley of the shadow of death, I will fear no evil.

—Psalm 23:4

Contents

Maps

Acknowledgments

Joe Galloway for his early support as I began my writing.

Bob Mason, John Duffy, and all who pushed, encouraged, and harangued me over the years to complete this book.

Patience Mason for her help in editing my manuscript.

Tom McKenna and Jack Heslin for setting the larger historical context for the battles I fought in, Tom in his book *Kontum: The Battle to Save South Vietnam*, and Jack for his marvelous website that presents a collection of impressive firsthand accounts of the fights that made up the Battle of Kontum (www.thebattleofkontum.com).

Ke Nghiem and Xanh Nguyen for saving my life.

Mark Truhan for not taking my life (as beautiful as his intentions were).

Pink Panthers.

Spuds.

Hawk's Heroes.

Colonel Morgan J. Cronin, my first battalion commander, for teaching me what it is to be a good officer.

Professors Norm Bender, Jim Sherow, and Harald Prins for helping open my mind to the intellectual wonder that surrounds us all.

Mrs. Taylor (Montrose Elementary, California) for giving me a glimpse of my own self-worth during a troubled youth; Coach Tiky Vasconcellos (Roosevelt High School, Hawaii) for teaching me to never quit; and Coach North (Palisades High School, California) for impressing me with the importance of team and how to be a "hard-nosed" competitor.

Boy Scouts of America for giving me skills in the outdoors, a love of hiking, and confidence in myself.

United States Army for showing me my destiny and giving me the tools to face it and survive.

Prologue

I played army as a kid and loved it. It was shortly after World War II when we played in the vacant lots and fields in the rapidly expanding San Fernando Valley, outside Los Angeles. We used stuff from our veteran fathers or gear from the war surplus stores that had popped up after the war. My dad had been in the Navy, so I used a clunky army helmet my grandmother picked up for a dollar at the new surplus store on Victory Boulevard.

We played with gusto. Sometimes we'd get wounded. Other times we'd die dramatically, only to come back to life again when we got bored being dead.

One day we were playing with a group of older boys, five- and six-year-olds against eight- to ten-year-olds. One of my friends, wearing his dad's leather flying helmet, climbed a tree. He waved me up and we scooted out onto a low branch. He made airplane noises, held both hands up as if gripping a machine gun, and went, "Rata-tat-tat, rata-tat-tat."

As the bigger boys got closer, I joined in, "Rata-tat-tat, rata-tat-tat."

We shouted, "You guys are dead! We're in an airplane and we shot you all."

A couple of the older boys came under us, snatched our legs, and pulled us to the ground with a thud. "We shot you down," they said. "Now you're our prisoners." They dragged us off to a deep depression near the middle of the field. In the bottom were several large cardboard boxes.

The older boys said, "This is our prison. Into your cells!"

I crawled into a big cardboard box. They shut me in. I panicked. Closed in the dark, I felt like I couldn't breathe. I shouted, "Let me out of here!"

Nothing.

"Please let me out of here! Let me out! Please get me out!" I shouted. Then cried, "Let me out of here. I don't like this! It's scary! Let me go!" I began sobbing and screaming.

I heard my mom coming from the direction of our house. She yelled at the boys. How could they do such a thing? She tore the box open and pulled me out, holding me close as I cried and cried.

I played war lots of times after that. No kids ever again tried to take me captive. But the terror of those moments in that closed-in darkness never left me.

THROUGH
THE VALLEY

CHAPTER 1

Secret Commandos

My flying gear was stacked on the ground beside me on the flight line at Camp Holloway, an Army airfield outside of Pleiku in the Central Highlands of South Vietnam. I was waiting for an instructor pilot to give me my in-country check ride (flight evaluation) in the AH-1G Cobra attack helicopter. I'd gotten to my new unit some days earlier and was anxious to get into the fight, afraid I'd missed whatever was left of the war. At the end of 1971, we thought the Vietnam War was about over. We'd won. We'd beaten the Viet Cong and were passing everything over to the South Vietnamese Army so we could leave. President Nixon called it Vietnamization.

With my check ride, I would be cleared to fly operational missions as a Pink Panther, a member of the 361st Aerial Weapons Company. We provided gunship support for highly classified special operations missions like the insertion and extraction of elite Special Forces teams, sometimes far behind enemy lines. The cover name was MACV-SOG, Military Assistance Command Vietnam–Studies and Observation Group. SOG teams did deep reconnaissance, raids, prisoner snatches, and downed pilot rescues

I had already completed a tour of duty in Vietnam flying armed fixed-wing OV-1 Mohawks on secret missions deep into enemy territory along the North Vietnamese coast, all over Laos, and into parts of Cambodia.

I was back in Vietnam for a second tour, a senior captain at the ripe old age of twenty-five. I was full of myself, ready for anything the war had to throw my way. I had lots of combat exposure but wanted to experience a whole new perspective as a Cobra pilot.

I stood there shifting my weight and crossing and uncrossing my arms. *Where the hell's my IP? Let's get this show on the road.* My instructor pilot was out on a mission with most of the unit. Time passed slowly. My impatience turned to concern. *Wonder what's up?*

A young lieutenant ran from the operations shack. He saw me standing there.

"Hey, new guy! Want to get a medal?"

Even though he'd been around for a while and I was brand new to the unit, he left it at "new guy" instead of the more common FNG (fucking new guy). I figured that was respect.

"Sure. What's up?"

"Pick up your shit and follow me. You'll be flying my front seat."

"But . . ." I wanted to explain that I hadn't yet had my required check ride, but the guy was gone. I chased after him, climbed into the front seat, and strapped in. Before I had my seat belt and shoulder harness fastened, he had the engine started. The rotor blades were turning.

As I tried to run through the aircraft checklist, the helicopter was dragging sideways out of its protective parking revetment. My first lesson in tactical operations in Vietnam: a fully armed and fueled Cobra was sometimes too heavy to hover on a hot day in the Central Highlands. The pilot had to use what power was available to drag the helicopter from the revetment and slide down the ramp to the runway. We skidded down the airstrip until we reached translational lift, the speed at which the rotors begin to function most efficiently at about twenty knots of airspeed. We were off the ground, climbing to altitude.

As we left the traffic pattern and headed north, the pilot, Mike Sheuerman, made a couple of radio calls. Then he came up on the intercom.

"All set up there?"

"Yeah."

"Smoke 'em if you got 'em. This is going to be a hell of a mission."

"OK." I lit a cigarette with my Zippo, a gift from my brother. In the small mirror mounted on the side of my canopy, I saw Mike seated behind me. His helmet was painted black. His nickname "Hunter" was lettered on the front. He was one of the most experienced pilots in the unit.

"A recon team is trapped. Tries at getting them out have been fucked. We're gonna join in and get this thing done."

"Roger." I shifted in my seat to get my chicken plate, a curved armored shield that covered my front from waist to neck, more comfortable. It sat heavily on my lap, held in place by the shoulder straps. The bottom edge dug into the top of my thighs. Most experienced gunship pilots put the plate on the floor and held it in place under their knees until they got close to their battle area. Some never used them. I endured mine for my entire first combat mission.

"We going over the border?" I asked.

"Yeah, we are. Laos. The team is out of NKP, Nakhon Phanom, Thailand. A couple of guys are still alive—maybe. The guy calling is not speaking English very well. Could be everyone's dead and the NVA got the radio. Could be a trap."

"Roger. Just let me know what to do."

"Keep your eyes open. Go hot when I tell you. Look for enemy fire. Shoot when you see it. Shoot any bad guys you see. We'll get more info when we get closer."

"Roger."

We flew north through a mountain pass. A broad green valley opened before us, dotted with tribal villages, each with a high-roofed communal house in its center. A river flowed north to south. After several miles, we flew over a city and big airfield.

"That's Kontum, capital of Kontum Province, the next province north of Pleiku."

"Roger."

We flew up Highway 14 another twenty miles to a town sitting at the intersection of two big roads. We banked left and headed west toward the triborder area, twenty-five miles distant, where the borders of South

Vietnam, Laos, and Cambodia came together. A large military compound lay under our wing after we turned. It sat on rising terrain, overlooking the town below.

Mike announced, "Tan Canh, home of the ARVN 22nd Infantry Division. ARVN, that's Army of the Republic of Vietnam. Got about a dozen American advisors down there, too."

"What's the town?"

"Tan Canh. Same name."

A few miles further, off the south side of the highway, was Dak To. Two Cobras and two UH-1 Huey helicopters were parked to one side of the airstrip.

Mike landed and hovered to a refueling point beside the runway. I held the controls. He got out and refueled the Cobra, the engine and blades still running. A big, badly shot-up CH-53 helicopter was sitting off the western end of the runway. Several crewmembers scurried around it. I gawked.

Mike finished fueling and climbed back in. I asked, "What happened to him?"

"Jolly Green. Air Force helicopter. The first attempt to get the team. Looks like he got the shit shot out of him."

"Roger that."

I had a mix of emotions. Helicopter warfare was going to be a much closer fight than what I'd known. A rush of nausea and light-headedness was countered by a sense of exhilaration. I was getting back into the fight in a Cobra attack helicopter! *Get ahold of yourself. Focus!* I told myself. *Concentrate on the tasks at hand.*

Mike hovered over and parked the Cobra by the other helicopters. He shut the Cobra down and we got out and joined the other crews in a short briefing. The Hueys were from the 57th Aviation Company, call sign Gladiator, also out of Camp Holloway. The Cobras were from our own Pink Panthers. Captain Dennis Trigg, the Cobra flight lead and overall mission commander, gave the briefing.

"Radio freqs. We'll be up 123.50, Victor. Understand the team is on 44.25 Fox Mike, but we'll also try emergency push. Monitor that. Covey is up 233.00. Fly at altitude en route. Drop low level on arrival. Lots of triple-A out there. Be careful." Triple-A was antiaircraft artillery. He had my attention.

We cranked the aircraft and took off as a flight of five headed into Laos.

As we approached the border, Mike pointed out the old Special Forces camp of Ben Het. A few hundred Vietnamese rangers occupied it with a couple of American advisors. Two Cobras were shut down on the airstrip. Mike flew over low and slow. I looked. They'd been shot full of holes. Good-sized chunks of airframe and rotors were missing from one. How had it had been able to fly at all, let alone get back across the border? *Lucky crew!*

"That's Smitty's bird. All the aircraft took hits. These two are out. You saw the Jolly Green." Mike paused as if to let that register, and then continued. "Third time's a charm. We've got to make this one work."

We sure as shit do. I was wondering why I'd ever believed becoming an Army aviator was such a great idea. Why in hell had I pushed so hard to get back in the fight on my second tour of duty?

As we crossed the border, the chatter on the radios died down. Each transmission was all business. No more bullshit. This was big-time serious stuff. Our lives were on the line.

The Cobras dove to the jungle canopy. Yellow smoke rose from the trees part way up a hillside, marking the location of the survivors. The three gunships set up an oval racetrack right on the tops of the trees, covering each other, placing the bulk of our fire all around the billowing yellow smoke. After the run in, we broke in a tight left turn to come back around the racetrack again for another attack. Tense calls snapped over the radios. Covey, the Air Force forward air controller, was overhead directing a flight of A-1 Skyraiders, propeller attack planes. They dropped 250-pound bombs, napalm, and lethal cluster bombs on both sides of our pattern and all along the upper slopes of the hillside where the most intense fire was. Mike maneuvered our Cobra through a canyon walled with exploding bombs.

Bullets came at us from all directions. With the nose turret, I aimed the minigun and grenade launcher at the source of the tracers. A few NVA soldiers were visible through breaks in the trees. Mike was unleashing pairs of rockets from the Cobra's stubby wings. We were taking hits. The sound of bullets cutting through the thin metal skin of our aircraft was like popcorn hitting the lid of a pan. I didn't have time to think or pray. I had to do what I'd been trained to do: identify targets and fire.

The racetrack was established. The A-1s bombed everything around it. One of the Hueys entered the pattern, flew toward the yellow smoke, and then rocked back steeply into a rapid deceleration unlike anything I'd seen before. He came to a stop, hovering over the treetops while his crew threw ropes out both sides. Enemy fire erupted all around it.

I worked the Cobra's weapons to cover the Huey and the other gunships. For a moment, I felt as if I were seeing it all in slow motion, a well-choreographed ballet. The performers moved with graceful precision, each perfectly executing his part. A close explosion wrenched me back to reality.

We shot as close to the Huey as we dared. After an eternity of taking enemy hits, the helicopter finally pulled up, with one guy hanging from the end of a rope. The other rope flailed in the rotor wash as the crew hauled it back in. The Huey turned and climbed for altitude, flying back out through the racetrack, while the Cobras continued to suppress the enemy fire. Then we all turned and followed the Huey, climbing as the A-1s dropped their remaining bombs on the jungle.

The guy dangled from the end of the rope all the way back across the border, and the Huey set down briefly at Ben Het. They got the survivor off the rope into the helicopter and took him to the 67th Evac Hospital at Pleiku. One survivor, one indigenous soldier, out of a special operations team was saved. The others were dead, their bodies claimed by the enemy.

We flew into FOB II (Forward Operating Base II), the SOG compound outside Kontum, for the mission debrief. A postflight walk-around showed a number of bullet holes in our helicopter. I looked at Mike, shook my head, and said, "I thought the war was supposed to be over."

"It is pretty well over inside South Vietnam," Mike said, "but not across the border. They're all over the place out there and up to no good." Mike finished the inspection, noting the results in the aircraft's logbook before we went into the operations hut. After dissecting the mission with the aircrews and special ops staff, we cranked up the three Cobras and flew back to Camp Holloway in tight formation. During the flight, I thought about how I came to be back in Vietnam.

At the concluding ceremony of Cobra school, with our families watching, the director had said, "After you receive your graduation certificates and pick up your flight records, stop by admin and get your amended orders. Most of you who thought you were going to Vietnam have had your orders changed."

Out of our class of twenty-four, only five of us went on to Vietnam. President Nixon's policy of pacification, Vietnamization, and withdrawal was under way. It seemed to be working well. More than 400,000 U.S. personnel had already gone home. Only American advisors, support personnel, and a number of Army aviation outfits remained. They, too, were ending operations and heading home.

I spent a thirty-day leave with my family driving across the country visiting relatives. We stopped at every national park, monument, and historic site along the way, the routine we had established in our frequent moves. Separation was part of the job. Everyone kept up a brave façade, but I knew the sadness it created. I'd have to deal with the demands of combat. My wife, Amy, had to run the household as a single parent while worrying about me. Our marriage had been troubled for some time, which added to the tension. My four-year-old son, Spencer, tried hard to be brave and help his mom and his sister. Only baby Vicki escaped the emotional pain, but even she sensed the stress around her.

From Utah, where I left the family, I flew to the San Francisco Airport, then rode a bus to Travis Air Force Base, where I would catch a military contract flight to Vietnam.

I strode through the doors of the flight terminal wearing a shiny nylon Army flight jacket, pilot's wings on one breast, a large Cobra patch on the other. The Mohawk patch just below identified my unusual combination of aircraft qualifications. The 1st Aviation Brigade patch on my right shoulder, with its golden eagle and silver sword, showed that I was a veteran of a previous tour of duty in Vietnam.

I checked in, dropped off my duffel bag, turned and scanned the room. Forrest Snyder, one of my classmates from Cobra school, stood up as I walked toward him. Forrest was a smart, well-spoken, polite lieutenant, not the image of a flamboyant attack helicopter pilot.

"Hey, Forrest! I'm on the flight leaving in three hours. How 'bout you?"

"Yeah, same flight. It's kind of ominous, heading out on Pearl Harbor Day."

"Hadn't thought about that. Don't worry. Everything's good."

———————

We boarded the plane and sat with Bill Davies, another Army aviator who had managed to smuggle a fifth of Jack Daniel's on board. We asked the stewardess for three Cokes. When she saw the whiskey, she was quick to bring refills. We drank our fill and passed the bottle around the plane. After it was empty, the flight attendant stuffed it upside down into the magazine rack at the front of the cabin. There was a spontaneous cheer.

In Honolulu, we spent the layover drinking Mai Tais. Back on the plane, I passed out and slept most of the rest of the trip, waking with a hell of a headache when we landed at Tan Son Nhut airbase in South Vietnam's capital city, Saigon. I survived the bureaucratic processing through the Long Binh replacement center nearby, where the assignment officer had said, "War's over, son. Not much going on anymore. We need your experience at headquarters, not in the field. Units are standing down, going home."

"I want to get to a tactical unit that's still in the fight," I said. "I've trained to fly Cobras in combat. That's what I want to do. My dad and uncles fought in World War II. I had a cousin in Korea. This may not be much of a war, looks like it's about over; but it's the only war we've got."

He stood up and said, "Hang on a minute; let me see."

When he returned, he said, "Lucky day for you. There's an attack helicopter company doing special operations work in the Central Highlands."

"Great!" I said, grinning.

"You depart at 0700 tomorrow morning with another new Cobra pilot, Lieutenant Forrest Snyder. I'm sending you both to the 361st, the Pink Panthers."

"Forrest's coming with me? Outstanding!" But I remember thinking, *Hope I haven't gotten him into something I shouldn't have.*

We made it to Camp Holloway in a series of unnerving flights, the first in the belly of a C-130 propeller-driven cargo plane with no seats. We sat strapped to the metal floor with a long piece of two-inch nylon webbing across our laps. We transferred to the back of a CH-47 Chinook, a tandem-rotor medium lift helicopter. At Holloway, we were run out the back ramp like so many cattle.

Map 1. North and South Vietnam

CHAPTER 2

Pink Panthers

The Army's airstrip at Camp Holloway, 2,500 feet above sea level, had been carved out of the fields and forests outside Pleiku in the Central Highlands. The camp was dirty and, depending on rain, either dusty or muddy on any given day. Luckily, it was a bit cooler than most of Vietnam because of its elevation. Tin-roofed huts and hangars clustered along both sides of a five-thousand-foot runway constructed of perforated steel planking, or PSP as it was called.

One side of the runway was a regular little town for aircrews and support personnel. The rest was taken up with maintenance hangars, operations shacks, a refueling area, and scores of revetments to protect the parked helicopters. Off a ways was a rearming point and ammo dump. While I was there, the ammo dump was blown up occasionally by rocket or mortar attack. It was always quickly resupplied. The attacks rarely affected combat operations.

On the rust-colored expanse of the base, nothing grew thanks to constant applications of defoliant. A perimeter of earthen berms, pillbox-like fighting positions constructed from sandbags and recycled PSP, and rows of concertina wire surrounded the camp. Guard towers rose above the stretched coils of razor wire. We were an isolated protected enclave, having little contact with the world outside, except for flight missions day and night.

Our crude, tin-roofed sleeping hooches were crammed with stereo tape players, big speakers, small refrigerators, and, most importantly, air conditioners. We had headquarters, mess halls, supply rooms, a medical clinic, a barbershop, and even a small gift shop. U.S. car manufacturers' representatives clustered around a central store, the PX, ready to help us buy a car at wholesale prices while in Vietnam, to be delivered at home at the end of our tour. We had an officers' club, too, a necessary place for young men to unwind after flying in the face of death each day.

In addition to the main club, the 361's small officer's club, the Stickitt Inn, featured a bar, a few tables, and a hole in one wall so you could dive into a sandbagged bunker during rocket or mortar attacks. We loved it. Camaraderie grew from our flights on SOG's secret operations. We cemented those bonds at the Stickitt Inn, drinking way too much, telling tall tales, and acting crazy.

Several days after my first combat mission, I was sitting in the Stickitt Inn, drinking and telling war stories with Forrest and a couple of other new pilots. We had flown a few more missions, none as harrowing as the first, which I was recounting.

One of them said, "That must have been a hell of a day. Scary?"

"Not really," I boasted, but instantly corrected myself. "Yeah, scary as shit, actually," I admitted. "Scared the fuck out of me. But I did OK. I did it. We do what we've been trained to do. No time to think. Just have to do. You know how and you do it."

I slammed my glass back on the bar. "I survived some hellacious missions on my first tour, too. I was shot up lots, and shot down once."

Somebody asked, "What happened?"

"Took a thirty-seven-millimeter antiaircraft hit in the right wing attacking a fuel depot hidden under the trees. Classified mission in Laos over the Ho Chi Minh Trail. As I pulled up from a rocket run, wham, the whole right side of the aircraft seemed to explode. We tumbled out of control. The right wing shattered and was on fire. Worked it hard. Got back some ability to fly. Got the fire out. But we were descending fast. Could not hold altitude. I gave the command to eject. The observer went out. I pulled my seat handle right after. I had a very short parachute ride. Got only partial chute deployment before hitting the ground with a thud. We were crashing through the treetops by the time I punched out."

"Wow."

"Yeah. Then I was nearly captured. I ran through the jungle for forty-five minutes while my wingman put down suppressive fire. That earned me the nickname Lightfoot. Got plucked out of the jungle by an Air Force helicopter from the 20th Special Operations Squadron out of Thailand, call sign Pony Express. Spent some time in the hospital there. Eventually I returned to the unit, back to flight duties. We'd lost fifteen airplanes at that point out of eighteen. Thirty crewmembers shot down. Not many of them ever recovered. I was one of the few. Lousy odds. I was scared then, I'll tell you. If you don't get scared in combat, you're a liar. Or nuts."

I continued. "Only after a tense mission is over does the real fright come. When there's time to sit and think, you watch it all play in your mind and wonder how the hell you lived through something like that." I looked at them and grinned. "Enough to drive a man to drink."

Forrest said, "I thought the war was over. Thought we'd missed the combat and would be bored to tears. The press claims that Nixon's Viet-namization is working. The Viet Cong guerrillas are beaten. The U.S. is going home. All is quiet in Vietnam. The war's won!"

"All true. Just not across the border—not in Laos and Cambodia. We've seen that the regular North Vietnamese Army is thick over there," I said.

Someone asked, "What do we do if the NVA come across? There aren't any American ground units left in the highlands." I had no answer. I thought, *If the shit hits the fan, I'll be fine. Other guys get killed. Not me. I'm the lucky one.*

Across the room, pilots began chanting, "Panther piss! Panther piss! Panther piss!" Two guys came up beside me, grabbed my arms, and led me to a bar stool in the center of the room. They filled a bizarre-looking mug with booze from most every bottle in the place, topped it off with a large plop of unknown gunk from a jug pulled from the refrigerator. The mug was passed around so anyone could add whatever they wanted to the mix (except lighter fluid, brass polish, or any known or suspected poison). The thing was handed to me. The guys by my side grabbed me and stuck their wet tongues deep into my ears. A commanding voice ordered, "Drink the piss of the Panther."

I stared at the awful looking brew. Pubic hairs floated on top of putrescent goo. All eyes fixed on me. I guzzled. I almost puked, but I chugged it down as they chanted. When I was done, they cheered. Guys patted me on the back. Now I was in the brotherhood of the Pink Panthers. Forrest and the other new guys followed, each downing a mug of Panther piss. One bolted from the room spewing vomit as he ran. I kept mine down, but I felt like shit. The room began to spin. Faces got more surreal with each whirl.

Great guys, these guys, I thought. I ricocheted out of the club back to my hooch, fell into bed, and passed out till morning. This would not be the last of my drunks in Vietnam, but it would be by far the worst.

The next morning, I was front seat to one of our best pilots, Capt. John Debay, on a SOG mission to insert a reconnaissance team. After the insertion, we would stand by at Dak To in case we were needed for a TAC-E (tactical emergency) extraction.

I felt like crap after the previous night, but my head cleared as we did our preflight. We flew to the SOG compound outside Kontum along with another Cobra, and we joined three Gladiator Huey crews who had landed moments before. In the operations hut, we got a detailed briefing from the recon team leader, the One-Zero in SOG parlance.

Three Americans and nine indigenous Montagnard tribesmen, all experienced and dedicated special operations soldiers, made up the team. Montagnards were some of the fiercest, most capable fighters on earth.[1] Besides the One-Zero, the Americans were the One-One, the assistant team leader, and the One-Two, the radio operator.

We were going to insert the team on the backside of a hill a few kilometers from an NVA headquarters. They'd gather information for two days, then snatch a prisoner if they could, and call for extraction. SOG recon team strength: twelve. NVA HQ and combat units in the immediate area: several hundred. It sounded insane. Everyone in the room took it as a matter of course.

We loaded up, cranked and lifted off from FOB II, the base for all SOG operations from the central part of South Vietnam.[2] We began along the same route as my first mission. When we approached the border, our course arced farther south. We dropped down into the racetrack, but didn't shoot. The two Hueys fell through into a small clearing. They pulled out in two seconds, the team already gone and invisible, putting distance between themselves and the landing zone. We moved a few miles eastward and orbited for several minutes to be sure the enemy had not immediately discovered the team. All was quiet.

We flew back to Dak To, refueled, shut down, and waited, ready to launch in two minutes if needed. We played spades, ate C-rations, soaked up some sun, and talked to push back the boredom. Eventually a fresh flight of Cobras and Hueys arrived to relieve us, allowing us to return to FOB II for a debriefing before calling it a day. Afterwards, one of the Huey pilots said, "Hey, Panthers! You guys want a string ride before we head home today?"

My wingman, CW2 Dan Jones, explained, "You put on a harness, clip onto the end of a 120-foot nylon rope, and dangle under the Huey while he flies you around the countryside. It's what we do with the teams we pull out of the jungle. It's exciting. You oughta do it. Come on. I'll go with you."

"Why not?" I said. Two others joined us. The helicopter hovered overhead. The crew chief leaned out the side and watched us. We put on harnesses and clipped ourselves to the end of the rope. The Huey rose. As the slack came out of the ropes, the harness straps tightened unpleasantly in my crotch, but I pulled them further to the side. Slowly, the helicopter lifted us off the ground and into forward flight. We locked arms to keep from banging into each other. It was terrifying and sensational at the same time. There was nothing between me and the ground a thousand feet below, nothing.

A celebration was taking place on the central street of a village, possibly a wedding. The Huey headed directly toward the village. By the time we got to the edge of town, we were close to the rooftops. Everyone on the street looked up, smiling. They waved, and we waved back as we hovered over.

That string ride around the countryside showed me how far pacification had progressed in the Central Highlands. Had there been any enemy in the area, we would have been an easy target. Most of South Vietnam was secure. The Viet Cong had been defeated. The war was just about over.

As we headed back to Kontum, the sun shone brilliantly in the blue sky low above the mountaintops, glistening off the rich green jungle and the paddies and fields below. It remains one of the most beautiful sights I've ever seen.

———————

A few days later, Captain Barfield, the 361st Aviation Company commander, sat behind his desk, scowling at me. He launched into a rant about an issue I was totally unfamiliar with. I knew something really terrible had to be coming next. Then he leaned back in his chair and smiled. "Come with me."

The company had assembled in formation outside, the company flag, our guidon, held proudly in front. As Captain Barfield approached with me, bewildered at his side, he turned to face the assembled group. "Today we have a new platoon commander in the 361st. Captain Reeder will take over third platoon effective immediately."

Barfield turned to me and said, "I know you'll do well. Come see me later and we'll talk. Congratulations. Now take your post."

I moved to the front of my platoon. Once I was in position, Captain Barfield commanded, "Officers fall out! First sergeant, take charge of the company!"

The day's missions were done. We headed to the Stickitt Inn. My 3rd Platoon pilots sat around in their usual comfortable spots, looking me over, wondering how I might affect their lives in the days to come. At the same time, I looked into their eyes, hoping I would give them the leadership they deserved.

"I'm Mike Kieren." A young-looking, handsome, blond first lieutenant offered his hand.

"Pleased to meet you, Mike." I would come to know him as enthusiastic, fun loving, and a great pilot who was always reliable.

Capt. John Debay stepped forward and shook my hand. "I'm still your assistant platoon leader for now, but I'm moving to become the company maintenance officer." I'd flown with him several times already. John was in a tough spot. He had been platoon leader until I, the senior ranking captain, was chosen to replace him. John was a good guy, a prince. He had extended his combat tour a number of times, well beyond the obligatory year in Vietnam. He gave up command to me graciously, continuing to fly with the platoon and serving as our instructor pilot. He taught me more than anyone else about our missions and getting the most out of the Cobra.

CW2 Dan Jones was the senior warrant officer in my platoon. Dan was tall, serious, and a bit older than the others. Solid as a rock, he was always where he was supposed to be when he was supposed to be there. He had a great attitude and worked as long and as hard as necessary. He flew well, placed fire accurately, and demonstrated sound judgment. We'd already flown together. I always enjoyed being on a mission with Dan. I felt confident when he was in the flight.

Mike Pasco introduced himself. "I'm the company signal officer, but assigned to 3rd Platoon. I'll be flying missions with you." Mike was a captain who had been given the additional duty of taking care of the unit's radios and other communications equipment because his branch of service was Army Signal Corps. Those duties kept him very busy, but he always met his flying responsibilities with courage and skill.

The youngest of the group, a warrant officer one, stood to introduce himself last. "Hi, PL. I'm Steve Allen. They call me Flame." His bright red hair left no doubt about the source of his nickname. He'd refer to me as PL, his term of endearment for platoon leader. Youthful and cheery, he'd always give me a bright greeting of "Good morning, PL," "Yes sir, PL," "Can do, PL." He was a courageous pilot with a great attitude, and I was grateful he was in the platoon.

CHAPTER 3

Easter Offensive

I flew missions almost every day as a front-seater, but I coveted the back seat. The front seat, also known as the bullet catcher, was the copilot and gunner, responsible for aiming and firing the 7.62-mm minigun and 40-mm grenade launcher, the chunker. The front-seater relieved the pilot on the flight controls when asked. In the back seat was the pilot-in-command, responsible for the aircraft. He made the radio calls and shot the 2.75-inch rockets from pods on the helicopter's stubby wings. He also fired the awesome 20-mm Gatling gun on the birds that had them. He was in charge. I had proven myself in the front seat. I was ready for the back.

I flew daily for two months. I worked hard at my front-seat duties. As platoon commander, I could have made myself a back-seater, but the unit instructor pilots normally said when a pilot was ready. I wanted the legitimacy of the IP's endorsement.

When some "old-guy" pilots completed their tours of duty and headed home, I was elated to be moved to the back seat. I wanted to be the best I could be. As platoon leader, I got the ship of my choice. I took tail number 295, one of the few Gatling-gun birds, a most awesome killing machine.

All Special Forces operations had been publicly declared over in Vietnam. In reality, the SOG teams replaced their berets with Army baseball caps and continued to conduct missions, some of which involved

17

training South Vietnamese special operators to take over for them. Our classified missions remained intense.

SOG missions often ended in a firefight, the team surrounded by a hugely superior enemy force. A prairie fire emergency was declared whenever the survival of the team was in question. Every available military asset was sent to support the extraction. We shot next to the guys on the ground and under them as the Hueys lifted them out. It was crazy. Team members sometimes suffered minor wounds from fragments of friendly fire. We shot where they asked. They were always thankful for Cobra support.

As spring came to the Central Highlands, the enemy moved along the range of mountains that formed the border with Laos and Cambodia. They also infiltrated further eastward, across the high country north of the highlands into the lesser mountains ranging north-south between the highlands and the coast. The North Vietnamese Army had long planned this move into South Vietnam from base camps in Laos and Cambodia. They probed and then launched outright attacks on a scale not seen before in the Vietnam War.[1] The 1972 Easter Offensive had begun.

I became AMC (air mission commander), leading missions made up of two to four Cobras, Hueys from our sister company, the Gladiators, or a variety of other aircraft. I was responsible for all the helicopters in the flight and their actions in battle. This made me part of something larger than myself, and I felt an increasing commitment to a greater cause. In my first tour I grew from a boy to a man. On this second tour, slammed right back into the cauldron of war, I was learning much more what that man was made of. The war was changing into something none of us could have imagined. We would soon face the greatest challenges of our lives.

In late March 1972, I was in a flight of two Cobras diverted to support an ARVN patrol with an American advisor operating west of Rocket Ridge. Rocket Ridge overlooked Highway 14 from south of Dak To to northwest of Kontum. From the ridge, the Viet Cong used to launch rockets onto the highway and villages below. A string of firebases spaced along the ridgeline had stopped that.

The ARVN patrol had been on routine reconnaissance to the west of one of the firebases. Now they were fighting desperately to break contact with a strong NVA force, withdraw to the east, and get back inside the perimeter of Firebase 5. We heard the American advisor, 1st Lt. Terry "Buddha" Griswold, on the radio. "In heavy contact. Large enemy force, at least a company. We are withdrawing back to Firebase 5. Enemy moving to flank and cut us off. Need help."

I radioed, "This is Panther Lead. Flight of two Cobras, inbound. Pop smoke."

"Roger. Look for orange smoke."

We crested the ridge over Firebase 5, and I called, "Got your smoke."

Buddha responded, "Roger, Panthers. Enemy is to the west and south of smoke. Moving in on us quickly."

I replied, "Got your position. Got the bad guys. In hot." We made several runs, expending our ordnance. My 20-mm was devastating, blasting small trees to oblivion and decimating the attacking force. The patrol broke contact with the enemy and withdrew back to the firebase. We'd saved their bacon, but we had witnessed an unusual display of enemy strength within South Vietnam.

In the weeks ahead, we got more and more in-country missions as enemy activity inside South Vietnam increased. On March 27, an urgent request came to launch on a mission to rescue a VNAF (Vietnamese Air Force) helicopter crew shot down west of Firebase Charlie, near the center of Rocket Ridge. A Gladiator Huey was with us at Tan Canh. The pilot, CWO Larry Woods, laid out a plan to surprise the enemy, get in, pick up the downed crew, and get out.

Larry, his copilot, door gunner, and crew chief loaded up and cranked the Huey. I flew with Dan Jones in my front seat. My wingman and I started our Cobras. My right hand held the cyclic stick, which controlled the tilt of the rotor's axis. My feet were positioned on the pedals that maintained the direction of the aircraft's nose. My left hand gripped the cylindrical collective, which made the helicopter rise or settle and adjusted speed in flight. I was one with the machine as I pulled the collective steadily and eased the cyclic ever so slightly forward, bringing the Cobra off the ground behind the departing Huey. The other Cobra followed closely on my right rear.

We headed southwest, angling toward Rocket Ridge, flying fast just above the trees. A little south of Firebase Charlie, we rose up the hillside together in formation. Near the top, we slowed. We floated up and over the ridgeline, banking sharply to the right, sliding back down to the tops of the trees, picking up speed. After changing course about ninety degrees, we moved north, accelerating just above the jungle along the west side of the hills.

Woods spotted the downed VNAF helicopter. I confirmed it by smoke rising from a clearing on the hillside ahead. Larry's Huey swooped in and rapidly decelerated to land next to the downed aircraft. Small arms fire erupted as the Huey slowed. The streak of a B-40 (40-mm rocket-propelled grenade) found its target and detonated. I watched in disbelief as the entire helicopter exploded in a violent burst of orange and yellow flame. It hung there for an instant, the tips of the rotors still visible, turning through the fireball. Then the whole ship slammed into the ground, and rolled on its back, continuing to burn. My heart sank. I loved the Gladiators and respected their courage. We covered the scene, searching for survivors until another flight of Cobras replaced us on station. We flew home to Camp Holloway, our spirits crushed.[2]

On April 1, a Chinook was shot down outside Firebase Delta on approach to the camp. The firebase straddled the crest of Rocket Ridge about a mile and a half south of Firebase Charlie. The crew got inside the firebase, but the enemy repulsed every effort to extract them. HQ put together a plan to rescue the crew at first light on the third day. We launched before sunrise. John Debay was flying in my front seat. The rescuers included every available Cobra gunship from Camp Holloway.

A thousand NVA soldiers launched a dawn assault against Firebase Delta that morning. As we approached the firebase, my transmission oil pressure light came on. I had to abort. If we lost all oil pressure, our transmission would seize, and we would fall out of the sky like a rock. The rest of the Cobra crews repulsed the attack and killed more than three hundred of the enemy.

A few days later, we had a heavy fire team of three Cobras that linked up with a small fixed-wing spotter airplane to form a hunter-killer team. We searched for enemy reinforcements building up inside Laos. Bob Hutchinson, our company executive officer, was in my front seat. Debay and Jones piloted the other two Cobras. We headed out.

"Headhunter Two-Six, this is Panther Three-Six," I radioed.[3]

Capt. Ed Smith, the spotter pilot, replied, "Panther, Headhunter Two-Six. I've got several trucks out here and a bunch of troops along the road. I can put you guys right to work. I'm at five thousand feet in a left-hand orbit over Route 110 just across the border. Call when you see me."

"Two-six, we've got you in sight. Where are the targets?"

"Watch me, Three-six."

Smith rolled the single-engine O-1 Bird Dog light-observation plane onto its back and dove steeply, firing a rocket. White phosphorous smoke billowed where it hit the ground.

"That's it Panther. Right there. Trucks and a bunch of gomers."

The trucks fled down the middle of the dirt track. Dozens of soldiers scurried into the jungle as we dropped to the treetops. Bob raked the NVA troops with the minigun and grenade launcher while I did my best to hit the trucks with rockets, a challenging task.

My first pair of rockets hit short of a truck and off to one side, exploding in the midst of a group dashing for cover. They were blown to bits, and others nearby were surely wounded badly. We banked hard left, coming around for another pass. I was flying way too slow for my heavily laden Cobra, dragging the skids through tree limbs scaring the shit out of my front-seater. More turret firing. Another pair of rockets. A hit. Right on the hood. *Hallelujah!*

We kept attacking, taking enemy fire, until we'd shot all our ordnance. "Headhunter Two-Six, Panther Three-Six. We're done. You can count the trucks damaged and destroyed. Not sure how many we actually hit. Killed lots of people. No idea how many. Looks like Charlie is really building up over here. Up to no good. I've never seen anything like it before."

"Roger, Three-Six. Thanks."

On April 11, NVA forces in the northern reaches of the highlands swung into action along Highway 19, below An Khe Pass. The area was far to the east of Pleiku, but the highway connected Pleiku to essential ports along the coast. The enemy overran South Vietnamese and Korean outposts and closed the highway. I led a fire team in response, and we joined others already working the battle. It was a day of hard fighting, rapid reversals, and confusion on the ground.

The enemy tried to do what they had done in 1954 against the French. French Group Mobile 100 was nearly wiped out at Mang Yang Pass, thirty miles east of Pleiku, with 500 killed, 600 wounded, and 800 captured out of a force of 2,500. Southern Vietnam was cut in half right through the Central Highlands. That war ended after this debacle was added to the French defeat at Dien Bien Phu. The French signed an armistice a month later and withdrew from Indochina.

The South Vietnamese, Americans, and Koreans fought unsuccessfully to reopen Highway 19. Henceforth, resupply of bases in the Central Highlands would be exclusively by air, and we Pink Panthers engaged in actions along the length of the highway as fighting continued. On each of these missions, we flew over the Mang Yang Pass. I reflected on that long-ago fight. I'd read about the battle in Bernard B. Fall's book, *Street Without Joy.* All those who died with Group Mobile 100 had been buried in a cemetery in the hills above the pass, standing up facing France. Returning from a mission one day, I circled it, taking pictures of the white markers on the hillside. I talked about it at the club that night. One of the old hands said, "Bad luck to take pictures in the Mang Yang!"

"Bullshit!" I said.

———————

On April 14, we received a radio call that Firebase Charlie was under attack by two regiments, three thousand soldiers, of the 320th NVA Infantry Division, and 130-mm artillery shells were pounding the position. It was defended by 470 South Vietnamese paratroopers and one American advisor, a Special Forces infantry major named John Joseph Duffy.

Dan Jones, the most seasoned pilot in my platoon, was within a couple of weeks of going home. He led the flight. I was his wingman. Dan pointed our flight toward Rocket Ridge, and we coaxed as much speed as our Cobras would give.

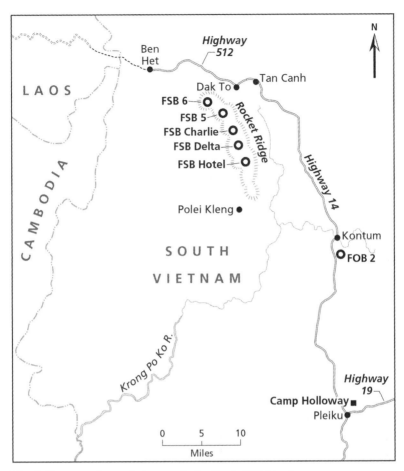

Map 2. The core of our mission area in the Central Highlands

"Firebase Charlie, this is Panther One-Three."

"Panther Lead, this is Dusty Cyanide. I have multiple targets for you. All .51-caliber machine guns."

"Oh shit!" My front-seater remarked over the intercom.

Oh shit? How about, Oh fuck! I thought as I set my weapons for combat. The .51-caliber machine gun seemed designed specifically to shoot down helicopters. They'd done plenty of damage over the past weeks.

Dan calmly acknowledged, "Roger, Dusty Cyanide. We're inbound. Give us the positions when we get there."

We made several passes on enemy guns. Bullets streamed past our cockpits as the NVA gunners tried to bring us down. Rolling in on a .51 position is always dicey. Tracers come at you and miss by a few feet. You try to get rockets onto him before he gets lucky and blasts you out of the sky. We took small arms hits. My knees vibrated like a sewing machine, but I focused on controlling the helicopter, lining up the gunsights and shooting. I was scared but had no time for it.

Dan radioed, "Dusty Cyanide, Panther One-Three. Be advised, running low on fuel. Out of ammo. We're breaking station for rearm-refuel."

"Roger, One-Three. Four gun crews destroyed, four guns taken out. Good work. Hurry back!"

By the time we got back, the situation had deteriorated dramatically. Other teams of Cobras had worked while we rearmed. VNAF A-1 Skyraiders and U.S. jet fighters dropped napalm and high-explosive bombs on the advancing enemy as well, but the NVA attack was intensifying, pushing back the South Vietnamese defenders. One of the A-1s was shot down and the pilot killed. The enemy overran outlying posts and breached the perimeter of Charlie itself. As dusk settled in, fires and chaos raged across the hilltop.

"Panther, the battalion commander is dead, acting commander wounded. Enemy broken through on the southwest. Put it there first. Then all around us—but real close."

"Roger, Dusty. We've got 'em," Dan said.

After a number of Cobra attack runs, Duffy called. "Panther Lead, this is Dusty Cyanide. You have broken the enemy attack, for now. Hundreds of bodies in the wire—maybe a thousand. But we cannot hold." After a short break, he continued, "We are leaving Firebase Charlie, now. Stop them from following us. Whatever it takes. Put your stuff right on top of the firebase, NOW."

Another Cobra team joined us, with Forrest Snyder in one of the front seats. We finished laying waste to Firebase Charlie and made our way back to Camp Holloway. The flight picked its way through hills and valleys below a worsening layer of low clouds in the pitch black of night.

The next morning, the badly wounded and exhausted advisor was rescued from the valley below Rocket Ridge along with 36 survivors of the 11th Vietnamese Airborne battalion. The remaining 434 members of the battalion had been killed or captured or were missing in action. Some would infiltrate through the enemy and later return to friendly lines. Major Duffy was recommended for the Medal of Honor. He would receive the Distinguished Service Cross for his actions on Firebase Charlie, our nation's second-highest award for heroism. The battle remains an icon in Vietnamese folk culture, the subject of film, song, and poetry both in Vietnam and among the expat community in the United States.[4]

1st Lt. Tim Conry, a new pilot, was assigned to my platoon a day later, on April 16. He was immediately impressive: great bearing, well-spoken, intelligent, an exceptional aviator, and a really likeable guy. He was engaged to be married. I knew this young officer would go places in the Army. As his platoon leader, I made him my front-seater. We grew close and became a great fighting team.

The war raged in the Central Highlands. The North Vietnamese launched all-out conventional attacks with every unit its army could muster. They assaulted across the demilitarized zone into the northern portions of South Vietnam. They attacked from Cambodia thrusting toward Saigon. They came out of Laos and northern Cambodia into the Central Highlands. Three months before, most of us thought we'd won.

Toward the end of April, long-ranging NVA 130-mm guns sent a thousand artillery shells into the 22 ARVN division headquarters at Tan Canh. Wire-guided Soviet Sagger antitank missiles destroyed the few South Vietnamese tanks at Tan Canh and Dak To. The enemy launched Soviet SA-7 heat-seeking antiaircraft missiles against U.S. helicopters.

At dawn the next day, April 24, the North Vietnamese attacked Tan Canh and Dak To with an infantry division, a tank regiment, and supporting artillery and sappers. Outmanned and outgunned, the South Vietnamese defenders at Tan Canh were overwhelmed within two hours, and those at Dak To succumbed shortly after. North Vietnamese tanks rolled inside Tan Canh, onto the runway at Dak To, and along the highway between the two.

Tim and I saw plenty of action that day. A Gladiator Huey that had rescued five U.S. advisors was hit by enemy fire and fell from the sky in flames. Advisors escaped from Tan Canh, the Dak To airstrip, and the district headquarters in Dak To village. Helicopters rescued most of them later in the day. Two remained missing in action.

Hundreds of ARVN soldiers lay dead and wounded. Others tried to evade the enemy and work their way to friendly positions. Some succeeded, but others were hunted down and killed or captured. It was the first time a South Vietnamese division had been overrun. The division commander and his entire staff were missing.

During one run back into Kontum to rearm and refuel, I got a call to land at the military headquarters and shut down.

Tim asked, "What's up?"

"Somebody wants to know what's going on at Tan Canh and Dak To, I guess."

I shot an approach to the HQ helipad, landed, and shut down. An American captain escorted us into the dining hall. A number of folks were finishing their breakfast.

Tim muttered quietly to me as we walked in, "What the fuck?" I shrugged. Some contrast.

Officers, all senior to me, sat at one table. Must be visiting staff from the headquarters at Pleiku, I surmised. They offered us a cup of coffee. Neither of us sat down. We stood, enjoying the hot brew.

"What's going on at Tan Canh?"

"They're overrun. Tanks and infantry. Probably more than a regiment. Maybe two. Could be more. Lots of antiaircraft fire, also."

"You sure there's tanks?"

"Yes. Absolutely sure. We saw them."

One of the staff colonels asked, "Are you going to get back out there?"

"As soon as we get out of here, get some gas and bullets." I added, "In spite of the twenty-three-millimeter and thirty-seven-millimeter triple-A threat."

Another staff officer said, "Large caliber antiaircraft? Nothing like that in South Vietnam. Never has been."

"Well, there is now. Antiaircraft is all over Dak To and the road to Ben Het, including thirty-seven millimeter," I said.

"How would you know it was thirty-sevens since we've never seen it before?"

"I've seen it, plenty of times. Used to fly Mohawks over the trail and saw a bunch of twenty-threes and thirty-sevens. Got shot down by a thirty-seven and had to punch out in an ejection seat for a very short parachute ride into Laos. We also see it sometimes on our FOB missions across the border. I know my triple-A. There are twenty-threes and thirty-sevens at Dak To right now."

He responded glibly, "OK, Ace. Got it."

I glared at him. He continued, "Come up on our radio push and stay with us. Keep us up to speed on what's going on."

We cranked our aircraft and returned to the war.

In spite of the war protests at home, I felt proud of what we were doing. I believed in preserving the South against communist aggression from the North. We all fought hard to quell the North Vietnamese advance. By the end of the month, the 23rd ARVN Division was deployed from Ban Me Thuot to replace the decimated 22nd. Only a few places in the highlands remained in government hands: Pleiku and Kontum, Camp Holloway, and the outposts: Polei Kleng, twelve miles due west of Kontum, and Ben Het at the triborder.

CHAPTER 4

Ben Het

Polei Kleng was tucked into a small valley, nestled against rising terrain to the west. Big hills loomed in most other directions. The old Special Forces camp had been built on the site of earlier French fortifications. The typical three-sided defensive perimeter of fighting positions sat inside concentric rings of concertina wire with minefields in between. A small airstrip lay outside the camp's defenses. The land was cleared of vegetation for a couple hundred meters all around.

Two ARVN ranger battalions defended the camp. Thousands of North Vietnamese artillery shells pounded them day after day and night after night for a week, while NVA units surrounded the camp, greeting all helicopters in the area with bursts of .51-caliber machine-gun fire. The defenders heard tanks nearby.

The decision was made to evacuate the two U.S. advisors on the ground. I could imagine the impression that must have made on the ARVN ranger battalions. "Too dangerous for us advisors, but you guys fight on in the face of what we fear will be certain annihilation."

On May 6, 1972, right after dark, we covered an OH-6 aircraft from the 7/17th Cavalry on the mission to extract the advisors. The OH-6 helicopter was always referred to as a "Loach" for the acronym LOH, or light observation helicopter. The pilot, Capt. Jim Stein, was one of the gutsiest scout helicopter pilots in the Army. Tim Conry was in my front seat. Jim dropped down onto the deck and dashed in with lights out except the beacon on the top of the helicopter, which let us keep visual contact with him. We stayed higher, firing to suppress sporadic small arms fire on his way in.

By the time Jim's Loach got to the helipad in the camp, he was receiving heavy fire and taking hits. Fifty-one-caliber machine guns opened up at him on the ground. The advisors jumped in, and Jim started outbound. The world erupted. I fired rockets and 20-mm rounds in front of and beside the Loach. Tim worked the nose turret, placing protective fire from the minigun and chunker all around it. My wingman was doing the same. Together we cleared a path for the Loach through some of the most intense fire I'd seen. Mission accomplished. The advisors were evacuated from Polei Kleng.

Three days later, it was barely light as I got up and headed to the 361st showers, a concrete slab under a high tin roof, open on all sides. One row of horizontally placed plywood sheets formed a sort of half-wall around the edges. An open doorway led to a bank of sinks and mirrors running along the inside of one wall. Meandering water pipes and scattered showerheads hung from the rafters above. I stood under one of the showers, rinsing the soap from my body. Water streamed onto the last of the Head & Shoulders in my hair. With my eyes tightly closed, I felt the warm spray on my face. It was good. The last of my sleepiness melted away.

"Tac-E! Tac-E! Third platoon, launch!" Someone running through the company area yelled.

I raced back to my hooch, drying as I ran. I pulled on my underwear, T-shirt, and socks. I dragged on my flight-suit pants and stepped into my boots and tied them. I threw on my shirt and grabbed my hat and CAR-15 automatic carbine, snatching two bandoliers of ammo as I bolted through the door, still wet from the shower.

Tim and I met WO1 Steve Allen in front of operations. "Flame" Allen was one of my best pilots. He exuded enthusiasm about most everything in life, this morning being no exception. Steve was going home in two weeks. I had taken him off the flight schedule, but I was short of pilots. Apologetically, I asked if he'd mind taking one more mission.

"Sure, PL. No problem." I was glad that Steve would be flying my wing. We scrambled with no idea yet what the mission was, but we knew it couldn't be anything good. The enemy had been clawing into the high-lands for several weeks now, almost at will.

The pilot I'd scheduled to fly Flame's front seat had not yet gotten to the flight line, but Capt. Bob Gamber, commander of 2nd Platoon, had arrived. He wanted to know if his guys would be needed to launch behind mine. They would be arriving shortly. Gamber was not in the schedule himself. He was available.

"Bob! Would you mind flying front seat with Flame this morning? I'm short a pilot."

"No sweat. Got my stuff right here."

Inside, John Mayes, our operations officer, was contemplating his ceiling fan, leaning back in his chair with his cowboy boots on top of the desk. A bank of radios sat on a shelf behind his head. Ops was the source of all knowledge and controller of all missions. John, an Oklahoman, engendered calmness and confidence that made you feel all was unfolding in a reasonable manner that could be sensibly tackled. Things made sense even in the midst of utter chaos. He was the perfect operations officer.

"Tanks in the wire at Polei Kleng. Launch now and call me en route for their radio freq. Hawk's Claw will get up later. You'll be covering him too. You have tail numbers 053 and 682. Go!"

I stuffed a small emergency radio into one of the pockets of my survival vest. No time to perform the normal check on the radio. I ran to my aircraft with Tim. My regular bird was down for maintenance. This one didn't have a 20-mm cannon. I stowed my carbine and ammo behind the pilot's seat, climbed in, dropped into my seat, flipped a few switches, and cranked the engine while Tim was strapping in. Canopy hatches closed and radio calls made, I hovered out and took off. Steve and Bob came up on my wing, tucked in close in tight formation. The Cobra was heavy with fuel and ammo, but it climbed well in the cool morning air. Once airborne, I turned the controls over to Tim and fastened my own seat belt and shoulder harness. I lit my first cigarette of the day before calling operations for an update and the radio frequencies and call signs we'd need when we got to Polei Kleng.

About ten miles from Polei Kleng, I initiated a call. "Ballsy Butler, Panther Three Six."

No response.

"Ballsy Butler, this is Panther Three Six."

Still nothing. Two Vietnamese army battalions defended Polei Kleng, a Montagnard border ranger battalion and the ARVN 22nd Ranger Battalion, which had been sent as reinforcement. Someone should be on the radio.

One more try, "Ballsy Butler, this is Panther Three Six, over."

A broken, accented voice reminded me there were no longer American advisors on the ground at Polei Kleng. "Panther, this Ballsy Butler, over."

"Roger, Ballsy. This is Panther Three Six. I have a fire team of two armed AH-1G Cobras inbound to offer assistance."

"Good, Panther. Thank you. We need help. NVA attack with tanks and beaucoup infantry. We withdraw to south. Please hit all over camp and toward tree line to south for cover for us. Do not hit trees. We south of camp in jungle."

"Wilco, Ballsy. Can you give me a current enemy sitrep? How many forces? What kind? Doing what? From what directions?"

He spoke rapidly, "Roger, Panther. Beaucoup infantry, many tanks. Many thousand NVA. I think regiment. Maybe ten tanks. They attack from north and west."

"Roger, Ballsy. We'll be there in a few minutes."

Thick dust and smoke hung over Polei Kleng, evidence of the hard-fought predawn battle. I could see enemy infantry running all over the camp. A couple of NVA tanks sat between the northern tree line and the camp's concertina wire, not firing. Some of the South Vietnamese rangers continued fighting from the southern tree line outside the camp.

We dodged .51-caliber tracers on every gun run we made. We took no hits. We shot our entire load of rockets. Tim fired the minigun and 40-mm grenades from the turret. We departed for Kontum, twenty minutes away, to rearm and refuel.

"Thank you, Panther. Big help. Please come back?"

"Roger. Need more fuel and ammo. Will be back soon."

We did a rapid turnaround at Kontum, hot refueling and loading our own ordnance. I peed, with one hand devoted to that and the other gripping the fuel nozzle, pumping gas into the aircraft. Tim had to hold the controls during fueling. He relieved himself at the rearm point. Back in the air, I got a call on the radio.

"Panther Lead, this is Hawk's Claw."

Hawk's Claw, a classified prototype system, was kept under wraps in a guarded hangar at Camp Holloway except when conducting missions. The aircraft was an old UH-1B model Huey that had been upgraded and specially modified to test a new wire-guided missile system. It could acquire, fire, and hit targets more than a mile away with an armor-piercing antitank missile.[1]

"Roger, Hawk's Claw. This is Panther Three Six. Go ahead."

"Hey Panther Three Six, this is Hawk's Claw. Was told you'll be covering us."

"Roger that. Where are you?"

"Passing 200 degrees off Kontum at about twelve miles, just north of Plei Mrong. On the way to Polei Kleng. Understand they've got some tanks there."

"Sure do. We were there earlier. We're coming back out from Kontum. Will join on you en route."

"Roger."

Hawk's Claw did not fly, even on training runs, unless it had Cobra gun cover, and today we were it. This would be their first engagement against the enemy.

"Hawk's Claw, Panther Three Six. Have you in sight. Will catch up before we get to Polei Kleng."

"Roger that. Let's go get some tanks!"

When we got to Polei Kleng, we were surprised to find it quiet. The NVA infantry had occupied defensive positions within the camp. I couldn't see any tanks at all.

"Ballsy Butler, this is Panther Three Six back with you. Don't see any tanks. Can you give me a situation update?"

"Panther, this Ballsy Butler. Infantry occupy on Polei Kleng camp. Tanks pull back to jungle. We still fight from here and cover withdraw. We go Kontum. VNAF A-1s coming. Please fire on enemy in camp."

Since no tanks could be seen, Hawk's Claw remained high to one side. We Cobras fired rockets on the NVA positions in the camp. After one run, Hawk's Claw called us on the VHF radio. The guys on the ground could not hear our VHF transmissions. They only had FM radios.

"Panther Three Six, Hawk's Claw. Have a report of tanks in the wire at Ben Het. Situation sounds pretty bad. Two Americans still on the ground there. Think they need our help."

"Roger Hawk's Claw, let's go." Then back on the FM radio, "Ballsy Butler, this is Panther Three Six. Diverting to Ben Het. Tank attack there. Will get back with you as soon as we possibly can."

"Understand, Panther. Please hurry back. Situation here not good. Need you to cover. Let us get away."

"Roger, Ballsy. Will come back as soon as we can. Your A-1s should be on their way."

We headed to Ben Het. As we crossed the last ridgeline, the entire valley before us was filled with smoke. Tracers streamed outward from the defensive positions inside the camp. Enemy tracers replied from outside. Two jet fighters bombed next to the camp. NVA artillery, rockets, and mortars exploded in the camp. Enemy tanks breeched the perimeter. One, inside and partway up the hill, looked like it had been killed already. I couldn't be sure. An Air Force AC-130 Spectre gunship was leaving. He'd worked the area over with 20-mm Vulcan Gatling guns and 40-mm cannons, probably hitting the tank. Enemy infantry moved through openings in the jungle canopy. I could see groups assembling to join the attack.

Ben Het, another old Special Forces camp, sat on a hill. The command post bunker was near the top, a small helipad nestled next to it and ammunition bunker positioned nearby. Several other bunkers and a number of now destroyed buildings were scattered across the camp. The defensive fighting positions had been reinforced over the weeks that the NVA offensive had raged through the highlands.

Two American advisors remained on the ground at Ben Het. Neither Capt. Bob Sparks, advising the 71st Border Ranger Battalion, nor Capt. Mark Truhan, advising the 95th, had asked to be evacuated. Both ranger battalions were filled with Montagnards but had ethnic Vietnamese officers. There had been dissatisfaction and a near mutiny by one unit the day before, but today they were pulling together, fighting ferociously against their common enemy.

"Sundance Rocket 88, this is Panther Three Six, inbound."

"Panther Three Six, this is Rocket 88 Nutcracker. Glad to see you guys! We're in some deep shit here."

"Roger. I am on station with two Pink Panther Cobras and one Hawk's Claw UH-1 with antitank capability. We have a visual on a number of tanks and will engage."

"Roger, Panther. Several tanks already dead. Spectre did a job for us.[2] Go after any still in action. Also have NVA in the tree lines. Hit those heavy with rockets if you would."

"Roger. Will have Hawk's Claw work with you directly on your push. We'll cover them and hit your targets."

We flew two thousand feet above the ground, what should have been a safe altitude. Near the camp, we could see .51-caliber tracers arching below us. I saw streams of much more threatening fire from ZPU 14.5-mm and ZU 23-mm antiaircraft weapons, a threat even at two thousand feet. I'd seen them in Laos, but never inside South Vietnam until two weeks before at Tan Canh/Dak To.

I radioed, "Take care, guys. I've got ZPU tracers and some zoo twenty-three airbursts. Watch out. That's some nasty shit."

Hawk's Claw fired on a number of the tanks. After he expended his missiles, we began shooting at enemy soldiers along the tree line and into the jungle. After we fired all our rockets and most of the 40-mm grenades from our turrets, I radioed, "Nutcracker, we're breaking station and returning to Kontum for rearm and refuel. Will be back as soon as we can."

As we turned, I saw several big white airbursts explode close to Hawk's Claw.

37-millimeter! Fuck me! A 37-mm blew my Mohawk out of the sky my first tour.

"Hey guys, that big stuff you see coming up is thirty-seven mike mike antiaircraft. It can eat your lunch. We're outta here."

We returned to Kontum. Once our rearm/refuel was complete, we took off, airborne again as a flight. We headed back to the fight and met Hawk's Claw en route.

On our way back to Ben Het, we could see the battle continuing at Polei Kleng. Vietnamese Air Force A-1 Skyraiders dove, dropping bombs. We passed close enough to see one as it trailed smoke and flame and went into the ground in an awful explosion. I saw a parachute, and a mayday call came over the emergency frequency on the radio. I called headquarters to tell them I was diverting for a few minutes to help recover the downed VNAF pilot. "Negative, Panther Three Six. Permission denied. Proceed direct to Ben Het. Out."

I tried again. Same result. *Assholes!*

As we got closer to Ben Het, the weather deteriorated. Under a solid overcast of darkening clouds, we flew right up against the bottom of the stuff at a thousand feet. Bad altitude. We were prime targets for every weapon at the enemy's disposal, especially .51-calibers.

I got a call on the radio. "Panther flight this is Rocket Four-Four, over."

Who the hell is Rocket Four-Four? I wondered. I keyed my mike, "Rocket Four-Four, this is Panther Three Six, go."

"Roger, Panther Three Six. I've got a Huey load of small arms and antitank ammo for the guys at Ben Het. They need this badly. Can you cover us going in? Over."

"Roger that. Standby."

I came up with a plan. "Rocket Four-Four, weather is getting worse and pushing us down under a thousand feet. There is significant triple-A threat, twenty-three and thirty-seven mike mike. Suggest we go in on the deck, same as we do across the border. Right on the trees. Come in from the east and depart in a different direction, to the south."

"Roger. Sounds good. Over."

"There is so much crap out here that I don't want to spend time in our usual racetrack. You guys lead in. We'll cover you. Kick off your shit, and we'll cover you out. How's that sound?"

"Sounds good, over."

"OK, let's get this done."

I smashed my cigarette out in the ashtray, sat up straighter in my seat, adjusted my chicken plate, and keyed my mike again. "Hawk's Claw, hold well to the east, at altitude. We'll pick you up after we run this resupply and help you get some more tanks."

I spotted Rocket 44's Huey inbound and maneuvered my fire team to his rear. Flame kept a little behind me and slightly to the left. The Huey dropped down, speeding toward Ben Het from the southeast, hugging the treetops. We stayed right with him, suppressing enemy fire along both sides of his flight path.

Tim called out enemy positions and weapons firing as he saw them, using the minigun and chunker as he talked. I fired pairs of rockets just in front and alongside the Huey. My wingman did the same. Tracers and antiaircraft airbursts appeared everywhere. We had jabbed a stick into a big angry hornet's nest.

The Huey came to a low hover near the command bunker. The crew kicked out the ammo boxes. The helicopter did a left hovering turn and took off. I began a sharp left turn so I could continue shooting suppressive fire for him. The enemy opened up on our two Cobras with everything they had. My view left, right, above, and below was filled with tracers.

Tim fired continuously on those firing at us. We took large-caliber hits all over the aircraft (.51- and 14.5-mm ZPU). Rounds came through the cockpit. Hits from small arms always felt something like Jiffy Pop popcorn popping against its tinfoil cover. These seemed like a jackhammer slamming into the aircraft, beginning in the rear, working up the side and then into the cockpit.

The tail rotor was shot off and the engine was shot up. Every system on the helicopter was damaged in some way. Without the tail rotor, the aircraft began to spin. Fuel lines ruptured and we were burning. I keyed the microphone. "This is Three Six taking fire from four o'clock. Taking fire, everywhere. Taking fire, taking hits, going down. Panther going down."

The engine quit. The rotor rpm caution light flashed. The audio warning sounded, announcing that my rotor blades were turning dangerously slowly. I slammed the collective down hard to autorotate. Under optimal conditions, this is a controlled emergency descent. Under these conditions, I could only hope to lessen the severity of the crash. We corkscrewed down in flames. As I wrestled the aircraft, I radioed my wingman, "Flame, you better get in here quick and get us out."

No answer.

They were fighting for their lives. I learned years later that when I called taking hits, Flame had banked his Cobra and fired rockets onto the positions shooting at me. As he did so, a big, ugly .51 round came through the cockpit and tore into his chest, high on the left side. Bob took the controls and headed for help, flying from the front seat.

My Cobra came down spinning and burning. It hit the ground hard, nose low on the left side. It bounced back into the air, spun another turn and a half, and crashed. It settled nearly upright. Fire engulfed the cockpit. I called Tim on intercom.

"Let's un-ass this motherfucker!"

"Roger that."

As narrow as a Cobra is, it often ends up on one side or the other in a crash. Since the front-seat canopy opens to the left and the back seat to the right, if the helicopter lands on its side one crewmember would be trapped. But we could both get out. We were lucky.

I was badly dazed and barely conscious. I remember smoke and flames and heat. I remember opening my canopy and unfastening my lap belt. I tried to climb out, but I was hung up by something. I dived out the canopy opening. My feet tangled in straps or cords. Wasn't sure exactly what.

Inside Ben Het, one of the American advisors, Mark Truhan, watched us get shot down and crash. He saw Tim exit the aircraft. He saw me hanging out the side of the Cobra, head down with my feet stuck in the cockpit, the helicopter burning. He'd seen a truck driver die in agony in a blazing semi wreck years before and had sworn he would not let that happen again. He raised the sights of his M-16 rifle to my body. As he began to squeeze the trigger to put me out of my misery, a cloud of smoke billowed from the exploding aircraft. It obscured me from his view. When the smoke cleared, I was gone.

CHAPTER 5

Evasion

I came to a short distance from the wreckage. I floated in and out of consciousness several times in the minutes, or maybe hours, that passed. I remember the heat from the burning Cobra. I heard and felt the explosions from the fuel and ammunition on board. Then I would fall back into oblivion. When I was finally aware of the world around me again, all was quiet at the aircraft. I could hear the battle raging in Ben Het, a few hundred yards away.

I was dazed. I knew I was hurt badly. I had no idea where I was or what had happened. At first I thought I'd just been shot down in a Mohawk and survived an ejection seat ride. I was back in 1969. I worried about my observer.

I was also paralyzed, numb from head to toe. I could feel back pain through the numbness, but I could not move my arms or legs. I couldn't budge at all.

Hurt bad. Need to be in a hospital.

My mind was stuck in a time three years earlier, skipping through confusing illusions for some time while I tried to will my body to move. Eventually, my arms began to respond. I worked my hands to the radio pocket on my survival vest. I groped the pocket for a long time before I finally got the radio out. I was about to transmit, but I couldn't think of my call sign. I tried to form the words. I hit a blank. I tried again. I blurted out, "Panther three-six."

In that instant, I remembered I was not flying Mohawks. I was a Cobra pilot in the 361st Pink Panthers. I had been shot down at Ben Het. I didn't have a right-seat observer to worry about. I had a front-seat copilot/gunner.

Tim. Got to find Tim! I keyed the emergency radio, trying to formulate a coherent distress call, but the radio was dead. I kicked myself for not taking the few seconds to check the battery before we launched that morning. I had never had a problem with a battery before. Now I did. The Air Force always carried spare batteries. In the Army we felt lucky to have a radio at all. There were no spare batteries.

Rescue was going to be tough.

Got to find Tim. I struggled to move. My arms worked better, and I fought to get my legs in motion. I rocked onto my belly and got my knees under me. A piece of jagged metal was sticking through the side of my right boot into my ankle. I pulled it out with one swift motion, like pulling off a Band-Aid. Then I pushed up onto my hands and knees and tried crawling. It worked!

I slowly, painfully crawled around the wreckage looking for Tim. No luck. I heard a Huey nearby and rolled reluctantly onto my back, giving up all the progress I'd made to that point. I fumbled with my survival vest to find the signal mirror and flashed some mirror flashes toward the Huey. Nothing. I got back onto my hands and knees and crawled around the wreck some more. Couldn't find Tim. I hoped he'd be OK. He had a radio. I had no doubt that his battery was fine. He was probably talking to aircraft already.

I crawled farther from the wreck and collapsed under a bush, exhausted. It rained and I got soaked. I lay there and shivered.

Late in the day, I heard the enemy moving and shooting around me. Air strikes increased in frequency and came closer. I heard the Spectre AC-130 gunship ripping the jungle to pieces not far away. If I stayed where I was, I'd be killed or captured. I had to do something. I rolled onto my front again, got in my crawling stance, tried pushing up onto my feet, and was surprised to find I could stand stooped over. I took a few small steps in terrible pain.

I shuffled around, tried to come up with a plan. To get into Ben Het, to the command bunker and safety, I'd have to move through hundreds of attacking North Vietnamese soldiers and tanks, go through multiple rings of concertina wire and mine fields, not get killed by the enemy, and hope that the friendlies would not mistake me for an NVA soldier and shoot me before I got to them.

The Montagnard hamlet of Plei Mrong, forty miles away, lay a bit southwest of Kontum City. That would be a good shot. I could walk there in a couple of weeks, even in my current state. The pain in my back was intense. It was broken. The fire had burned the back of my neck, and I had lesser burns on my face. My hair was singed. I had pulled a shell fragment out of my ankle. Superficial lacerations covered my face and forehead, bleeding badly. I was a mess, but I was motivated. I wanted to get away. I staggered from the crash site and headed southeast, toward Kontum, as it was getting dark.

I had not gone far when I heard helicopters approaching. Cobras came in low, shooting. They set up the familiar racetrack above the trees right over me. I heard a Loach screaming in at a low level, like a hummingbird possessed. I grabbed my strobe light and slipped the blue tinted cover in place over the bulb to make the bright flashing light appear blue, rather than white, so it wouldn't be mistaken for muzzle flashes. I held the light over my head, pointed toward the aircraft. It flashed a few times. The gunner in the lead Cobra opened up on me with his minigun. A stream of tracers came right at me.

God damn!

I dropped the light and rolled away from the bullets. They missed by a few feet. The stupid strobe light, attached to my survival vest by a cord, was lying there still flashing into the dirt. I fumbled with the switch and got the damned thing shut off before it got me killed. I was badly shaken. I hurt like hell, but I was elated, too. I had heard the Loach hover down to the ground and sit there for a moment. Then it climbed back up and left the area.

They got Tim out. Thank God.

I got back onto my feet in pain and gave thanks. I had not just been killed by friendly fire.

In survival school, they taught us to stay off trails, travel at night, and avoid people. That's what I did. I pushed my way through the jungle southeast by my compass. Every step was agonizing. When I had to bend or squat to get under a branch, the pain was excruciating. I had to be quiet, but at times I would groan, "Ahgg!"

I don't think I went far that night. I was still dazed and I tired quickly. The pain was disabling. Fighting my way cross-country through the jungle was taking its toll. *This off-trail, at night, in the jungle, is shit. This is impossible!*

Rain began to fall, and I shook uncontrollably with cold and fatigue. I found a bush up against a small tree and worked myself under its cover. I collapsed on the ground and fell asleep instantly.

An AC-130 Spectre gunship had been shooting for much of the time I'd been traveling, along with frequent strikes by jet fighter aircraft. Spectre departed and the fighter air strikes slowed. I slept soundly for the first moments.

Armageddon wrenched me awake. I raised just my head. I felt the first distant rumble of bombs. *Oh shit! B-52 strike!!* Terror gripped me. The thundering came toward me, louder and louder. The ground trembled. The earth shook. Hundreds of bombs fell almost on top of me. Then it stopped. Silence.

Pieces of debris crashed close by. Floating residue of the earth-churning explosions drifted down around me. My nostrils filled with the acrid smell of explosive. I trembled again. How many times that day? I laid my head back down on the dirt and fell back asleep thinking, *Whatever is going to happen will happen. May live. May die. No sense in worrying about it.*

Other B-52 strikes intruded into my uneasy dream state as the night went on, none as close as that first. I rested fitfully. At dawn, a flight of jets struck a target close enough to instantly snap me from slumber. I jerked awake, but lay still. I thought through the sequence of events that had brought me to this place and point in time. I was a mess. My face was covered with crusted blood. I could feel some pretty good lacerations, particularly one on my hairline above my right eye. I hurt all over, especially my back. I was stiff and had trouble getting my arms and legs moving again. After some effort, I rolled onto my front. I struggled onto my hands and knees, then back up on my feet. My back screamed as I stood. I was bent over like a very old man. On my left forearm, a squiggling worm-like thing was standing on its head, a leech. I grabbed it and tore it away. I discovered another on my arm, one on my neck. I ripped them off.

I thought about finding a better place nearby and hunkering down for the day. One tenet of my evasion training was to travel only at night. I decided to accept whatever increased risk there might be traveling during the day. It would be too hard to do what I'd done the night before. I checked my compass and headed southeast, continuing toward Kontum or Plei Mrong, forty miles away.

Before long, I came to a stream. I dropped slowly and carefully to my knees, cupped my hands, and raised water to my lips. I was really thirsty. I'd had nothing but a cup of coffee since the night before I'd been shot down. I guzzled the water. The taste of cordite didn't deter me from quenching my thirst. Afterward, I wondered if it was poisonous. I came upon the B-52 strike. I dragged myself through and around craters and shattered trees for half a mile before I was back in the jungle again.

Later that morning, I came to a trail that was running southeast. Another principle of my evasion training was stay off trails. Exhausted and in pain, I took the trail anyway, rationalizing that I would remain alert and take cover if I heard or sensed anything. *Besides, I've got a lot of distance between Ben Het and me by now. Shouldn't be any NVA this far out.*

The trail was easier going. I felt optimistic. *Keep moving southeast. Get around or over Rocket Ridge. Get near Kontum and find friendlies. Plei Mrong is good. That'll work. This is gonna be OK.*

A large grassy area opened to my right. The trail was still in the trees, but I could look out onto the open field. I heard the sound of a light airplane. I stepped into the field and looked up. A VNAF O-1 Bird Dog spotter plane was approaching the field. *Thank God.* I pulled out my pen flares. I mounted one onto the launcher as quickly as I could. The plane was heading past the edge of the field. I pulled back the spring-loaded firing mechanism and let it go. The flare shot into the air and burst into a bright red cluster. I held my breath, hoped, waited. Nothing. The plane kept flying. No wing-rocking, nothing. He hadn't seen it. I turned back to the trail, my head not as high as before.

Small arms fire erupted from across the field. Voices shouted in Vietnamese as eight or ten uniformed NVA soldiers came running across the field. The Bird Dog had not seen my flare, but they had. They rushed, hot after me. My hands patted my hips and survival vest. *Oh, crap.* For the first time since being shot down, I realized I had no weapon.

I had been issued a .38-caliber revolver, the same weapon I'd had on my first tour. When I was shot down then, I'd drawn my pistol, looked at the stream of rifle and machine-gun fire coming from my pursuers, and reholstered it immediately. I would not die hopelessly in another Custer's Last Stand. Instead, my wingman covered my forty-five-minute run through the jungle to a helicopter rescue, a dash that earned me the nickname of Lightfoot. A .38 wasn't worth a shit. I had wangled a CAR-15 automatic carbine from one of my special ops friends, which I carried instead. The CAR-15, with my two bandoliers of ammunition, was still behind my seat in the Cobra. I hadn't thought about it as I'd struggled to get out of the burning aircraft. There hadn't been time to get it even if I had.

I shuffled down the trail as quickly as I could. After a curve, I dropped and rolled under a patch of thick bushes to my left and lay there as quietly as I could. I was breathing heavily. I was sure I'd soon be dead or captured.

The enemy soldiers came down the trail at a fast run, yelling among themselves, probably shouting commands to me as well. I knew about five words of Vietnamese, so I had no idea what they said. I held my breath when they ran past me. The noise died down, I took several deep breaths. They ran on down the trail. I had made it. There was still hope.

I was cocksure. If anyone could survive this, it was me. I had been a Boy Scout. Though I was one of the troublemakers in my troop, I'd learned a lot. I'd backpacked sixty-five miles through the mountains in five days and practiced survival skills.

My troubled youth got me suspended from school a number of times, but it also taught me lessons. I learned to street fight, take care of myself.

I had boxed, played football, and run track. I majored in forestry, worked cattle ranches, rode broncs in small rodeos, fought forest fires, worked construction, and was an electrical lineman for Southern California Edison.

Survival, escape, and evasion training were part of officer candidate school as well as flight school. Navy jungle survival school in the Philippines gave me additional training. Being shot down and evading capture on my first tour made me about as ready as anyone could be for what I now faced. I only needed some luck and, I damn well knew, a little help from something beyond myself.

I remembered a little ditty my mother had taught me. "The Lord helps those who help themselves." I knew I could depend on its absolute truth to help get me through this. *The Lord helps those who help themselves. God, I'll do that. Do all I can. Muster every bit of what's inside me. I'll do my part. I'll do all I can to help myself. So please, please do yours. I need your help!* I said it to myself again, drawing comfort and strength. *The Lord helps those who help themselves.* I would repeat it often, as I set my mind to doing all I must to survive.

I crawled out from the bushes and left the trail, back into the tangled jungle toward high ground to the south. There I turned to my southeasterly course again. I would get up out of the valley and work across the hills. Never again would I risk using a trail.

Thirst took hold of me. Every painful step toward the hills made me thirstier. You'd think there would be an abundance of water in the jungle. Not so. I hadn't crossed another stream since that morning. My mouth was dry as dust. I tried to cup rain in my hands during a shower. That rendered only a few drops. I came upon some plants with large, horizontally lying leaves with small amounts of rainwater puddled on each. I drank eagerly, moving from leaf to leaf. I got no more than a couple spoonfuls of water for my effort.

I found myself in an astonishing place. I stood under high, dense jungle canopy as in a large, dimly lit room, quiet, serene save for the sounds of the jungle. The air was filled with bird songs. Another strange yodel-pitched sound was almost like some creature singing out, "Fuck you. Fuck you." It was the exotic call of a Tokay lizard.

The tops of the largest trees formed layers of canopy like a protective ceiling, a hundred or even two hundred feet above. Smaller trees and a variety of bushes and other shrubs spread across the decomposing duff of the forest floor. Thick vines hung from the dome.

I felt a sense of security here. I used this almost spiritual place to collect my wits and gather my strength for whatever lay ahead.

I knew I had to eat. I hadn't eaten for two days. Another wilderness survival technique helped me find edible plants. I identified a plant that I'd seen in abundance. I took a piece of leaf, rolled it into a pea-sized ball, and ate it. There were no ill effects after several minutes, so I ate a larger piece. Still no ill effects after a short while, so I figured that plant was fine. I ate a bunch of the leaves.

While I was chomping on leaves, I spied a large ant mound nearby. I walked over and placed my hand on the mound. When my hand was covered with ants, I raised it, looked at them for a second, and then started licking ants off the back of my hand. Pretty acrid taste. I could feel their tiny pinchers trying to bite as I chewed. It was a source of protein, though. If I could find water and eat plants and ants, that would sustain me for the two to three weeks it would take me to get to Kontum.

Moist warmth ran along the inside of my thighs. I looked down. I noticed my whole crotch was more soaked than the rest of my rain-sodden flight suit. I was pissing myself. I reached behind me and felt a gooey mess in the back of my pants. I had lost control of my bowels as well. *Must have something to do with my back injury*, I thought. *Well I'm a hell of a mess.*

I left my sanctuary and headed for the hills, my goal for the day. It was getting dark. I drank my fill at another stream and found a spot above the bank to lie down and sleep. Off in the distance, bombing continued through the day. Sporadic strikes came much closer, some not far ahead of me.

I fell asleep, exhausted. Occasional rumbles and rain showers kept waking me. Morning came just as I was finally comfortably sleeping. Sunlight and animal sounds woke me. I struggled up, shivering, got a drink from the stream, which now had a definite cordite taste, and continued my journey.

I moved diagonally upward, to the left, along the first hillside. The jungle thinned and I was on a slope covered in grass taller than me. Two-thirds of the way up the hill, I came to a large bombed-out area with no live vegetation, only big craters and churned-up earth dotted with boulders, tree stumps, and shattered trunks and limbs. It was a long way around either side. I kept going straight across.

Somewhere near the middle of the devastation, I heard an airplane. A small U.S. Air Force O-2 forward air control airplane was droning across the sky a couple thousand feet up. I stopped, took off the top of my two-piece Nomex flight suit, and began waving the shirt over my head. The aircraft continued to fly by. My head and my heart fell again. Then the droning sound of the engine changed. I looked up. The plane began a left turn right over me and circled twice as I waved my shirt more energetically. Then he left. I was excited, sure he'd be back shortly with a rescue helicopter. Thoughts of a hot shower and beer at the officers' club filled my head. My heart pounded.

I heard the O-2 returning. He stayed off to one side. I looked for the helicopter. Instead I heard the wailing screech of a jet fighter in a steep dive. I squinted. An F-4 fighter-bomber was diving right at me. I fell into a crater and stood in the bottom, fixated on the plane as it plunged toward me.

Time slowed. The plane plummeted straight at me, releasing two bombs. The plane pulled up. The bombs continued, gliding along a line that had been invisibly drawn to my head. They grew bigger and closer. I fell to my knees, covered my head, and waited. Kaboom! The earth shuddered. I was alive. The bombs struck a nearby crater, not mine. A second F-4 dove. Its bombs fell farther away. The planes left, and I sat there, badly shaken. After a while, I crawled out of the hole, finished crossing the bombed area, and continued on up the hill.

Near the top, the jungle gave way to an expanse of grassland that covered the gently sloping ridge. My southeasterly course would take me right across the middle. The route around was long and thickly jungled. I was physically and mentally drained. I decided to chance the open field. With much care, I slowly stepped out onto the grass. I scanned the tree line, stopping frequently to listen. I hadn't covered more than thirty yards when I heard voices across the field. I saw movement in the trees just beyond.

Oh, shit, I muttered to myself. *If they see me out here, they'll shoot and I'm dead.* Blood pounded in my head. Why in the fuck had I thought I could get away with such a dumb-shit move? I found myself repeating, *The Lord helps those who help themselves.* Then I made a pact. *God, get me out of this one, and I owe you. Anything. You name it. I'll become a rancher and raise cattle. No more Army. No more war. OK?*

I turned left, away from the voices, stealing back toward the cover of the jungle at the edge of the field. With each step, I expected to feel a bullet rip into me. Surely they'd seen me out there. I thought I heard a couple of distant shots, but it was more likely my imagination. I got back to the tree line, stepped in, and breathed a sigh. I hadn't been seen. *Thank you, Lord.*

Pushing my way through the thick jungle, I continued away from the field. My course would keep me well clear of the soldiers there. The hill dropped away on the back side. I stumbled slowly downward. I heard air strikes, but they were far away. Hope returned.

I came upon a small cultivated field with banana trees along one edge. No sign of habitation or recent human activity. The bananas were little green things. They didn't look ripe. I peeled one and ate it anyway. Not real good, but it was food. I ate another and stuffed several into my pockets. I continued down the hill and back into the jungle.

I reached the bottom, worked my way up the side of another hill, and then went back down again. The going was difficult. The jungle was so thick I almost couldn't see my hand if I held it straight out in front of me. I was not going back onto any more trails, though. I was done with any more idiotic meanderings in large open fields. I was doing everything right with one exception. I was traveling during the day instead of at night. Night was too tough.

I felt confident. I had several bananas. For the next few days, they would supplement my leaf diet until I found more bananas, ants, or something else. I was good to go. My wobbly steps took on a little more bounce. I continued pushing through the jungle, down the hillside.

Then, out of nowhere, I heard excited voices.

"Cái gì vây?"

"Tôi nghe cái gì çó."

"Có phäi çó là con thú?"

"Không, tôi không nghĩ như vãy! Chúng ta hãy đi!"

Shit. People! I crouched down and kept absolutely silent. I could feel my heart pounding in my chest, hear it in my ears. *Maybe they'll think it was an animal and go back to whatever they were doing.*

What if they didn't? What if they found me? *Could be Montagnards. That would be great. I'd be saved.* I couldn't tell if the language was Vietnamese or a tribal dialect. I could only hope. I breathed as shallowly as I could. I felt for my weapon that I knew wasn't there. I brought my hand back onto my knee.

A lot of crashing around came from the direction of the voices. I looked up and saw uniformed NVA soldiers pointing AK-47 rifles at my head. They shrieked something and motioned for me to stand up. I did. I was captured. I felt indescribably sick in the pit of my stomach as my world fell away. I'd been struggling for three days to stay alive. I was in miserable shape, but I'd been free and I had options. No more. My soul was awash with anguish. I was no longer a free man. In that instant, I had become a captive of the communist North Vietnamese Army, a prisoner of war, another American POW in the long Vietnam conflict. I had no idea how long they might let me live, or if I was about to die.

CHAPTER 6

Captive

Five young North Vietnamese soldiers nervously pointed their rifles at me. A couple of them were shaking. We stood in utter silence for a moment. They glared at me. I glared at them. For that tense instant, I didn't know if I'd be riddled with bullets or be allowed to live. One barked something I could not understand. Another joined in, then a third. I looked right into their eyes. I was an American. I would show them the best American fighting man that I could.

I tried to stand proud, as straight as possible. Even so, I was badly bent over. God, how I hurt. How miserable I must have looked. Three days in the jungle with no food and little water. Three days' growth of beard over a face crusted with caked mud and dried blood, topped with singed and unkempt hair. Three days of pissing and shitting myself. I must have stunk.

One motioned his weapon and commanded, "Đi. Đi đi mau!" They'd come upon one of the very few Vietnamese phrases I understood. Go. Go quickly!

Two of them led. I followed, and the other three fell in behind. After only a few feet, we came out of the dense jungle. The foliage thinned, and a stream flowed a few yards from where I'd been captured. The soldiers picked up canteens they'd been filling when they heard me crashing down the hillside. One motioned me to go up a trail on the opposite side. They followed me. The first two held their weapons on me, their fingers on the triggers. I moved with difficulty. They seemed annoyed with the slow pace.

About halfway up the hill, we rounded a curve. A soldier, coming down the trail, was less than ten yards ahead. He grabbed a stick grenade from the pouch on his belt and arched his arm back to throw. One of my captors shouted something, and the startled soldier stopped his toss, looking rattled and absolutely confused. We moved past him, coming into an area of huge columns, the trunks of towering jungle hardwoods. Their highest limbs reached out and interlocked with others, forming a dense canopy roof a hundred feet overhead.

Concealed under the jungle canopy, hundreds of NVA soldiers were at work, while others sat in small groups, talking. Large bunkers were scattered around. Tunnels opened into larger underground spaces, each reinforced with narrow logs. Some positions were little more than wide trenches covered with logs and a few feet of soil. Some had defensive fighting positions incorporated into their design. Most simply offered protection from air strikes. This was obviously a major staging area for the attack on Ben Het. I'd unknowingly been headed right toward it. None of it could be observed from the air. I doubted even infrared systems could have detected the small cooking fires I'd seen walking in.

I smelled a distinct odor—foreign cooking, unbathed enemy combatants— unlike anything I'd ever experienced. It wasn't foul. It was simply different.

My captors led me deeper into the encampment. They had a short conversation with someone in authority, then backtracked several yards and sat me next to a large tree. They jabbered among themselves for a minute. One gave me some water. I guzzled it. Another offered a cigarette. I took it, inhaling deeply with each long drag.

They looked curiously at their prize. At first they seemed concerned about my sorry condition. Then they started laughing and pointing. I had no idea why. Others gathered and began laughing as well. I flinched as one came up and thrust his hand toward my face. He reached toward my nose, grabbed something, and pulled hard, ripping it out of my nostril. He held a squirming leech and squished it between his nails. He sneered, turned, and left.

Someone barked orders. The crowd around me dispersed. Seasoned soldiers took over as my guards. They took my survival vest, wallet, everything in my pockets, my watch, wedding band, boots, and my socks.

They rifled through the survival vest. It became clear they were asking about my weapon. All I could do was shake my head.

If I'd had my CAR-15 with me, I could have put up a hell of a fight for a few minutes before I was killed. Would've lived a shorter time yet if I'd had only my pistol. I thought, *Probably best I'm unarmed. At least I'm still alive—for now.*

A couple of hours passed under the steady stare of my guards. They never moved more than a few feet from me. After a while, I heard some commotion nearby. Two people moved purposefully toward me. One was a young man wearing a clean, creased uniform with insignia on his collar. *Must be an officer,* I thought. An older soldier, a rumpled mess, came with him.

The officer approached, looking at me for a moment before hunkering down right next to me, his feet flat on the ground, knees apart, bent until his butt was nearly touching the dirt. He had a look of deep concern on his face. "How are you? Are you hurt?"

I was surprised at how good his English was.

"Yeah. Hurt. My back hurts a lot. Think I injured it badly."

"Are you a pilot? Were you shot down in an airplane?"

I sat there in silence, recalling all I could from the Code of Conduct. *I am an American fighting man prepared to give my life. I will never surrender of my own free will. If captured, I will continue to resist and make every effort to escape. If I become a POW, I will keep faith in fellow prisoners and obey the orders of senior officers. When questioned, I will give only my name, rank, service number, and date of birth. I will never forget that I am an American and will act accordingly and will trust my country.*

He repeated the question, still in a kindly tone. "Were you shot down in an airplane?"

"My name is William Spencer Reeder Junior. I am a captain in the United States Army. My service number is O5424128. My date of birth is 22 December 1945, 12/22/45."

He smiled. "All right. I understand. I am only trying to help you. We will get a doctor to look at your back. We want to be sure you are OK."

He looked at me. He seemed worried over my pitiful state. "Are you hungry? Would you like some food?"

I took a breath. "Yes. I am hungry."

"I'll be back."

He left. His sidekick remained, scowling at me. The guards still watched me. The young officer returned with a U.S. canteen cup filled with hot rice. He handed it to me with a spoon.

"Eat."

I ate. Even near starvation, the flavor of plain boiled rice was not appealing. I forced down spoonful after spoonful because I knew I needed it. It must have shown.

"Here. Try this." He handed me an open can of sweetened condensed milk. The canteen cup and can of milk must have come from the stocks at Tan Canh.

After mixing the sweet thick milk with the remaining rice, I ate the resulting goo eagerly. A couple of weeks before, the ARVN 22nd Division had been overrun at Tan Canh. I flashed back to the meals I'd had in the Tan Canh mess hall and the American advisors there. Some of them were dead or missing. I was eating their food with their utensils. It was not right. Just not right. I ate every last bit from the cup.

"Now, do you feel better?"

I said nothing. Only looked at him.

"The people of Vietnam want to show you the humane and lenient treatment. All you have to do is obey the rules. You follow rules, you get good treatment. We take good care of you. Understand?"

"Can I have some more water?"

"Yes." He handed me a canteen and watched me drink. Then he asked, "Are you married? Do you have children?"

I said nothing. He then added, "We found pictures of a pretty lady with children in your wallet. Obviously your family."

"Yeah."

"I know you miss them and they are very worried about you. You follow the rules and you will be home soon. You will receive the humane and lenient treatment. You will be allowed to go home."

Then an awful thought struck me. *Found pictures in my wallet? Oh fuck. They must have found my calling cards in my wallet, too. If they read them, I'm in deep shit.*

The Pink Panthers had calling cards to drop over areas we'd hit in the Cobras, but I never knew anyone who had actually done that. Mostly we had them to impress some nongunship pilot, an Army nurse, or a Red Cross Volunteer Donut Dolly. The front of my cards had a small Cobra patch in the upper left corner, the words "The Pink Panthers" in the upper right, and my name and call sign printed prominently in the middle. Other places on the card boasted phrases like "Call us for death and destruction, night and day" and "Killing is our business and business is good." The back of the card boldly stated: "Congratulations! You have been killed through the courtesy of the 361st Aviation Company. Yours truly, Panther 36." That boastful calling card could now mean torture or death. Astonishingly, nothing was said.

"I know you are married. You have a family. You follow the rules, and you will be treated well and you will go home soon. You understand?"

"Yes."

"First we must tie you. You understand? Necessary precaution for security. Understand?"

He spoke to his shabby assistant, who fetched a length of rope and returned. He tied my arms loosely behind my back as I sat.

"Now you must answer some questions. It is required." He still had a friendly air, but his tone became more businesslike. "Where is your weapon? I must have your pistol. Surely you understand. We did not find it. Where is it?"

"I don't have a weapon."

"You must. Everyone does."

"I didn't have one."

"Very well, please tell me your unit. Where is it located?"

I stared straight ahead and said nothing.

"Your unit. Are you army, navy, or air force pilot?"

No response from me.

"What did you fly? What kind of plane? F-4 Phantom?" His voice became more determined, more intimidating. He looked intently into my eyes as if searching for my secrets. "You must tell me your unit. What kind of plane you fly. If you do not cooperate, you will not receive the humane and lenient treatment."

The threat had been made. I glared at him. I didn't speak. The line was drawn. He was becoming angry. I was angry too. His kindness had been nothing but a ploy. Now he was down to the business at hand. I knew I'd said too much.

"Where is your pistol? We know you have a weapon. Where is it?"

I glared. He became more agitated.

"Your pistol! We know you hid it. You plan to use it in your escape. Where is it?!"

I didn't answer. He stood up, bent down, and put his face right into mine. "We will find it and you will pay a price."

His expression twisted. He screamed, "Where is your pistol?!" and slapped me hard in the face. My head snapped to the side. Again, "Where is your pistol?!"

I glared at him with a look of utter hatred. I didn't know what would happen next, if I would live or die. I didn't care. I'd walked close to death for days. I felt numb, numb to physical pain, numb to mental abuse, numb to thoughts of living and dying. The only un-numb feeling I had was hatred for this son of a bitch. I despised him. He was not only my enemy, he had pretended to care about my plight. I had believed his act. It infuriated me.

He had to see the hatred in my eyes. I saw frustration and loathing in his. He spun around and stomped away, shouting orders as he went, his assistant scampering after him. My guards grabbed me up and led me away. It was already getting dark under the dense jungle canopy.

They pushed me into an abandoned bunker. I tripped and fell several feet into the hole. The pain! The place was dim and dank. Slimy mud covered the bottom. In the faint light, I could make out big centipedes and spiders moving across the ceiling and along the walls. The guards put logs across the entrance. I found myself sitting in slime, in darkness, my arms still tied behind me.

The gloom became thick velvet pressing in on me, heavy and suffocating. I couldn't breathe. Panic rose inside me. The closed space seemed to get smaller, tighter, and more intolerable. I could feel the weight of the darkness.

Terror grabbed hold of me. I fought it. I took control of my breathing and slowed it down. I made myself feel the air as it entered my lungs, which calmed me. I willed my trembling to subside. For hours, I sat there staring and thinking. I was careful not to let myself wonder what the morrow would bring. Finally, I lay down on my side and fell asleep.

I slept fitfully. Things crawled across me. At one point I thought a small animal scampered across my legs, maybe a rat. I couldn't be sure if it was real or if I was dreaming. After a night that seemed it would never end, I woke to the sound of a rooster crowing. My first thought was, *What are chickens doing here?* Then, *Must be dawn.*

I struggled to sit up. *Oh God, am I sore.* Pain moaned throughout my body. My jaw hurt from the blow I'd taken to the side of my face. I sat there and waited while hours passed and nothing happened. Finally, guards removed the logs covering the entrance above my head and pulled me out. It was still early in the morning. Camp was just beginning to stir.

The guards took me to an area on the edge of the encampment, obviously a latrine. They motioned. I was supposed to do something. I hadn't had a controlled bowel movement or urination since being shot down. I felt no need, but I tried to piss anyway. Voila. Success. I peed.

Back at the interrogation spot beside the big tree, they sat me down. One of them brought a bowl of steaming rice with a spoon. Another loosened the ropes on my arms so I could eat, and I was given water. Someone slipped me a cigarette and gave me a light. When I'd finished, they resecured the ropes.

Later that morning my interrogator and his underling returned. The officer carried an important-looking canvas satchel. He took it off his shoulder, laid it down, and took a seat on a log a few feet away. He looked at me for a while before he said, "You are a war criminal."

That set me back. *What does he mean, war criminal? Is this leading to some sort of jungle trial?*

"You are a war criminal and the Geneva Agreements do not apply to you. You have no rights. But we will still give you the deserved humane and lenient treatment. All you have to do is cooperate with us and acknowledge your crimes."

I ranted silently to myself. *What the hell does that mean? I'm not acknowledging shit!* I said nothing.

"Do you know the two-thousand-year history of the Vietnamese people?"

I looked at him, trying to figure out where he was going with this. I said nothing.

"Vietnam has existed for thousands of years. We have always been a very independent people, but others have tried to conquer and rule us. The Chinese, the Mongols, the Cambodians, the Japanese, the French, and now you, the Americans. All have failed. You will fail."

He went on for at least an hour, beginning two thousand years ago and coming forward to today. He told of an ancient Chinese conquest of the land of Vietnam and went through a series of Vietnamese uprisings that again and again threw off the yoke of that giant neighbor to the north. First the Trung Sisters rode elephants into battle in AD 40 and initially succeeded, though their uprising was defeated within a few years by Chinese military might. The sisters committed suicide to avoid capture, and they remain national heroes. He boasted that their example ensures the equal treatment of women in Vietnamese society and in the army.

He lectured me on the series of uprisings that followed over the centuries. All succeeded for a time. But each eventually succumbed to the power of another conquering force. There was Lady Trieu, who also killed herself in defeat, and Ly Bon, Ngo Quyen, Dinh Bo Linh, Le Hoan, Tran Hung Dao, and Le Loi.

The story shifted to French colonization, Japanese occupation during the Second World War, and Ho Chi Minh's role in fighting the Japanese and his struggle to expel the French afterwards, a struggle for independence, he noted, that now continued against the Americans.

This is indoctrination, not interrogation, I thought. *What's his point with all this?*

The officer spent a good deal more time detailing the exploits of Tran Hung Dao and Le Loi, then Ho Chi Minh, Uncle Ho. Hung Dao was important because he defeated far superior, better-equipped Mongol forces with a much smaller army of volunteer peasants, common men. He did this by avoiding Mongol strengths and attacking their weakest points. Le Loi led a successful revolt, defeated the Chinese, instituted land reform, and united Vietnam as a state that would remain independent until French colonization. My tutor told me that Le Loi used a magical sword like King Arthur's.

At the end, he focused on Ho Chi Minh. Ho formed the Viet Minh, the Peoples' Army, fought the Japanese, and then defeated the French. He was helped by the United States Office of Strategic Studies (OSS), precursor of the CIA, during the Second World War. The Democratic Republic of Vietnam, fathered by Ho Chi Minh, would now defeat the United States.

My anger rose. I knew better. *Ho Chi Minh was a sorry communist bastard. He was trained in Moscow. He was a puppet of the Soviet Union. Inspired by communist China. Supplied by both. He's no nationalist hero. He was a communist dictator suppressing his people and trying to overthrow South Vietnam and take over all Southeast Asia to become part of the Soviet bloc. He murdered thousands of people. Bad guy!*

The session ended with a tirade against the United States war in Vietnam and the criminal acts being committed against the Vietnamese people. "You bomb hospitals and schools. You kill pregnant women, babies, and old people."

Trying both to educate and to shame me struck me as a pathetic attempt at amateur brainwashing. At that moment, in my miserable state, none of his propaganda was having any effect. The dull dribble of words barely registered in my consciousness. I must have appeared catatonic.

He politely asked if I understood all that he said. Did I have any questions? With equal politeness, he said that I would now be expected to at least offer some cooperation. He said, "I must remind you that you are a war criminal. You could have a trial and be punished. If you cooperate you will receive the humane and lenient treatment. You will go home soon."

He went into a lengthy explanation of why I was a war criminal. He listed the most unimaginable atrocities he claimed the United States was perpetrating on the good people of Vietnam. When he finished, he pulled some papers from his canvas case.

"Here, please sign this." He handed me one of the sheets of paper and a pen.

I looked at the paper. It was typed in English. As I began to read the words, my interrogator interrupted, "This is simply a form that acknowledges your status. We need it so we can begin to process you for release. So we can send word to your family of your status. Please just sign."

I read the words. I could not believe what I was reading. There was a blank place to fill in my name. The text said that I was an American war criminal who had been conducting illegal acts against the Vietnamese people, including biocide, genocide, and ecocide. I had dropped fire bombs and chemical bombs. I had killed old men, pregnant women, and babies.

Biocide? Genocide? Ecocide? What a bunch of crap.

I raised my head and looked into his eyes. "No. I will not sign this." There, I had spoken.

"You must."

"I will not."

His agitation now returned. "You must!"

I glared at him. He got up and came at me. He smacked me across the face. "You must."

He turned to his sidekick and spoke quietly, and the man got up. At his direction, two guards dragged me up against the broad trunk of a tree. I'd been bent over since the crash, unable to stand erect. They forced me up into a straight sitting position and tied me to the tree. It hurt like hell. I couldn't keep my face from contorting in anguish.

"Now you sign."

"No."

More orders. They pulled on the ropes to bring my arms closer together behind me. The pain in my back increased. New pain was introduced in my shoulder joints. More demands to sign. More refusals. The ropes tightened further. They moved my elbows closer together. More demands, more refusals, ropes ever tighter, more pain. I was uncontrollably grimacing and cursing. I would not sign. I could never consider signing anything like that. The brutality made me angrier and more firmly set against giving in. I could have been broken and made to sign eventually, there's no doubt. No man can resist forever. But this interrogator would not bring me to my breaking point on that day.

His demands continued, and so did my refusals. The ropes tightened more and more. Pain screamed through me. My anger swelled against this asshole. I began grunting, an audible attack against the agony. The guards gave the ropes one huge last pull, which brought my elbows together behind me. I felt a pop as each shoulder dislocated. Pain shot through my torso, up my neck into my head, and down my back, through my groin and onto my thighs. I'd never felt such pain. My vision narrowed, and I nearly passed out.

"Sign."

I could only groan and shake my head.

The interrogator scowled angrily, turned, and left. His sidekick hung around for a time watching me. He smiled. The ropes holding my elbows together stayed as they were. I was in agony, my shoulders out of their sockets.

The assistant left, and the guards loosened the ropes. My arms rolled forward again. Eventually they returned to the proper placement in their joints. The pain remained for weeks.

After a while, the guards brought water. Later they gave me some rice. Once I finished eating, they took me back to that same abysmal bunker. I spent another night lying in the muck in absolute darkness while jungle critters crawled about.

Am I going to die? I prayed, thought of Amy and my kids, Spencer and Vicki. I felt bad. No one had any idea where I was or what was happening. I fell asleep, my head filled with thoughts of family.

Morning came quickly. I woke up tired. I started to stretch but was caught short by the pain. In time, a guard lifted the logs from the entrance. He grabbed me and dragged me from the hole as I tried to get my feet under me. Once out in the morning light, I could see my interrogator. He told me to sit on the edge of a freshly dug trench with my feet hanging inside. It was about the size of a grave.

He began his harangue. "We have given you every opportunity to cooperate and receive the humane and lenient treatment of the Vietnamese people. You have refused. You have one last chance to answer my questions and sign the papers. You cannot refuse. We are good people, but we have no more patience. You have this one last chance to cooperate. Will you?"

My head hung down, partly in exhaustion and partly in intentional rudeness, not paying him any attention. I looked up when he finished. I saw his sadistic minion standing a few yards in front of me, holding an AK-47 rifle at the ready.

"Your last chance."

The assistant raised the rifle and pointed it at me. I stared ahead and said nothing. No heroism was involved. I was wrung out, at the end of everything I had to give. I'd been so close to death for so long, was so angry, and so absolutely drained. A faint spark was all I had left. I felt numb, detached from what was happening. I was not resisting. I was just giving in to the flow of whatever was destined to be. That might be death. It might not.

I had seen an Army training film years before showing the mock execution of a Korean War POW. I remembered that scene. The action of the trigger being pulled went over and over in my mind. *"Click, click, click."*

"Bân!" I flinched as the soldier jerked the trigger back, but nothing happened. No shot. No loud bang. No bullet ripping my skull or chest. Nothing.

The soldier laughed. My interrogator smiled.

"I am done with you. You will be taken away from here."

He reached into his pocket, pulled out a card, and handed it to me. It was not much bigger than a business card. I was amazed to see it printed in English with the following:

"You are in the care of the People's Army of Vietnam. You will receive humane and lenient treatment if you follow instructions. You are being moved to an area that is safe from American air and artillery strikes."

With that, he and his assistant turned and left.

CHAPTER 7

Go Quick or Die

Two North Vietnamese soldiers approached. They didn't say anything. I suspected neither spoke English.

What now? I wondered.

One tossed an old rice sack to the ground next to me. Two ropes, fixed to it, served as shoulder straps.

The other threw down my boots. No laces and no socks, just boots. I looked, waited for a moment, and then pulled them on and sat there. It seemed like what I was supposed to do. The soldier handed me a full NVA canteen.

The two glared, shouted something in Vietnamese, and gestured with their AK-47s to get up. I had no idea what they said, but I knew I was to haul this sack on a trip of indefinite duration to some unknown location. These two were my guards.

I stood. It hurt to put the straps over my shoulders and the crude pack onto my back. I could feel grains of uncooked rice inside shift and scrunch to conform to the bend in my spine. The pack seemed heavy, but then I was weak.

Rifle muzzles poked into my ribs. The guards pointed me toward a trail and commanded, "Đi. Đi!"

I took my first painful steps, stooped like a hunchback, on a journey that would lead me deep into a hell that I could never have imagined.

Each step fired bolts of pain down my back. The heavy sack of rice jarred my spine and hurt every inch of the way. Going downhill was worse. My feet slid inside my loose boots, and the leather rubbed against raw skin. I could feel my face twist in agony. *God damn,* I cried to myself. I bit my bottom lip, the top pressed hard against it. As I walked on, I fought every hint of self-pity. *I can do this. I will do this.*

The trail went up. It went down. We kept on. I was tired, weak, hurt. I kept walking. I thought about my family, about Amy. I thought more about my two kids, Spencer and Vicki. I imagined getting home at the end of all this. I would get home. I had to survive.

God, help me do this. I swore a hundred well-intended oaths, most never to be fulfilled. I've wondered what price I'll pay at the end of my days for so many broken promises to the almighty.

The day wore on. One guard walked in front of me, the other right behind. The one behind held his rifle at the ready, his finger close to the trigger. I had no thought of escape. I was in bad shape and was trying, with all I had, just to survive the day.

I went as far as I could will myself to go, and then went some more. As dusk settled, we began a series of switchbacks down a long, steep hillside. It was dark when we reached the bottom and stumbled into a small encampment. A dozen soldiers were there already. Cooking fires burned. Voices chattered. My guards made small talk and seemed to answer questions about me. We found an open spot near the center.

I collapsed. The guards boiled rice and some unknown greens. I tried to eat, but it was awful. I gagged down some of it but could eat no more. I lay in the dirt and went to sleep. The North Vietnamese slept in hammocks they tied between trees. I was hardly aware of my captors tying my hands together at the wrists. A longer rope secured me loosely to a tree next to where I lay on the ground. I slept soundly through the night.

I woke in the morning to the smell of cooking fires. One guard held a small bowl of rice in front of me with a spoon. The other fumbled at untying my wrists. I tried to eat the rice. I got only some of it down.

For the first time since being shot down, I felt like I had to shit. Up until then, my crap had run out of me at will. I'd had no control. Now I felt an urge.

"I've got to shit."

The guards looked at me, expressionless.

"I've got to shit." "Got to shit." "Go to the bathroom." I pointed at my ass and made a face of straining. They got it. One guard led me a short distance from the camp. The other tagged behind. He pointed his rifle in my direction. My feet screamed in pain, rubbed raw by my unlaced boots. I hobbled to the designated spot, dropped my flight suit pants, bent over, and spread my legs, and the deed was done. Under my breath, I muttered, "Hallelujah." My eyes filled with tears. A small positive thing had just happened.

The guard picked a couple of large leaves, made a wiping motion behind his butt, and handed them to me. I cleaned myself as best I could and pulled my underwear and pants back up. In the days ahead, I would learn to select the right leaves myself (large and not too coarse). This was how I would wipe myself for months.

Back in camp, I gathered from their gestures what I should do. I hoisted my pack on my shoulders. They did the same. We stepped out and began the second day of the trek. They wore Ho Chi Minh sandals made from the treads of old tires and rubber straps. I wore laceless boots on sockless feet. Throughout the day, my feet got worse. My back spasmed in pain. I was weak and tired quickly.

We moved downhill for an hour or so. I caught glimpses of a large mountain I knew well, Chu Mom Ray. We called it Big Mamma. It was massive, towering three to five thousand feet above any of the surrounding terrain.

We were moving south, headed to the west side of the big mountain. The trail eased into a broad basin. I thought it was the upper end of the Plei Trap Valley. Many a big fight had taken place here throughout the war.

This part of the valley was now nothing but defoliated tree spires and the dark skeletons of other vegetation. It had been poisoned and denuded by the aerial spraying of Agent Orange. It was surreal, a ghostly dead world unlike anything I'd ever seen.

The pathway scuffed into smoke-like billows as we walked. Dust covered us, and I choked as I breathed. We pressed on for a long time, silent, as if in mourning for the earth that had died around us.

We came to a dirt road and turned to follow it up out of the valley to the west. Tire tracks showed that there was heavy use of the road at night. Nothing moved on it during the day, nothing but us, two North Vietnamese soldiers and their American prisoner staggering up the steep hillside. The international border with Cambodia was at the top.

The guards sensed the nearness of sanctuary and pressed me to move swiftly. They had been saying a phrase for the past two days that I couldn't understand. I thought it was Vietnamese. "Gawk wik odai." As we pushed up the road, they walked behind me, poking their rifle barrels hard into my kidneys and ribs, shouting with increasing urgency, "Gawk wik odai. Gawk wik odai."

Then, for the first time, I understood what they were saying: "Go quick or die." They had been taught one short phrase in English. It was all they knew, and they had pronounced it so poorly that it took me two days to figure it out. I moved as fast as I could, but I was about at the end of everything I had. I struggled on.

The road snaked its way up a hillside shredded by bomb craters. Repair crews, working all night and hiding in the jungle by day, kept it open. I knew exactly where we were. Air strikes hit this area frequently. My guards wanted to get through it fast and cross into Cambodia. They pressed me hard. "Go quick or die."

About three-quarters of the way to the top, we heard the screech of diving U.S. jets, and my guards started running, dragging me with them as fast as I could move.

The first bombs hit close. We ran. A few yards farther on, cut into the bank, was a bunker entrance. They pushed me through the L-shaped passage and pressed in behind me. We crammed together in the small space. The air was dank, stuffy, and hard to breathe.

Being a few feet underground would protect us from fragments of bombs that fell nearby. I had no confidence, however, that we would survive a direct hit. I don't think my guards did either. I could feel their fear as we all three pressed closely against each other in that hole.

I found myself mentally reciting what I could recall of the 23rd Psalm. I repeated one line over and over in my head. *Yea, though I walk through the valley of the shadow of death, I will fear no evil; for thou art with me.* That wasn't the only time during my captivity that the 23rd Psalm came to my lips.

The earth trembled at each load of bombs. When the strike ended, all was quiet, all was still.

We crawled out into the lingering smoke and stench of explosives. The ruptured landscape was freshly convulsed by the new attacks. The roadway was demolished. It would be repaired again that night.

I pushed myself up the hill along the devastated roadway. The guards wanted to move quickly. I went as fast as I could. We crested the top of the ridge, where a crude sign on the left must have marked the Cambodian border. My guards seemed to relax as we crossed.

We left the world of churned earth. We walked on a well-kept, fairly level dirt road crossing a plateau. Big trees and lush vegetation overhung the roadway. The well-manicured trees interwove their branches to provide cover, while sunlight filtered through the foliage. The beauty and the clever camouflage captivated me. It looked like a lovely country lane, totally concealed from the air.

I stumbled on. My back screamed with pain, my raw feet burned, and thirst consumed me. My canteen was long empty. We crossed a small stream, and I pleaded for a drink. One of the few Vietnamese words I knew was water, "nước."

One guard pantomimed stomach cramps and sickness. I got the message, but I didn't care. I begged and he caved. I fell to the stream and gulped my fill. I got up and we continued.

We came to a truck park. Half a dozen trucks were pulled into dugout positions among the trees on the side of the road. They waited to run supplies into Vietnam during the night. One guard stayed with me while the other walked among the vehicles looking for the person in charge. He talked to few of the drivers and then came back. He spoke with the other guard before leading me to one of the trucks. We climbed in the back, the engine started, and we drove down the road in the same direction we'd been walking. After jolting along for some distance, we pulled off into an impressive-looking military camp.

Well-built structures crafted of split bamboo and tree limbs covered several acres. Each sat on stilts a few feet off the ground. A network of neatly tended pathways connected the dozens of buildings. Communications wires rising from one of the huts headed in different directions. The wires ran along tree trunks, fastened about fifteen feet above the ground. The camp exuded military efficiency, a headquarters of some importance.

I was taken to an empty hut. The bamboo-matted floor was clean, and for the first time I felt how filthy I had become. My wretched unwashed body was caked in blood, dried mud, and dirt. My unkempt hair fell over a face covered with more than a week's growth of scruffy stubble. My flight suit stunk of absorbed sweat, shit, and piss. I was a mess. A soldier (I suspected an officer) joined my guards and motioned for me to sit down on the clean floor. I did so with pain. I felt embarrassed over my filthy state.

Someone brought a bowl of rice. The officer took it, handed it to me, and said, "Ăn com. Eat."

My head raised and my eyes widened at the English word. I took the rice. Again, after a few bites, I began to struggle.

The officer spoke again. "You must eat or you will die. You must eat." I forced down the rice. I gagged, but I ate it all.

The next morning I ate more rice, and then my two guards and I climbed into the back of a truck and drove on. A few hours later we were let out at a road intersection. My torn feet screamed as we climbed out. We walked along the other road for a couple of miles. It began to rain and the dirt turned to muddy, oily goo. I was soaked. Even in the tropical heat, I felt chilled. The soldiers pulled plastic ponchos from their packs and stayed dry.

We left the road and moved onto a steep trail down a long hill. I slipped and fell several times in the slick mud, causing my guards to bark at me for my clumsiness until one of them fell. After that, they kept silent.

Near the bottom, the jungle opened into an expanse of grass and bamboo. I saw something among the trees on the other side, but I couldn't make out what it was until we got closer. An enclosure stood there like the wooden stockade surrounding an old cavalry post on the American frontier. Instead of being made of wooden posts, this stockade was made of tall bamboo poles lashed together. I could see a number of towers along the top of the bamboo wall.

We headed toward the entrance, a break in the stockade. Someone in one of the towers shouted to my guards. They answered. An NVA soldier came out of the camp and joined us as we continued toward the opening.

When we got to the entrance, I could see two concentric walls, one within the other, about ten feet apart. A moat had been dug between the two walls. The bottom of the dry moat, eight feet deep, was lined with punji stakes, pieces of bamboo sharpened on both ends. One end was dipped in human waste and the other was driven upright into the ground. A person who fell into the moat would not only be impaled by the sharp stakes, but his wounds would become horribly infected.

A single log, flattened along the top edge, bridged the moat at the entrance. We didn't slow down. I was weak and my back hurt. My feet were raw and bloody, my legs were tired, and I'd been stumbling. My balance was gone, but I was expected to continue walking right across that log. I worried about falling onto the punji stakes below. I thought of running the bayonet course in basic training. We'd had to cross logs to get to a life-sized dummy on the other side of a ditch to thrust our bayonets into it, screaming, "Kill!" The drill sergeants told us to look at the far side of the log and keep moving. "Don't slow down. Don't stop or you'll fall off."

I looked at the far side and didn't stop. I got across.

I was inside a prison camp. The jungle floor within the camp had been cleared away, but several gigantic trees remained, providing a canopy that extended over the entire camp. I was surprised by its size.

Bamboo cages spread out before me, some tiny, many others quite large, none very high. In the bad light, pairs of eyes set in gaunt, hollow faces peered out as I walked by.

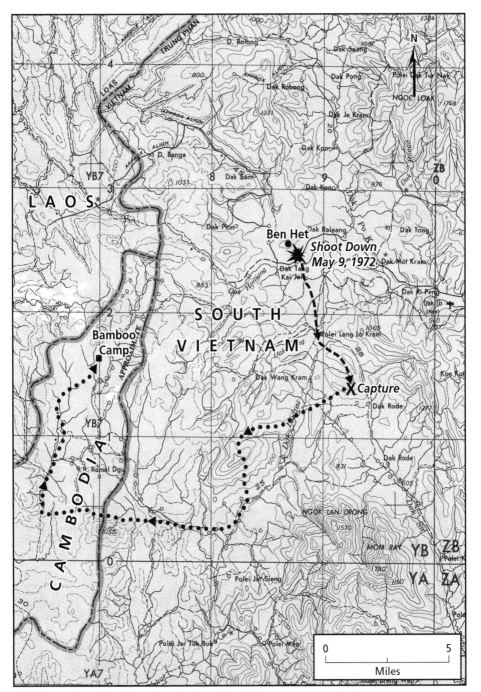

Map 3. Nine days in May—from Ben Het to jungle prison

We stopped in front of one cage and the door opened. A guard pushed me in and I stumbled over someone lying inside and fell, tumbling to the ground. Pain shot through me.

The cage was about twelve feet wide and twenty or so feet long. It could not have been more than four feet high. Twenty-six prisoners were stuffed inside, all South Vietnamese soldiers. Heat hung in the cage, heavy and stale. The air smelled of filth and putrid wounds. People moaned in a constant dull rumble. The occasional wail was met with sharp shushes and guarded whispers. The doorway was shut and secured. I lay there, thankful I'd survived the journey of the past three days. What would become of me now?

CHAPTER 8

Bamboo Camp

The prison camp, somewhere in the jungles of northern Cambodia, was free from routine air strikes and ground combat operations. The United States had gone into the border areas of Cambodia for a short time in 1970 to clean out communist sanctuaries. That caused riots across America and the tragedy at Kent State University. After that, combat operations in Cambodia were limited to special operations missions like those I'd flown with SOG. I knew if Americans ever found out about this POW camp, our special ops guys would be here in a flash to get us out. I also knew that our location would almost certainly never be discovered. I was going to be here for a very long time.

I lay among the prisoners inside the cage, waiting to see what would happen next. I asked quietly, "Does anyone speak English?"

"Shhh."

"I am an American. Does anyone speak English?"

"Shhh!"

The guy on the far side of me briefly put his hand on my arm and gave me a reassuring pat. He pulled his hand away quickly as we heard a noise at the doorway. The bamboo door opened. A uniformed NVA soldier came in with a hammer and chisel. He pulled my boots off and threw them outside.

I thought, *Oh my God. They're going to cut the bottom of my feet with a chisel to make escape impossible.*

The soldier barked something. Someone outside untied a wrap of twine and raised the upper half of a log that ran along the earthen floor, the length of the center of the cage. For the first time, I realized that all the prisoners in the cage had their feet in this giant wooden stock. Holes had been cut for their ankles. The holes in front of where I was lying were too small for me.

The soldier went to work with the hammer and chisel to make the holes larger for my big American legs. When he was done, he picked up my feet and laid them across the log. He checked that all prisoners' ankles were in place before ordering the stocks closed. The top of the log lowered and was tied fast outside the cage. The soldier left and the door was shut and secured.

The guy next to me whispered, "We no can talk. Bad thing if we catch talking." He paused. "You be OK."

I asked very quietly, "Where were you captured?"

He was afraid, but he whispered to me, "Some capture at Tan Canh. Other place too. Me at Firebase Charlie. Shot in chest. Not do good."

A blood-soaked bandage covered his sucking chest wound. Every time he breathed, air came into his chest through the hole, which made breathing inefficient. The bullet was still in his chest. The wound hurt. He labored for every bit of air.

"I Duc," he muttered.

"I'm Captain Reeder. Captain Bill Reeder."

"Reeto. OK, Dai úy Reeto." He hushed. We heard footsteps approaching.

Someone opened the door. I cringed. They handed a large piece of bamboo filled with water into the cage. A prisoner took it, tipped it up, and took a drink. He passed the vessel around. Everyone got some. As he handed it to me, the guy next to me whispered, "Water boiled. It OK." The last man placed the nearly empty container in the far corner of the cage.

A short time later the door opened again. This time, a guy handed in grapefruit-sized balls of rice. The door stayed open until we each had a rice ball. Then it closed.

I ate but had little interest. Again I forced down all that I could. I passed my leftovers to Duc. He'd already finished his and quickly devoured what was left of mine. He smiled through the pain and anguish on his dirt-smeared face.

It grew late. Everyone in the cage was silent, each absorbed in his own thoughts. An occasional whimper of pain or despair burst out. I was never sure which it was, from one groan to another.

Someone came close in the darkness holding a piece of wood with a glowing ember on one end. There was a shuffling among the prisoners in the cage. I couldn't tell what was going on until I saw a guy rolling a cigarette. The rustling sounds I heard were prisoners reaching into their pockets or hiding places for pieces of paper and any tobacco they had. I would find out later that some guards doled out a little bit of tobacco on occasion. This first evening, I had none.

The man with the stick stuck the ember through the bamboo lattice-work of the sides of the cage in a number of places. Prisoners lit cigarettes from it. Soon everyone with tobacco was smoking and sharing with others who had none. Their expressions became dreamy in the glow of the ember as they inhaled the smoke, a brief respite from the horror of their existence. Each smoked his homemade cigarette to a nub. One by one, they lay back and fell asleep.

Duc took a few drags from his carefully crafted cigarette and passed it to me, wet with his saliva. I put it in my lips and sucked in the delicious smoke. I held it in my lungs for a long moment and then exhaled. I tried to pass the cigarette back to Duc. He shook his head. I finished it.

My broken back screamed every time I tried to lie down. With my feet in the stocks, there was no way I could lay on my side. I couldn't lay straight back, so I sat upright in the dark in agony. I thought of my family, thought of my day, of where I'd been, where I was now, and what might lie ahead. I hurt badly. Still, I had hope. *I can live this way. I can do this. I can survive. I will survive.*

I sat there, thoughts drifting across the landscape of my life, shaped by these extraordinary circumstances. Eventually I fell asleep, sitting upright that night, dreaming of what might become of me.

I jolted awake. Something scampered across my legs. Something was on my feet. Something small, cool, and wet touched my arches and soles.

Little rat noses poked and sniffed my feet. Tiny teeth gnawed my pulverized raw flesh. My arms swung without command as I batted a large rat off my lap. Others scurried away. I screamed inside, lips pressed tightly shut, a muffled shriek of terror. I thrashed. My legs flailed but went nowhere. I wiggled my feet as well as I could in the stocks and got the rats off. They fled into the night, only to return when I fell back asleep. They would return to torment me nearly every night in that jungle prison.

Morning came, and with it the urge to pee. I had to go bad. I squirmed and made a face and gesture to Duc, who was already awake.

"Got to piss," I whispered to him. "Go to bathroom. Use toilet."

He said something softly that was repeated quietly across the cage. Someone passed a bamboo tube over to piss in. It wasn't easy from my sitting position, but I got it done. I handed the bamboo urinal back. It was passed to a guy who carefully stuck the end outside the cage and let the contents flow onto the ground.

We sat for hours, lost in thought. About midmorning, a guy approached our cage with a basket of rice balls and handed them inside. I had my second meal in the camp. I couldn't stand the rice, but made myself eat it.

We sat for hours more. My cage-mates, all ARVNs, appeared a ragtag crew. Almost everyone had been wounded, some gravely. Filth covered their tattered uniforms. The whole place stunk of sweat, blood, infection, feces, and urine. We all were hurting, and some would die. Some cautiously whispered to their neighbor. Most, like me, just sat and stared. That's what I did. I sat and stared at them sitting and staring at nothing. I wondered if I would go crazy here. Would I die here? What would happen first, insanity or death?

I snapped back to what little grasp I had on reality. *Hold it together. Focus. Spence and Vicki. We'll hike. We'll play. Get back home for those kids. You can do it. You can endure.*

I couldn't allow my thoughts to drift in dark directions. I forced myself into logical, structured thinking. I began planning a hiking trip with my family, a backpacking trip into the woods. I planned the route, the equipment loads for each. They'd be feather light for Vicki, a little more for Spence and Amy. I'd carry most of it. We'd eat dehydrated food cooked around a small campfire. *Delicious!*

"Đi đi vệ sinh!" a soldier called out as he came up to our cage. He opened the door and raised the split log. Everybody sat up straight and then raised their legs out of the open stocks. I did the same. My neighbor said softly, "We go shit now."

The guard barked, "Đừng nói chuyện! NO TALK!" He thrust his raised finger menacingly toward us. I got up with difficulty, partly stood, hunched over in the small space. We stumbled from the cage and marched single file toward one corner of the camp under the eye of the guards. As we moved through the camp, I got a good look at the prison compound.

Set on uneven ground, the stockade formed an irregular circle around the perimeter. Near the middle of the compound, one hut served as the kitchen. Inside, fire pits were dug into an earthen mound, vented from the back to reduce the possibility of heat detection by aircraft sensors. I don't know if the idea worked or not, but the camp had not been found.

A few dozen cages of different sizes and configurations were scattered around the compound, no two alike. They looked like they'd been constructed over time as more prisoners came into the camp.

The camp provided a miserable existence on the edge of madness. All was filth and disease and suffering. Moans and wails of pain and anguish cried from the enclosures as we walked by. I caught glimpses of sick and wounded men inside cage after cage, their eyes white orbs of desperation, peering from grimy faces through the din of the gray world inside.

I shuddered when we approached the area set aside for our business. The dying were collected by the open latrine lying in sorry hammocks strung between trees, a few steps from where they could squat and let the dysentery erupt from their bowels. The ones who didn't have the strength to rise from their hammocks lay in their own foul waste as they died.

Duc, shuffling just behind me, moved up close and said in a loud whisper, "All here die. They die very soon. They all die."

The dying prisoners left piles of shit all around the area, creating an enormous mound. They couldn't make it more than a few steps from their hammocks. Some of our group continued up onto the mound. I stopped at the edge, lowered my pants, and began to squat. A guard screamed and threatened me with his rifle. He motioned me to continue onto the heap of crap with the others, while railing in disgust what I took to be something like "filthy American pig."

I held my pant legs up and waded into the mess. I began gagging as I squished, open sores on my feet, through foul fecal muck. In the middle, I joined the others squatting over one of the few narrow deep holes, the official prisoners' latrine. No leaves remained in the area for wiping. They'd been picked and used long ago.

We returned to our cage with no way to clean ourselves. We stooped back inside the doorway, went to our spots, and put our filth-covered feet in the stocks. The log was lowered and the door shut and secured. Our daily outing was done. We would get out again sometime the next day. Any prisoner who couldn't accommodate his needs to the randomly changing camp schedule would have to crap in his pants in the cage, dealing with the disgusting situation as best he could. Sanitation was impossible.

The next meal came in the late afternoon. We got two meals of grapefruit-sized balls of rice each day, one in the middle of the morning and one in the afternoon. That was it. Someone delivered a bamboo tube of water at least a couple of times a day. We got to use the latrine once a day for a few minutes. That was the daily routine.

Badly wounded prisoners received minimal treatment, nothing more. Most of us were sick and got no care and no medication. Prisoners struggled to live. Some died. Just about every day, at least one body was carried from the camp for burial on the hillside outside the camp.

Sitting there, wounded, in stocks, in a bamboo cage, in an unknown jungle prison camp, with death all around me, I began to wonder, *How long can I endure this?* Then my voice said out loud, "As long as it takes."

I figured there must be close to three hundred prisoners in the camp, mostly South Vietnamese soldiers and some Montagnard tribesmen. Duc told me there was another American in the camp. I hadn't seen him.

One afternoon, a huge spider crawled up the inside of our cage. A prisoner grabbed it and played with it for hours, torturing the poor creature. Others laughed. I thought it was sick.

Our cigarette lighter, the guy with the glowing ember, came that evening. Duc had given me some tobacco and a small piece of paper. I did a shabby job constructing a cigarette, and my little rollup was coming apart. I licked the paper, held it tightly together in my fingers, waiting for my light.

The hot stick pushed into the cage. The guy playing with the spider put it on top of the glowing end of the stick. He left it for a few seconds, then gingerly lifted the roasted creature from the stick. He jiggled it in his hands, letting it cool. He took a bite, smiled, and passed it to a few guys close by. Others, not among the chosen few, groaned. I didn't get any, which was fine with me.

I sat there and fell asleep. In the night, rats woke me up again, gnawing my feet. I fought them off. As each evening passed, I became more terrified of the revolting creatures.

"Reet. Reet," a soldier outside the cage hollered as he opened the door. Another undid the twine and raised the log. I pulled my feet out of the stocks and stumbled outside. One grabbed my arm as I came out. He led me along a path inside the perimeter fence, up a short hill, and into a small hut. A neatly dressed soldier was seated behind a table. A bench stood in front.

"Sit, Reeto."

I was surprised to hear English. I sat on the bench.

"Please have tea." He poured from a small pot into a metal Army cup and handed it to me. I sipped the tea and listened.

"We have talk. It is good. You call me *bộ đội*. That mean soldier. You call all soldiers from People's Army *bộ đội*." He paused. "You know history of Vietnam people?"

"Yes, I do."

He stumbled through the story anyway, struggling with broken English, laboring to form sentences and find the right words. I interrupted him. "I know the history very well, thank you."

He frowned at me, but softened.

"I give news from war," he said. I waited for him to continue. "Yesterday, heroic people of Vietnam shoot down more than one hundred U.S. airplane. They kill one thousand U.S. and puppet soldier."

That was total bullshit, I knew, but I kept quiet.

He pulled an American military identification card from a folder, holding it so I could see it. "You know this man?" It was the card of Specialist Ed Wong, who had gone missing when Larry Woods' helicopter was shot down by Firebase Charlie.

"What happened to him?" I asked.

"You know him?"

"No, but I'm curious. What happened to him?" I got no answer. I assumed he must be dead.

"Cigarette?" He pulled a red and tan pack of factory-made cigarettes from his pocket and put them on the table. "Take one." He handed me a book of matches. I took a cigarette, lit it, and inhaled deeply, enjoying the quality tobacco.

He let me smoke for a minute before he said, "Now you write." He pushed a pencil and small booklet toward me.

"I will not write." I looked at him, expecting beatings and torture again. His face became red. He groped for words. "You go back. We talk later. You think. You write." He grabbed the pack of cigarettes and matches and left. He was frustrated and angry, but not violent. His crappy English helped me play stupid. This was not the end of it, though. He would pull me out of my cage every few days to repeat the process.

After I'd been in the camp about a month, I woke up one morning and looked over at Duc lying beside me. Something was odd, and it scared me. I knew it, but I couldn't believe it. Dreading what I had to confirm, I touched his arm and shook him. I whispered, "Duc?" He didn't move. His face looked like chalk under layers of dirt. He was stiff, dead. His struggle was over. I shuddered. I'd lost my only friend. Later that morning, his body was carried out for burial. I sat, staring at nothing, my world upended.

That afternoon, a guard got me from the cage and marched me halfway across the camp, where we stopped in front of another, much smaller, cage. He opened the door and motioned me in. I crawled inside, pausing in the entrance. I saw a gaunt, pale figure in front of me. I stared at him for a moment. He was an American. He looked awful.

"Hey. I'm Wayne. Wayne Finch," he said.

"Hi. Bill Reeder. I'd heard there was another American."

"Yeah, me. Been here for—"

The guard shoved me the rest of the way inside. The stocks rose. I put my feet into the holes next to Wayne's. These holes were already big enough for my American ankles. The stocks lowered. The door closed and I looked around.

The cage was tiny, only four other prisoners inside. Wayne introduced me. The man on the other side of him was an ARVN lieutenant, an Army doctor. He'd been a battalion surgeon. Next to me was a young ARVN paratrooper. An older Montagnard man, wiry and muscular in spite of his weeks, maybe months, of imprisonment, sat at the end of the cage. He was nearly naked except for the cloth wrapped round his loins. *Strange bedfellows,* I thought. *What an odd mix of humanity.*

I whispered, "It's OK to talk?"

Wayne answered, "Yeah. We've been together for a week. No one has stopped us."

"Wow. We caught shit in the other cage."

"Yeah, I did too. But not here."

I asked, "How long you been captured?"

"Two and half months. Captured on 30 March."

"How you doing?"

"OK. Had some problems at first, but doing all right now. How about you?

"OK." I breathed in and thought about it. "My back hurts. My feet hurt. I'm weak. I feel like shit. But doing OK."

He studied me, looking me over. His eyes scanned my body and settled on my face.

"How were you captured?"

"Cobra pilot, shot down at Ben Het on 9 May. Front-seater was rescued. Evaded for three days. Captured working my way down the side of a hill. Jungle was thick as shit. Couldn't see a thing. But they heard me." I paused, shrugged. "Had the crap beat out of me for three days, marched another three days to here. Been here for several weeks. Not sure. I've totally lost track of days."

Wayne said, matter-of-factly, "It's Tuesday, June 16th."

I was impressed. "How have you kept track since you were captured?"

"I didn't. Didn't know what day it was for a long time. Finally got it from one of the guards who isn't as mean as the others. He'll come by and give us tobacco sometimes. He's the best of them. Most'd just as soon beat the crap out of you. No love for Americans." He made a face. "Try to remember the day. Should be easier from here."

We talked for a long time. Like me, Wayne was married, but he had no kids. He was from the Alabama Gulf Coast, where his father worked in the oil industry. He'd say, "When I get out of this, I'm gonna get a boat and be a shrimp fisherman out of Bayou La Batre. The most beautiful place on earth." Wayne had been a scout pilot in B Troop, 7/17th Cavalry at Camp Holloway. He'd been flying a Loach when he was shot down, an OH-6 light observation helicopter, the same as Jim Stein, the gutsy scout pilot I'd covered on that dark night extraction mission in early May. At Camp Holloway, I'd heard that Jim had replaced the guy who had been shot down and was missing in action. We'd all heard about the incident. That was Wayne. Now here we sat together. Crazy world.

Wayne told me his shoot-down story. "So, I had a young observer. When we flew over a bunker complex, I asked if he got it on the map. He hadn't seen it. I turned the helo around, circled back over, came to a hover, pointed and said, 'There's the bunker complex. Right there.' The whole world erupted. We got shot down."

Wayne continued, "Think he got rescued. Heard him going up the hill. Couldn't follow, exactly. I had pieces of Plexiglas and blood in my eyes. Couldn't see. Wandered right into the enemy. I heard helicopters come in farther up the hill. Think they got him. Blackwood. Specialist Blackwood. Hope he's OK."

"Yeah, they got him out. You were the only casualty from that incident."

Things were better in the new cage. I had another American to talk to, a friend. The ARVN doctor turned out to be a talkative turd. The paratrooper next to me didn't speak much English, but he was able to make me understand that he was a gung-ho soldier who hated the communist NVA. The Montagnard was older, maybe in his sixties. He was quiet, mystical. I sensed a meditative spirit and wisdom about him. I felt comfort in his presence.

Wayne worried about my condition. I was in sorry shape. We talked a lot at first, but over time we settled into a routine of sitting, staring into nothingness, losing ourselves in long naps. I daydreamed a lot. I would daydream about what I'd do when I got home. I dreamed of getting home to Amy, Spencer, and Vicki, of hiking, backpacking, and camping with them. I began designing a house in my mind, every detail of every room. The process would continue throughout my captivity. And food. I thought of food every single day. I dreamed of particular dishes and whole meals. I put together menus for whole days. I strung days together into weeks. It was torture, but it felt so good. I was starving but would delight in savory thoughts of food. I could make myself taste flavors in the saliva around the base of my tongue, while hunger pangs tormented my gut.

I tried to stay hopeful. Still, gloom settled over the camp like a dank fog pushing our spirits down. Shadows of despair lurked in our minds. I fought hard not to let hope slip from my grasp. Each day became more difficult than the last in this hell.

One day I returned from another NVA indoctrination session feeling particularly low.

"What happened?" Wayne asked.

I answered, "No cigarettes. No tea. Not even hot water. Just grief."

"What kind of grief?"

"He wants me to write. I refuse. He gets less patient each time."

Wayne looked at me for a moment, then said, "Go ahead and write. I've been writing for a while. I don't see anything wrong so long as you don't give them anything they can use against our guys or for propaganda."

"You really think it's OK."

"Sure."

Next time I got called out, I took the booklet and pencil and wrote something trivial about life. My North Vietnamese minder wasn't happy with what I wrote, but he was thrilled that I had written something. I received cigarettes and tea that day, with promises of toothpaste when my writing became more enlightened. I never got toothpaste.

I wanted to escape. We could not survive forever under these conditions. Wayne and I worked out a plan. Wayne would put something next to his ankles when they opened the stocks. That way, when they closed it, the log would not clamp tightly on our ankles. We could slip them out, undo some of the lashings in the wall of our cage, push open a hole, and we'd be out.

We had seen a gap under the fence where it crossed a small creek that flowed through one corner of the camp. We could squeeze under it on a dark night. The only decision remaining was whether to travel east back toward Pleiku, or make the long trek westward toward Thailand. We favored going west.

Wayne insisted we wait. He thought I was too frail to make it. My injuries needed time to heal. My wounded ankle was swollen with a low-grade infection, my feet still hurt, and my back ached. I had lost so much weight, it frightened me to see my bare arms or legs. I had to mend and get stronger. We decided to wait, but we would go. We had to. We'd be dead in months if we stayed where we were.

As the days went by, I wondered about the Montagnard tribesman in our cage. He was silent except when muttering occasional words of encouragement. I assumed he spoke only a few words of English. I was wrong.

One day, when I was feeling particularly poorly, he turned toward me and said, "You find strength in our ways."

"What?" I replied, surprised.

"You find strength in our ways, power from the spirits of my people."

I looked at him in wonder. He was one with the jungle, all the elements of the wild within him. He represented a state of mankind that we all shared millennia ago. His being in this cage seemed so wrong, even more tragic than my being here. He was meant to roam free in this jungle, his home. As he spoke, I sensed a special aura about him. I said, "Tell me. I'd like to know."

In surprisingly good but strongly accented English, he began a tale. I listened in awe.

"I Sedang. We one tribe of what you say Montagnard. Vietnamese say Moi. Mean savage. Nine tribe in highlands. All different. We are one. Live in mountains here." He moved his arms in a big arc. "Relation to Bahnar tribe. Also not far." He pointed in the distance. "Have many spirits. Some good. Some bad. Kiak and Ong. You use good spirit. They help. Take care from bad spirit. Some very bad. They are demon. Some eat own liver. Some have swords for arms. They find you. Take your *mahua*, your soul. You torment forever." Now he frowned earnestly. "Must capture and kill enemy for bad demon ghosts. Keep demon away. Kill enemy with crossbow or knife. Big ceremony with dead enemy give to demon. Keep bad ghosts away."

I listened, perplexed. "How can this help me? I have no dead enemy to sacrifice."

"Good fight bad. Use this. Many good spirit. Dead people spirit from family. Spirit of lightning, water, rice. Most powerful, Mountain Spirit and Sun Spirit. Mountain Spirit give strength. Look at mountain. Take strength. Look to Sun. He protect you. Most good of all spirit, Sun."

He went on to tell me about his people, their culture, how they lived in their remote villages. Families lodged in longhouses, raised up on stilts. Each house accommodated scores of extended family members, sometimes more than a hundred. Young men and older boys did not live with their families. They slept in a large communal structure near the center of the village. There they stayed until they paired in marriage and went to live in a family's longhouse. The central communal house was also used for special meals and all village ceremonies. He went on about the ceremonies, the dances, the demons, the ghosts, and the spirits that filled his mystical world.

The Montagnard told me how his people hated the Vietnamese. In ancient times, the Viet migrations had pushed the indigenous populations into the mountains. Battles had been fought. He spoke angrily of the low regard the Vietnamese held for the tribes. There was also warfare among the tribes, the taking of slaves, even incidents of human sacrifice in years past.

I had to ask, "Did you ever fight for the Americans?"

He beamed and sat more erect. "Yes, I fight with Special Forces for many years. We kill many VC." As old as he looked, I suspected his fighting days ended some time ago.

"My village friends with Americans. Young men fight with Special Forces in Kontum. VC no like us. Kill many. Take some prisoner. Men and women. Village no more. All destroy." Hatred seared his face. I figured he was using the term VC to refer to both the Viet Cong guerrillas as well as the regular North Vietnamese Army (NVA) forces that held us captive.

Then he went on. "VC like tiger. He hunt you. He catch you. He eat you. Not always. Sometime you lift head and stare into face of tiger. Sometime he no eat you. He eat somebody else. He no eat you. You live. No one know why. Tiger not eat us. We lucky. Maybe." Indeed, I had looked into the face of the beast. The tiger could have eaten me any time over the past weeks. I had stared into the tiger's face. He had stared back. For some reason, he hadn't eaten me. I had prevailed, so far. *Of course, the tiger could be just saving us for a later meal*, I thought but didn't say.

The Montagnard was done. He held his knowing gaze on me for a moment, and then slumped, looking down. He never addressed me in that way again. I had been blessed, though, to have had that vision of a wise native elder, maybe an outright magical and holy shaman of the Sedang.

I looked past Wayne. The ARVN doctor sneered his disbelief. I could tell he didn't like Montagnards by the dismissive way he always dealt with our cage-mate. His racist attitude emphasized his arrogance and weak character. He never did anything to help anyone, certainly none of us in the cage. He played mind games, always asking stupid trivial questions and being happy anytime someone couldn't answer. At such moments, he'd boast about his knowledge. The asshole badmouthed the American effort in Vietnam and talked up the benefits of communism. He had caved quickly to the indoctrination efforts of the enemy. I never had any use for the sorry son of a bitch.

I sensed that a degree of the doctor's negativity was rubbing off on Wayne. I tried not to let it affect me, but this guy could get to you. Wayne became more pessimistic as time wore on. He was withdrawn, sometimes for days. He would get very depressed when we'd see bodies carried out of camp. He worried about getting sick. More than once, he said, "If we ever get malaria, we'll die. These guys live here, and they can't survive it." The mosquitoes were thick. We had reason to worry, but not to admit defeat before a fight.

Wayne and I weren't the only ones plotting escape. One night we heard a lot of shouting and screaming followed by several volleys of gunfire.

"They try escape," whispered the ARVN paratrooper.

We heard screams and moans throughout the night. At first light, I peered out of the cage. I could see people lashed to trees, tied to the trunks several feet off the ground, some barely alive, others obviously dead. The airborne soldiers captured at Firebase Charlie had fought bravely. Almost all of them were wounded. They had survived and endured captivity. With great courage they tried to escape, but they had failed. Now they hung on trees like so much rotting meat.

I looked at Wayne. He looked at me. We said nothing. We had our own thoughts about our escape plan, our hopes for success and fears of failure. Now those fears darkened our minds. *Is all hope lost?* I wondered.

Those paratroopers hung on the trees for days, their suffering an example to all who would think of trying such a desperate and foolish act. When the guards finally cut them down, they took the dead to the hillside and buried them. Those still alive returned to their cages. Some died later.

It was several days before Wayne and I talked of escape again. We had to try after I got a little stronger. We wouldn't survive these conditions forever. We waited for the right time.

That day would never come.

CHAPTER 9

The Journey Begins

The next morning, after our ball of rice, two guards stood in front of our cage. One commanded, "Reet, Fin!" The other unlashed the tie down and opened the stocks. Wayne and I pulled our feet out, crawled over to the doorway, and hobbled outside.

One guard led us to the center of the camp, where we stood in front of the kitchen area, joined by a couple dozen South Vietnamese prisoners. The ARVN doctor from our cage stumbled toward us, half dragged by one of the guards.

They lined us up. Wayne stood in front of me, near the middle. A guard went down the line, tying our arms loosely behind our backs. Another tied us to one another with a long piece of rope so there were four to six feet between prisoners. A dozen guards in fresh uniforms with bulky rucksacks carrying AK-47 rifles at the ready joined us. Talking excitedly with one another, they eyed us strangely.

One of the guards was the NVA soldier whose lame tries at interrogation and indoctrination had so annoyed me during my weekly sessions. I felt he hated me even though he tried to act polite as part of his indoctrination technique. His name was Dzu.

After being tied, we each got an old rice bag with ropes fixed to the corners, a sort of pitiful rucksack. They weren't heavy. A guard barked a command. The South Vietnamese prisoners turned and faced him. Wayne and I did too. The guard said something in Vietnamese. The prisoner beside Wayne spoke. "He say translate to you. Tell you what he say." I nodded and waited.

The guard began. "Điêu kiện xâu trong trại này. Chúng tôi sẽ chuyên ban dén một vị trí mới. Chúng tôi là về để tham gia vào một cuộc hành trình dài."

"He say we go far."

"Chúng tôi sẽ đi đến một trại mới tốt hon nhiều, đó là ở môt vi trí tốt hon nhiều với nước sạch và các điều kiện sức khỏe."

"He say we go to new camp."

"Bạn sẽ nhận được chăm sóc y tế tại trại mới. Bạn sẽ nhận được thư, gói, từ nhà. Ban sẽ được phép viết thu cho những người bạn yêu thương. Bạn sẽ nhân duoc nhung món an ngon với lúa gạo, rau quả tươi, cá và thịt."

"Things better there. Get mail and package from home. Can write letter. Get better food and get med-sin."

"Đây sẽ là một hành trình khó khăn. Nó có thể mất chừng mười một ngày. Bạn phải mạnh mẽ. Cuộc hành trình sẽ dễ dàng hơn cho bạn như mỗi ngày qua đi. Ban phải manh mẽ. Bạn phải cố gắng rất nhiều đê làm cho nó."

"Could take eleven days. Try hard to make it."

Wayne and I both nodded. I said, "OK."

No one got his boots back. We marched barefoot. *Probably a blessing*, I thought, remembering what my sockless, unlaced boots had done to my feet during my last trek. The string of prisoners headed toward the camp entrance and exited across the broad flattened log over the moat, still fearful of the punji stakes below. Instead of following the main trail up the hill, we turned left on another path, which went past where they buried the prisoners who had died. So many dead. I felt a flush of sadness. We worked our way along the base of the burial hill and on down a long, sloping valley.

As we walked, the guy behind me spoke. "What's your name?" His English was excellent.

I answered. "Bill Reeder. Captain Bill Reeder. U.S. Army."

"I am Lieutenant Nguyen Dinh Xanh. Vietnamese Air Force. Call me Xanh."

A VNAF pilot. Surely trained in the U.S. Likely spent a good deal of time there. No wonder the good English. I had my marching buddies, Wayne in front of me and Lieutenant Xanh behind.

We trudged out of the valley up onto a rising ridgeline. There wasn't much talking. When we began to climb up a long steep trail I was already exhausted. I had to push hard to make every step. My swollen infected ankle throbbed with pain.

I wondered, *Is anyone else having this much trouble? How long will I be able to keep going?* Only then did the words of the lead guard really hit me: "as long as eleven days. Try very hard to make it." My being revolted. *Eleven days of this! How in the hell am I going to be able to do that?* In two seconds, I answered. *Got to. As long as it takes. Reach down deep. Got to go. Keep going. God help me.*

On I went, step after agonizing step. I pondered what was meant by the part, "Try very hard to make it." *So what's the consequence if you don't?* I struggled with each step, wondering how I would make the next. Somehow I did it.

Wayne was stoic. He was in better shape than I was, but still it had to be tough for him. He just bore down and put out what was needed to keep on going. Some of the other prisoners did as well. Many, like me, had trouble. A number complained, and a few cried. Other prisoners berated them. A couple of them fell down and whimpered, and the guards yelled at them, slapping, kicking, and hitting them with rifle butts until they got up. I thought, *This is going to be a hellacious eleven days.*

Our guards got frustrated when it started getting dark. They jabbered among themselves and decided we would go no farther. We stopped where we stood, high on the hillside, to spend our first night on the trail. We'd had no food or water since we set out, and we'd get none tonight. The guards had army rations for themselves. The prisoners had nothing.

Someone barked orders. Guards untied us. Other prisoners translated instructions for Wayne and me. We were to make hammocks out of a length of canvas from our packs. We also carried a piece of plastic, a small metal rice bowl, and some rope. Other prisoners tied pieces of the rope to the ends of the canvas. The guards cut the rope as requested. Wayne and I did the same. We soon had hammocks.

I tried tying mine between two trees. When I sat on the edge, it came sliding down, and I hit the ground with a hard thud. I was ready to stay where I was, to roll onto my side and sleep right there on the ground, but the others protested strongly that dreadful creatures crept along the jungle floor. I had to be up in a hammock. I struggled to get mine right. I wasn't doing well.

Wayne had better luck. Once he was done with his, he came over and helped me. I could sense his concern. He could tell by my pathetic fumbling efforts that I was near my wits' end, physically exhausted and mentally drained.

We got my hammock up. It supported my weight. I collapsed into it. The stronger prisoners strung ropes a few feet above the hammocks. They collected the pieces of plastic from our packs to wedge between the ropes, creating a roof over us. They worried about rain.

We prisoners crammed as close together as the trees would allow, while the guards positioned their hammocks in a circle around us. They didn't retie us. Some of the guards stayed awake, with their weapons poised, ready to stop any escape. They worked in shifts through the night. I fell asleep, feeling like shit.

———————

I'd been backpacking for several miles. It had been a beautiful day. I pitched my Sierra Designs tent and set the rain fly over it. What a great tent! I had used it in extreme conditions at altitude while scaling high mountain peaks in California and Colorado. I loved to hike, rock climb, and mountaineer.

After a good meal of dehydrated beef stroganoff, I crawled into my Eddie Bauer down-filled sleeping bag and went to sleep. As the night wore on, I could hear thunder approaching. Rain pattered on the tent fly. The rain came harder and harder. It was nice to be cozy and warm inside my tent and sleeping bag.

———————

I jerked awake from my dream world. A steady stream of water ran onto my face. The plastic roof only collected the rainwater and funneled it off the drooping edges down onto us. I was soaked. I was cold. I could only lie there and shift, and shift again, to avoid the worst of it. I was miserable.

The rain stopped as morning finally came. I got out of the hammock with difficulty. Pain filled my injured leg as I stood. Wayne sat on the edge of his hammock, his shabby flight suit soaked and his wet hair a mess. Water drops glistened in his hair and beard. His face was gaunt, his cheeks and eyes hollow.

I smiled from deep within my own pitiful self and said, "Good morning. Aren't we a couple of drowned rats?"

Wayne looked at me and shook his head.

I helped, as much as I could, to get the ropes and sorry pieces of plastic down. Wayne helped too. We stuffed our gear into our packs and lined up for another day's march. We kept the same order as before, Wayne in front of me and the VNAF lieutenant, Xanh, behind me.

As I stood there, I reached down and pulled two leeches off my leg. *Fucking bastards*, I almost yelled. I was covered with the bloodsucking freaks in the days after my shoot-down. I hated them.

Ropes again bound our arms loosely behind our backs, but we weren't tied together. It had been too much of a struggle the day before. The guards probably felt we'd make better time if we weren't tethered to each other.

We set off, tired, hungry, and thirsty. My ankle hurt with each step. The swelling was worse than before. The guards walked among us, but two remained at the front and two at the rear of the line of prisoners. Every prisoner was within sight of two or more guards at all times. The guards always had their finger right by their triggers.

Today's march was shorter. Plenty of strenuous ups and jarring downs remained, but nothing like the day before. I wasn't as fatigued, though my ankle still throbbed. The swelling became worse. My broken back ached.

Early in the afternoon, our guards halted us at a trail junction on a hillside while some of the guards went ahead. We sat, mosquitoes swarming over us as we waited and waited. We couldn't swat them with our arms tied behind us. Hundreds matted onto my hands, neck, and head.

Some even scored hits through the fabric of my flight suit. Eventually, our guards took pity and untied our arms.

One of the guys broke small branches and handed them around. The guards didn't protest. We used them to swoosh the mosquitoes off us.

The group of guards returned and spoke with the others. We got up and tramped down a steeply sloping trail. In a quarter of a mile, we came to a big open structure on a level piece of ground. The walls were widely spaced bamboo with a doorway on each end. The shelter had a bamboo roof with room inside for all the prisoners. Posts positioned throughout would accommodate tying our hammocks.

Voices sounded from farther down the hillside, and most of our guards disappeared in that direction. Others guarded both entrances or walked around the outside. There would be no escape.

The guards came back with pots of rice and a tub of hot water. We used our small bowls to drink the water. The rice was dumped on a cloth in the center of the floor. We scooped up handfuls and ate. Even though Wayne and I were hungry, it didn't take much rice before we were done.

This way station for the NVA had a kitchen down the hill. From the sound of the voices in that direction, a lot of soldiers were in the camp. Our out-building at the edge of the site was probably where our first day's march was supposed to end, not the miserable open hillside we had camped on.

Under close supervision, we went out to pee and crap in the woods. I got into my hammock and went to sleep. I slept the whole night.

In the morning I felt rested but stiff. I swung my legs over the edge of my hammock. As my feet touched the floor, blood flowed down into my leg and pain surged in my ankle. I forced myself to stand. I looked over and saw Wayne already awake. I walked over to him, stuck out my hand, smiled, and said, "Happy Fourth of July."

He shook my hand and answered, "Happy Fourth of July. You remembered the date."

"I did." That was our Independence Day celebration.

We drank water, ate rice balls, collected our few things, formed up, and headed out on our third day's march. They did not tie our arms behind us. No more ropes. We probably seemed too sorry a band of half-dead souls to worry about. Still, the guards watched each of us, fingers close to the triggers. I had become fixated on their trigger fingers, the hell they could unleash in a quarter of an inch.

We came upon a large river that I was sure must be the one that flowed into the town of Attapeu in Laos to the west. I had flown over the area in Mohawks on my first tour and covering SOG missions in Cobras on my second. It was thick with NVA. Several aircraft had been hit and a number of SOG teams badly mauled very close to where I now stood. How odd to be walking the same ground I'd shot up months earlier. Strange world.

I looked for helicopters or airplanes. There were none.

The wide river ran swiftly and looked deep. We halted at the edge. A thick manila rope stretched across it. Two guards slung their AK-47s, grabbed hold of the rope, and started across. On the other side, they squatted, raised their weapons, and sighted on the crossing. Two guards on our side did the same. The message was clear. Any prisoner who let go to try to escape would be shot. So would anyone who lost his grip from exhaustion. Everyone struggled as we started across. We were weak and the current was strong. After every few prisoners, a guard crossed.

I was the fifth prisoner to cross. As I climbed out of the water on the far bank, a hand reached down to help me up. I took it. It was Xanh.

"Thanks."

"Glad to help."

We sat together waiting for the others to cross. Wayne was just behind me. A guard followed him. It was warm. We were wet but not uncomfortable. It was good to relax for a few minutes in the middle of the day.

I asked Xanh, "What aircraft did you fly?"

He answered, "A-1 Skyraider."

"Where were you shot down?"

"Polei Kleng."

"Really. I flew. . . . Wait. What day were you shot down?"

"9 May. Two month ago."

"No shit. I tried to rescue you. But they wouldn't let me divert back to Polei Kleng. I saw you get hit. Saw your parachute. I had to go on to

Ben Het where I got shot down. I was captured three days later. I really wanted to come get you at Polei Kleng, but they wouldn't let me."

I took his hand again. "Xanh, glad to know you. We have something in common. Both shot down on 9 May, very close to each other."

Xanh smiled broadly. I was smiling too.

The prisoners crossed the river without incident. No one let go of the rope. No one was shot. The last two guards pulled themselves across, and we continued the march.

Before dark, we came upon another camp. I could tell by the smoke and smells and activity that our bamboo shelter was within sight of the kitchen. The other shelters in the camp were empty. We were the only guests.

The scuttlebutt among the prisoners that evening was that we were going all the way to North Vietnam, possibly to Hanoi. Wayne's reaction was, "No fucking way! We can't make it all the way to Hanoi. That's hundreds of miles."

I countered, "If we can make it, we'll be able to get better food and medical care. We've got to make it."

Funny, for three days I'd been questioning whether I could gut out a trip of eleven days. Now I was enthusiastic over one that could take several weeks. *This is nuts*, I thought, but I felt good at the same time. That night I dreamt of family and home and smiled in my dreams.

We continued walking north. I got worse as I gouged the bottoms of my feet on rough roots and sharp rocks. I grew weaker. Every day Wayne helped me. He helped me get up in the morning. He helped me pack up my stuff. He usually tied up my hammock for me in the evening. I could not have survived without him.

In return, I'd crack stupid jokes at the most terrible times. Wayne never appreciated my jokes. I'm afraid they actually tormented him. One day, as we strained up a particularly steep hill, I hit him with this: "Hey Wayne. Did you hear that the United States is now buying medical supplies in the Orient?"

He looked at me, scowled, and shook his head.

"It's true. Haven't you heard of the Singapore sling?" I chuckled. He looked straight ahead and said nothing.

As the days continued, I became weaker and lost weight. Fevers followed waves of shivering chills. *Might be malaria.* I suffered from diarrhea. *Probably dysentery.* My festering ankle wound hurt more. The swelling grew worse, aggravated by the journey. Leeches plagued me, sucking my blood and adding infections of their own. My right leg became a heavy painful mass that I dragged along the trail. I must have been a sight.

Though my wounds placed me in a worse situation, Wayne was sick and deteriorating too. He had some sort of jungle fever and lost his appetite. He quit eating regular rice, preferring only the crispy layer that formed right next to the surface of the cooking pot, what the Vietnamese called *com cháy*, or fire rice.

Xanh was having troubles too: injuries from his shoot-down, decline from months in captivity, poor diet, disease, and the daily toll of this horrendous march north.

Every step of the way, our personal demons threatened our physical ability and mental willingness to press on. Everyone suffered. We looked like the walking dead, struggling to survive each agonizing mile of that march. Most of us stoically faced the challenges that beset us. Sometimes selfishness and self-pity erupted and tempers flared. Pain and suffering took its toll.

The senior ranking prisoner in our group was Pham Van Thanh, a major in the South Vietnamese Army. He tried his best to be a leader for twenty-five South Vietnamese officers and two American helicopter pilots under the most trying conditions. The enemy gave him no authority to lead. I had a lot of respect for what Thanh tried to do. I felt for the frustration he had to endure. Morale sunk lower and lower, bickering grew rampant, and prisoners died. Thanh was senior, but most dismissed his efforts as they struggled to survive.

Xanh tried to help him, but he could only do so much as a lieutenant, a junior-ranking member of the group. There was an outstanding young airborne officer, as well, Nguyen Hung Van, who had been captured in the battle at Firebase Charlie. Lieutenant Hung was a great guy, always helpful, hated the communists, and constantly worried about Wayne and me. But he, too, struggled and could only do so much. The responsibility of leadership rested with Thanh, but he was unable to lead. Perhaps no one could have led under those conditions.

For me, it was hard just to move my foot forward in the next step, and harder yet to take the next one and the next after that. Pain seared my ankle and lower leg like a hot iron. I cried inside as I walked.

Have to stop this, I thought. There was no way I could escape. Too weak, too sick, too many guards too close. Wayne had given up on the idea as well. He was more concerned with my daily survival. My condition troubled him.

With escape out of the question, I tried pulling my mind away from the pain, away from this moment in time, away from this place. I formed an alternate world inside my head, the California Riding and Hiking Trail, a place I could go even while stumbling along in agony. There is no such trail, but in my mind it was real as could be. It was a place I could be instead of where I was. I walked its meandering track with pleasure on a beautiful, wide, gently sloping path of smooth, hard-packed gravel. The pathway was dry. Each day on the California Riding and Hiking Trail was mildly warm with a soft, gentle breeze. Sunlight always streamed through the trees lining its side.

I jerked back to reality.

Captain Trần Hùng Việt had collapsed on the ground and called out, "Tôi không thể đi." He pleaded, "Tôi đang hoàn thành. Tôi đang thực hiện." He lay there and whimpered.

A guard screamed, "Hãy đứng dậy. Hãy đứng dậy hoặc mày sẽ chết." Việt cried helplessly. The guard jammed him with the barrel of his rifle. He kicked him hard and shouted. "Hãy đứng dậy, bạn đồng của phân. Đúng dậy và đi. Bạn kẻ yêu đuối lợn!"

The guards yelled back and forth to each other. They ranted at the prisoner lying on the ground. They barked orders to the rest of us. I didn't understand any of it.

Xanh said softly but earnestly to Wayne and me, "Keep walking. No stop." We continued. One guard stayed with the prostate prisoner where he lay. We walked on.

After a short while, BANG! One shot. Sometime later, the guard caught up. A dull sense of disbelief and shock overcame me. I had no doubt what had just happened. I kept walking as I cried.

That evening, everyone was quiet. Wayne seemed especially caring as he helped me get my hammock up and got me settled for the evening. I lay there for some time before I fell asleep. It was clear. If you could not march, you would die.

The journey was a nightmare, a horrid, soul-wrenching nightmare. It grew worse. Others fell out and died. Each step, every day, wracked my body with pain. My infections became worse; disease was taking me. I knew I was sliding closer to death, but I kept fighting as hard as I could. To keep my spirits up, I thought continuously of my family, of things I would do with Spencer and Vicki when I got home. Thinking of those two kids always gave me strength, always bolstered my hope.

Other things lifted our spirits as well. Toward the end of a particularly tough day's trek, when we thought we should be done with it, we started a long steady climb up a high hillside, a tough task late in an exhausting day.

One of the prisoners started to whistle. Others slowly joined the tune. Those who couldn't whistle hummed. After a while, I recognized it. It was the "Colonel Bogey March" from *The Bridge on the River Kwai*, a movie about Allied POWs of the Japanese held in western Thailand during the Second World War. The tune was well known to Americans. I didn't realize it was also popular among the South Vietnamese.

We whistled with gusto, adding new spring to our steps. We looked knowingly at each other as we moved up the switchback trail. The NVA had no idea of the significance of the song. They had no clue what was going on. Surprisingly, they didn't interrupt us. We continued through several iterations all the way to the top of the hill. We all felt something extraordinary had just happened. It never happened again.

My leg was now swollen to twice its normal size, dark colored, filled with pus. Long splits formed in the skin. Pus and bloody, stinking fluid oozed from the cracks. I dragged it along like a sodden club. Every movement lashed me with searing pain that kept my face contorted. I shrieked a silent cry within. Pain burned a blackened scar deep in the center of my soul.

Gangrene set in. My bloody dysentery worsened. I had chills and fevers. I would find out later that I had three different kinds of malaria, several intestinal parasites, and tropical sprue (malabsorption syndrome).

Each morning I fought a battle to stand. As I put weight on my feet, I'd moan or scream through clenched teeth and pressed lips. Pressure built in my leg as I raised myself up. Standing brought a surge of pain. Gravity pulled blood and bodily fluids down into my decaying limb, and pressure grew. My leg was rotting.

I'd assemble my gear into my pitiful pack and pull it onto my back. I'd take the first few agonizing steps, then I would fight all day to reach the end of each day's journey. We had to cover six to ten grueling miles every day. It was horror, a nightmare come true.

Wayne and Xanh suffered badly themselves, but they always helped me. Xanh encouraged me with stories of how things would be when we were free once again. As we ate our rice one evening, he told me this was not how Vietnamese ate. "We eat fine food in my home. Vietnamese meals very good. They are delight. Do not judge food by what communists give us to eat."

I wanted to believe him, but all I could think of was steak and potatoes, or a Big Mac, or macaroni and cheese, or a milkshake, or a chocolate éclair. *How I'd love a chocolate éclair.*

I tried to maintain a sense of humor. It was hard, but it was necessary. Spirit is the most important factor in survival. A sense of humor, even under the very worst conditions, helps maintain spirit, and in spirit lives hope.

I was determined to survive. Still, I owed so much to Wayne and Xanh. They helped me through the worst and were always concerned about me. They did all they could to help me. Xanh especially helped me remain positive, to be hopeful. As bad as things got, I never gave up hope.

I mustered all my will each day just to wake, stand, and take a step. Then I fought hard for the remainder of the day to keep going, to keep moving along the trail. I could barely walk, but somehow I did. I survived each day to open my eyes in the morning to the gift of one more dawn.

The realities of my miserable world were clear. Death, our constant companion, stalked us, waiting for us to give in to its relentless temptation. That would be an easy thing to do. In normal life, you have to take some overt action to die. You have to kill yourself. As a prisoner of war, under these circumstances, that is reversed. You have to reach deep within yourself and struggle each day to stay alive. Dying is easy. Just relax, do nothing, give up, and peacefully surrender. Stop gagging down food, stop struggling to walk, stop fighting, and you will die.

Many did. They died in that jungle prison camp we'd left. They died along the trail. Some completed a day's journey and then lay down to die. Others collapsed on the trail and could not continue. The group marched ahead; a rifle shot or shots rang out. The pitiful suffering prisoner was not seen again. We lost half a dozen of our band of twenty-seven as the days turned into weeks.

The worst day of my life came a few weeks into the trip. I fought hard to continue the march, but I faltered. I dug deep inside myself for strength. There was nothing there. I dug deeper. I staggered on and faltered again. I struggled more. I reached deeper yet. I prayed for more strength. There was none. I collapsed. I got up and stumbled along. I collapsed again and again, and I got up again and again. I fought, fought with all I had in my body, my heart, and my soul. I collapsed and couldn't get up. I could not will myself up. I was at the end of my life.

The guard looked down on me. He ordered me up. He yelled at me. I could not. It was done. I knew my life was ended. Here on this miserable muddy jungle trail, it was over. Would my family ever know what had happened to me?

Then Xanh was there, looking worried, bending over me. The guard yelled at him to stop. Undeterred, Xanh reached down to help me. The guard yelled louder, but Xanh's face was set with determination. In spite of whatever threats the guard was screaming, Xanh raised me up, turned, and pulled me onto his frail, weak back. He wrapped my arms around his neck and clasped my wrists together in front of him. The rest of the day, he pulled me along, my feet dragging on the ground behind. Part of the time, he was helped by Lieutenant Hung. Nông Le, a big impish brute, helped briefly, but it was Xanh and Hung who carried the burden that day. It was Xanh who risked his own life to lift me from death. It was Xanh who carried me, and cared for me, until we completed that long day's struggle at another wayside camp.

The next morning, I went through the normal agonizing ritual of waking up, standing, and feeling the rush of painful pressure in my leg, of dragging my leg through those first determined steps as I willed myself to walk. It was more of a struggle than ever before. I reached within myself and mustered the will. I went on. At the edge of the encampment a broad log spanned the rapids of a river. I started across, trying to balance, in pain, weak, unsteady. I had no sense of balance. My worthless leg made it worse. I slipped and fell onto the rocks in the rushing water below.

The impact nearly knocked the life out of me. My world exploded in pain. I tumbled a short distance down the rapids and was smashed against a big rock, held there by the pressure of the current. I was on my back, face up, my right side underwater, my left side above, pressed in place like a squashed bug in a specimen display.

Xanh and Wayne came off the log and down the high steep bank to my rescue. They waded into the torrent and pulled me onto the bank. With Wayne shouting in English and Xanh in Vietnamese, they pleaded for the group to stay at the camp until I was able to travel again. They were ordered away. They wouldn't leave me. Guards dragged them away and forced them across the log bridge at gunpoint. They marched off with the rest of our prisoner group. Everyone believed I was left at that camp to die.

CHAPTER 10

The Road

The road must be trod.

—J. R. R. Tolkien

I asked my NVA guard, "What is it?"

He talked with the medic who wore a white coat over his NVA fatigue uniform.

The guard turned back to me. "It help you."

"What is it?" I repeated, eyeing the large needle sticking out of a fat syringe.

"Anta-botic."

"What kind?"

The guard spoke with the medic again. He replied, "Pen-silin."

As I feared. "I can't take it," I said. "I'm allergic to penicillin. It could kill me."

I'd gotten a penicillin injection years before for a strep throat. It put me in the hospital for a week because of a severe reaction. I had large welts all over my body. The doctor had said, "Don't ever take penicillin again. It could kill you."

My guard was the asshole Dzu, my poorly skilled interrogator from the jungle prison camp. He was assigned to stay behind with me because he was the only one who spoke any English. He was the one-man security force ordered to stay with me until I recovered enough to continue the trip and catch up with the group . . . or until I died.

Dzu looked at me with that superior air I despised. "You no take med-sin, doctor cut off leg. No med-sin, you pretty sure die. You take med-sin, still maybe have to cut leg. Better chance you live then, with med-sin."

The medic said something else. Dzu translated. "Doctor say you have med-sin maybe have problem." I nodded assertively. He continued. "Doctor say you no have med-sin, you die for sure."

"OK. Give me the shot."

For some reason the communists had decided not to kill me. They were not even going to let me lie there and die of neglect. The North Vietnamese saw the value of American POWs as bartering chips in nego-tiations. It would be to their advantage if I lived. An official at this camp clearly understood that. They gave me medicine for the first time in my captivity. They let me rest. I had penicillin injections for the next few days. I did not have a reaction.

I lay in a hammock, strung under a lean-to, not far from the spot Wayne and Xanh had pulled me out of the river. I was by myself, at the edge of the camp. I lay there, alone, save for a rotating guard squatted nearby and the daily appearance of the camp medic, frowning disap-provingly at the progress of my wound. In a few days, I was able to stand. As soon as I could walk again, I was put back on the trail.

The first miles were really difficult. Each step was still extremely pain-ful, though the pain was not nearly as bad as before. The swelling was slowly decreasing, the hurt becoming less soul-wrenching as I struggled through each successive day.

I had my own personal escort, Dzu. We traveled with groups of North Vietnamese soldiers moving north. I moved slowly, at a pace that pissed off my NVA traveling companions. They'd move on ahead, and I'd stumble along with Dzu. He'd rant and push me with his rifle as he cast the most hateful looks at me. We would reach each day's camp late.

Rocks, sticks, and protruding roots on the trail slashed gashes in the bottom of my feet. I smashed my toes, and most got broken. Compared to my leg and my back, however, my feet caused the least of my agonies. I dealt with that part of my discomfort and pain.

Dzu would lambaste me. "Take care. No hurt feet. Take care with walk," as if I was intentionally bashing my feet to tear them apart and break my toes. I'd look at him and scowl. Sometimes I'd mutter so he couldn't hear, "Right, you asshole." I watched him stride easily ahead. I was angry. I stumbled and struggled.

Dzu strutted along, strong and confident. He had a big rucksack and carried his weapon and ammunition. But he was healthy. He wasn't wounded. He ate adequate food. He had no problem with his feet. Some days he wore a pair of olive-green Soviet or Chinese made sneaker-like combat shoes. Most of the time, he wore Ho Chi Minh sandals.[1] My feet were bare. My back was broken. I was sick. I was weak. I fought to survive.

I knew I was both a massive, burdensome responsibility and an annoyance to him. If something happened to me, or if I escaped, he'd be screwed. But I was also his ticket back to North Vietnam. He must have been happy about that, but he never let it show, not to me anyway.

Sometimes we ran into NVA soldiers carrying wounded from some distant battle. They struggled with litters that were nothing more than a hammock attached to a long pole. The wounded man lay in the hammock. A soldier grasped one end of the pole. Another soldier took the other end. They lifted it onto their shoulders with an "Ugh." Other soldiers carried their weapons for them.

Travel was difficult for them. One particular group was moving up a steep hill behind us. After we stopped on a level spot on the hillside to catch our breath, I looked back down the trail. They came up at a slow, steady pace, straining with every step. They stumbled frequently, causing the wounded to grimace. Some cried with each jolt.

The group rested when they reached us. Their curiosity about the American prisoner barely kept their anger in check. Some shook their fists at me. One walked up and spat on me. Others yelled what were surely obscenities. As they ranted, I could see the blood-stained bandages wrapping the wounded. Flies buzzed around their faces and danced on their dressings. One soldier pointed at a legless man in a litter and shouted, "Cobra máy bay trực thăng! Cobra!" Dzu's translation wasn't needed. "He say Cobra helicopter do this."

I felt a flush of pride and remorse. I was proud, knowing how effectively we supported our American Special Forces teams and South Vietnamese allies. I was proud of the disdain the enemy had for our Cobras. At the same time, I was sad for the human suffering we caused. Cobra gunships had maimed and ripped apart these bodies. This was what I had done to scores, probably hundreds of human beings over my months of combat. Many had been evacuated like these. Others lay dead, their torn and dismembered corpses left where I cut them down on the battlefield.

That image stayed with me for a long time afterward. It made me think a lot as I continued my journey along the trail. I felt for those I'd killed or maimed, their suffering, their families' loss, of human lives I'd ended.

I reminded myself I'd always fired on military targets and had never engaged civilians or shot into villages. Never. I had killed or crippled those trying to kill me. I came to see it like a deadly game of chess between military opponents. I knew the rules. They knew the rules. We each maneuvered against each other. They were soldiers doing their duty. They were trying to kill me. I was a soldier doing my duty. I tried to kill them.

Man had played the deadly game of warfare throughout history. Now I was part of it. True, I'd been dealt a bad hand and might not survive, but there was hope I would. I would never let go of that hope. I would continue to do all I could to live through this day and see the next.

I held these thoughts and so many others as I moved up the Ho Chi Minh Trail. There was a lot of time during the journey to ponder, and that was about all I did. Think. I had no friends. I was a captive of my enemy. I had only myself and God for conversation. I thought of life, of my kids, of hopes and dreams for the future. I imagined food. I continued creating menus, planning a house, drawing blueprints in my head.

As I walked, I frequently let my mind transport me to the California Riding and Hiking Trail. There I'd hike in pleasure with long, easy strides. I enjoyed the beauty and fine weather of that magical, make-believe place, so far from the awful reality I lived.

One day on the trail, my trance was broken by Dzu frantically screaming just behind me. I didn't know what he was shouting about. I turned around to see him coming at me swinging a big long stick. I didn't know what I'd done. I cringed as I prepared for the beating that was whirling toward me.

Dzu halted and started hitting the ground between us with the stick, no more than eight feet from me. He smacked the ground a dozen times, then poked at something in the trail. He raised the stick to show me a small green snake hanging on the end. The snake was very dead.

Dzu's voice still quivered with alarm. "You die. You die. Snake bite, you die. Very bad snake. Have strong poison. He bite, you die quick."

Dzu paused, breathing heavily. "You walk over snake. He no bite. You lucky." He shrugged in exasperation, showing from his expression that he regarded me as a stupid fool. He looked at me like that often. His emotions seemed to shift from hatred to frustration to annoyance to fury. Regardless of his mood, he always seemed to loathe me.

It was the monsoon season. Rain poured from the sky almost every day. The trail was a slimy swath of thick mud hiding toe-breaking roots and sharp, sole-ripping rocks. In places, it was slick as grease. On steep sections it was impossible to keep your footing no matter how much care you took. I slipped, Dzu slipped, other NVA soldiers slipped. Once, one plunged past us, sliding down a particularly treacherous slope. He bounced down the steps that had been carved into the steep hillside, careening all the way to the bottom. When we reached him, others tended him, his body limp and lifeless. We marched on.

The monsoon rains made the jungle more mystical and foreboding. Gloom hung in the dank air, making it thicker, more oppressive in the wetness. The light was dimmer, colors darker. Leeches were more numerous. They twisted up from soaked leaves and branches, or from the sodden jungle floor, searching for ripe flesh to latch onto. Pulling those bloodsuckers off became an instinctive reaction, repulsive nonetheless.

I felt that whatever lurked in the soggy recesses of the shadowy, waterlogged jungle could not be good. Best not to dwell on the black murky gloom all around. I had to remind myself of better things, pleasant things. I wouldn't get drawn down into the dark mental abyss of despair. I would never let go of hope. Not for a moment.

The Reeder Family in the mid-1950s: My parents, Helen and Bill Reeder Sr., along with me (with baseball bat) and my brothers Don, Wes, and Greg. *Author's collection*

Mark Karvon's painting of the airplane I flew on my first tour of duty in Vietnam, the OV-1 Mohawk. *Mark Karvon*

AH-1 Cobra attack helicopters "Heading for Trouble" as we did so many mornings in the central highlands of Vietnam in a painting by William S. Phillips. Heading for Trouble, ©*William S. Phillips. The Greenwich Workshop®, Inc.*

Me as a Mohawk pilot on my first tour of duty at Hue-Phu Bai, Vietnam, 1968–69. *Author's collection*

Forrest Snyder, Cobra School classmate and fellow Pink Panther. *Snyder family photo collection*

Mike Sheuerman, Cobra pilot extraordinaire. *Sheuerman family photo collection*

Dan Jones and me beside our bullet-riddled Cobra. Some of the bullets came far too close to Dan's head as he flew in my front seat that day (bullet holes circled). *Jones family photo collection*

Maj. John Joseph Duffy, hero of the battle for Firebase Charlie. *Duffy family photo collection*

Tim Conry of the combat crew "Conry and Reeder." An exceptional officer, gentleman, and gunship pilot. An extraordinary young man. *Conry family photo collection*

Me a few days before the action at Ben Het.
Author's collection

American advisors Mark Truhan (on the gun barrel) and Bob Sparks sit on a disabled North Vietnamese PT-76 tank in the wire at Ben Het—just after the battle. *Truhan family photo collection*

Melvin Wayne Finch, aeroscout platoon leader, B Troop, 7/17th Cavalry, and fellow POW. *Courtesy of Vietnam Veterans Memorial Fund*

Lieutenant Colonel Nghiem Ke, 22nd ARVN Division Engineer Officer. *Nghiem family photo collection*

My kids, Spencer and Vicki. My inspiration for survival. (Photo taken shortly after my return from captivity.) *Author's collection*

Special Forces sergeant Dennis Thompson in Vietnam before his assignment to the camp at Lang Vei. *Thompson family photo collection*

The Armed Forces Vietnam Network (AFVN) TV station crew in Hue. From left, two unidentified soldiers, Don Gouin, Harry Ettmueller, John Anderson, Courtney Niles (NBC engineer), Lieutenant Dibernardo, and an unidentified soldier kneeling. *Ettmueller family photo collection*

Inset: me (on the left) and Al Kroboth looking out of our big cell in the Little Vegas section of the Hanoi Hilton shortly before our release in 1973. *U.S. Department of Defense*

My release at the Gia Lam Airport in Hanoi, 27 March 1973. *Author's collection*

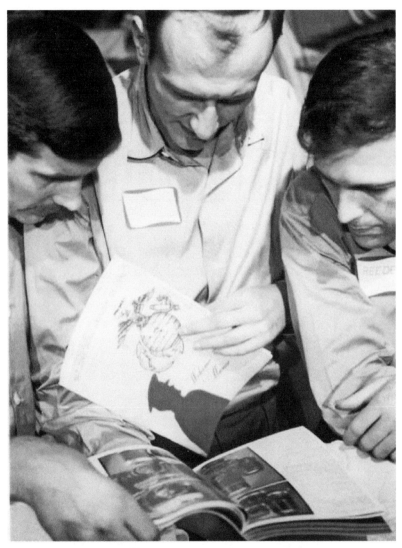

Cellmates Dave Mott, Al Kroboth, and me on board the Air Force C-141 airplane from Hanoi to the Philippines. *Author's collection*

Returning home after hospitalization at Fitzsimmons Army Medical Center in Denver, Colorado, with five-year old son Spencer in hand. *Author's collection*

At a reunion of former Vietnam POWs in San Diego. Ke Nghiem, me, Jim Thompson, Melanie, Ke's wife Bé, Thanh Van Pham's wife, and Thanh. *Author's collection*

For decades, I could not determine if Xanh Nguyen had survived. Finally, I found him in 2008. This is the occasion of us first seeing each other again after thirty-six years. *Nguyen family photo collection*

POW statue at National Prisoner of War Museum, Andersonville, Georgia. I influenced the sculptor, Donna Dobberfuhl, to have this figure looking up in hope instead of down in despair. *National Park Service Photo*

Added joy. Chad and Chelsea. *Author's collection*

Melanie and me at the end of the story. *Author's collection*

One thing I did to raise my spirits was sing. I'm not sure when it started, but I'd often find myself singing some tune inside my head. I sang mostly to myself. Sometimes, though, I'd risk a small, audible but quiet voice or hum. My two favorite songs for marching along the trail were the Beatles' *Yellow Submarine* and Burl Ives' *A Little Bitty Tear.* Don't know why. The songs were just there for me.

I'd march through the mud and the rain for miles. I was soaking wet, wrapped ineffectively with the small sheet of plastic from my sack. I'd feebly strut along caught up in one of those two songs. I got by most of my trek up the Ho Chi Minh Trail by mentally removing myself to the California Riding and Hiking Trail and by singing to myself. Strange, I know, but somehow so very helpful.

Despite the gloom of the monsoon season, moments of magnificence arose along the way when the rain stopped and the sun beamed. I would catch a glimpse of a mountain peak, the quilt-work of glistening green hillsides, or the sight of spectacular karst formations jutting like craggy fingers from the earth.[2]

I remember marching along a steep mountain trail one day just as the rain stopped. Sunlight streamed between parting clouds. Steamy water vapor rose from drenched foliage. I saw a rickety-looking cable and wood-planked bridge far up the valley ahead. It was like a scene from a primordial lost world movie. As I crossed the narrow, unsteady structure, I looked down, in awe at the beautiful river, its powerfully rushing rapids far below.

There were few such moments of magnificence. Their splendor is fixed in my mind forever. The images remain especially vivid because they were wonderfully real in the midst of an otherwise horrible nightmare.

Occasionally, at the end of the day, we'd stop at an established wayside camp where there was shelter for us, with a roof. Mostly, there was no structure available. We'd camp as we had that first night of the journey, my hammock strung between two trees in the jungle, the rain pouring down.

One thing I learned from watching Dzu was how to make a sleeping shelter using my sheet of plastic. I ran a rope line between the same two trees as my hammock. It sat about eighteen inches above my head.

I pulled it tight. That served as the center line for the plastic. I pulled the four corners of the plastic sheet away from the center, keeping them spread with short pieces of twine pulled taut.

The result was a small, pitiful plastic tent suspended atop my hammock. It did a pretty good job of keeping me somewhat dry through the night. My tattered flight suit stayed damp for the whole monsoon season, though. The Nomex material was designed to be fire resistant, not quick drying. It soaked up moisture and stayed wet for days. I suffered a constant chill.

As my journey dragged agonizingly on, I'd occasionally catch a glimpse of some feature I recognized. I'd flown over the entire length of the Ho Chi Minh Trail on the reconnaissance missions on my first tour of duty. I now saw distinctive mountains I remembered. I crossed rivers I knew. I kept rough track of my progress north. I knew how much ground I'd covered and how much remained ahead if we were going all the way to Hanoi. There was still a very long way to go.

We traveled high along the western slopes of the Annamite Mountains, the spine of the border between the two Vietnams and Laos. The highest peaks are more than eight thousand feet. Going through the mountains was tough but more secure than the lower reaches. Below was the heavily trafficked road network of the Ho Chi Minh Trail, which was heavily bombed. U.S. intelligence didn't know of the narrow foot trails we followed, or believed them to be so insignificant that they weren't attacked.

In fact, large numbers of fresh North Vietnamese soldiers moved steadily down this trail. We encountered group after group, some numbering in the hundreds, replacements for NVA units engaged in heavy fighting in the South.

Strings of porters hauled supplies on their backs. They were strong and moved with purpose, hardened by months or possibly years of such labor. Some were Vietnamese, while others looked like indentured tribal Laotians.

I saw bicycles too. Every one bore a load like a pack animal, with more gear and rice-filled bags than I ever imagined could be put on a bike. Each was pushed by a porter walking beside, straining hard into the handlebars.

One day we encountered a tall, dark-skinned man who intrigued me. His skin was bronze and clean, his eyes metallic, projecting a dark energy as they fixed on mine. His uniform was a mixture of NVA fatigue and the dress of a mountain tribesman. Instead of an army hat, he had a head-dress of dyed cloth and fine-looking leather, stained red and blue. Tiger teeth adorned the front, and fur covered the top. It gave anyone a sense of the power and prestige of its wearer. He had an AK-47 strapped across his broad back. He traveled light, barefoot and without pack.

The man looked different than any Montagnard I'd ever seen. He was taller; his tribal dress was unique. He had an air of confidence, the appearance of a respected leader even though he was a younger man, not an elder in his tribe. He stopped only for a moment, holding my eyes intently in his gaze. He turned and moved swiftly across the mountain.

"Pathet Lao?" I asked Dzu.

"Yes, Laos fighter," he said, a note of disdain in his voice. I could tell Dzu didn't like him, but he wouldn't want to get into a confrontation with him either. The NVA ran the Ho Chi Minh Trail right through the spine of Laos. They did so with the consent of the Laotian communists, providing them some assistance in the war they waged against their own government. The level of distrust and animosity between the two, how-ever, was evident that day as the two cultures brushed briefly by each other on that mountainside.

Further along the trail, we passed a house with a couple of small out-buildings, all perched on stilts raised eight feet or so off the ground. It appeared to be a family farm, sitting alone, carved out of the towering jungle around it.

I stopped and feebly turned my head toward Dzu. "Wait. They have corn, and pigs and chickens. Can't we get any?"

"No."

"But . . ."

"No," he barked with finality.

Days later, we descended a long steep hill, stopping on the bank of a broad river where it made a pronounced bend. I knew where we were. The Xe Kong River flowed out of the high mountains to the east, wid-ened, gained strength, and turned south. Nearby was a major junction of two branches of the Ho Chi Minh Trail road network, dirt tracks labeled

Highways 92 and 923 on maps of the region. If we were going all the way to Hanoi, we were less than a quarter of the way there. Hundreds of miles lay ahead, a long, long way yet to go.

We stood in a vulnerable spot where air strikes were common. A shudder shook me as I scanned the sky. After all, I was traveling with a group of NVA soldiers. What a target we'd be.

We moved along the riverbank to a small camp, where three soldiers grudgingly emerged from underground bunkers. After a brief discussion, a thin, muscular, older man slipped into the water. He pulled a dugout sampan from under foliage growing along the bank. His pant legs were rolled above his calves and he wore an unbuttoned tattered tan shirt and large-brimmed hat. His sunbaked skin was like dark, dry, cracking leather.

This sinewy man got in the boat and stood in the back, our helmsman. We climbed in after him. He stood solid as the boat rocked. He worked a single large rudder-oar at the rear of the craft, expertly propelling us out into the current. He angled well upstream and worked the rudder energetically to get us to the far side of the river. We landed almost directly across from where we'd launched.

A wide, well-worn path led away from the river up a valley covered by jungle canopy. Underneath was wide open except for the huge trunks of the massive trees. About half a mile from the river, we came to a large encampment.

What's this? I thought. *Civilians. What the hell are they doing here? Looks like a Boy Scout camp for families.*

In addition to a garrison of uniformed North Vietnamese soldiers, I saw groups of smartly dressed people moving about. Some were men, but the majority were women and children, mostly young boys, ten to fourteen years old. Well-constructed long rectangular single-story wood huts sat atop timber pilings a couple of feet high, aligned in widely spaced rows with broad pedestrian avenues between. A small river ran down the valley just behind the camp.

Dzu and I left the group we'd been traveling with and moved into a building, a combination bunkhouse and dining hall. Individual bed-like structures lined the walls, each fitted with bamboo mats suspended across the low frames. Tables and benches filled the center of the room. This was the nicest place I'd seen since being shot down.

"Hello. What your name?"

I was startled to hear the young voice behind me speaking English. I turned. A twelve-year-old boy stood there, curiosity beaming from his face. He struggled to maintain the composure of the seasoned young man he wanted so badly to be.

"What?" I said in surprise.

"What your name? I Chinh."

"Reet. I Reet." I gave him the Vietnamese butchering of my name. My captors couldn't pronounce Reeder.

Dzu said something to him. His eyes brightened and he began sharing a story he truly believed. He was an educated young man but naïve in his enthusiasm for utopian communism—not the cruel oppressive regime that was actually in place in North Vietnam.

"I live in Phu Binh in the south of Vietnam. Progressive men come to my village. Help us plenty. I learn much. I help them. Now my family go to North. We learn more. We become better Vietnamese. Have better life."

I was standing in some kind of way station where the North Vietnamese political machine brought "enlightened" South Vietnamese who showed potential to become really good communists. They were clothed and fed, given an intensive education program, and prepared for the journey north. Some walked. Others went by truck. I wondered how many survived the trip, and how many of those would make it south again to be placed as agents or shadow government cadre. North Vietnam was making a substantial investment in this program.

I ate well. The rice was free of the rat droppings, white wormy weevil larvae, and tiny pieces of rock that I'd been accustomed to. I'd already broken two teeth on unseen rocks in rice. I would break no more this afternoon. I also had a real treat, some bamboo shoots and a piece of manioc. I savored a rusted cup of hot tea, cradling its warmth in both hands, letting the aroma fill my nostrils, swishing the flavor delightfully in my mouth. It was a small feast. That night, I fell into deep sleep on a comfortable bamboo mat inside a completely dry hut.

The next morning we got back on the trail early. In spite of the comforts of camp, Dzu had had enough of the blabbering civilian youth who seemed to take a liking to me. Dzu was also pushing hard to catch up to the group of prisoners I'd started with.

We hiked for days, then for weeks more over challenging terrain. We moved close to the crest of the Annamite Mountains, with peaks ranging from four thousand to over six thousand feet. Farther north they would get to nearly nine thousand feet. We trekked through pine forests instead of tropical jungle. The trails were always steep, exhausting going up or treacherous coming down. I got stronger as my leg continued to heal. But the journey never got easier. It only got steeper the farther north we went.

We continued day after day after miserable day. The journey was taking its toll, stretching my will to press on. Each day's trek demanded more than I thought I had to give. I was able to go on only by scraping up the few remaining bits of grit that remained in the most obscure recesses of my heart and soul. I prayed, I commanded, I willed myself to take step after impossible step. That effort itself fed an agony festering within me, which swelled and gnawed at my core as week followed wretched week.

Malaria attacks and bouts of bloody dysentery tortured me. The pain of my broken back pierced me every day. The soles of my feet were mosaics of raised welts and open, bleeding gashes and punctures. Previously broken toes throbbed as I broke them again; and always there were the pesky leeches. But I was still alive and for that I thanked God.

Often, as we'd come toward the finish of a day's march, I'd hear a rooster crowing in the distance. Many camps had chickens for feeding the soldiers, but never a prisoner. When I heard a cock crow, I knew we were getting close to a camp, the aim of our day's journey.

Bless the Lord, I'd mutter to myself.

At the end of one especially brutal day, we came to an encampment set on a level shelf of land, high on the side of a steep mountain.

"You go," a soldier ordered me, pointing into a storage building. Dzu watched, surprised at both the English and tone of authority.

The structure was the size of a tennis court. The walls were framed with thin, widely spaced logs, lined with something like chicken wire. The floor was hard-packed dirt. I didn't know what had been stored there, but it was empty now.

"Put bed there."

I strung my hammock across one corner, between two of the posts. In the other corner, in my end of the rectangular building, was another hammock. Somebody lay deep inside the fabric, hidden from my view.

I called out quietly, "You all right? How are you doing?"

No response. I tried once more, a little louder. I gave up.

That evening I got rice, as always. A soldier took a plate of rice to the lump filling the other hammock. Nothing moved. The soldier persisted for a moment. Someone yelled from a distance, and the soldier turned and left, still carrying the untouched food.

That night there was a pathetic moan from the hammock. "Xin đi cầu."

I yelled to the guards in the darkness. "Man need dee cau. Man have to shit."

Soldiers shouted. Finally Dzu entered, annoyed that he had been disturbed.

"What you want?"

I pointed, unnecessarily, at the only other person around. "That man asked to shit."

"You take him. You carry him. He shit there." Dzu pointed to a far corner.

Right, I'm going to pick this guy up and carry him. Fat fucking chance.

I got out of my hammock with difficulty. I hobbled over to the other hammock.

"Can you get up if I help you?"

In the darkness, I could make out his hollow, dark eyes looking up helplessly from the cocoon he had pulled around himself. He began to cry.

"Here, I'll help you." I put my arms under his back and head to help him sit up. He wasn't able, but surprisingly, I lifted his torso with ease.

I shifted my one hand down, under his buttocks, and lifted him out of the hammock without difficulty. He was light as a feather in his sickly, emaciated state.

I carried him to the far corner, put his feet down, held him, helped him with his pants, and wiped his ass with leaves from a stack that had been piled there for that purpose. I carried him back in his hammock, and he wheezed a barely perceptible, "Thank you, Reedo."

I was taken aback and asked, "Who are you?"

Forming his words slowly and with difficulty, he muttered, his voice but a thin wisp. "I Zinh. I die. I die."

I remembered him from the group of prisoners. I wondered, *How are Wayne and Xanh doing?* I started to ask, but I couldn't. I simply said to him, "No, you'll be fine. You rest here for a few days. Get your strength back. Then you can finish the journey. You'll be fine. You will get better." I left it at that.

He whimpered a bit more as he fell mercifully into the sanctuary of unconsciousness. *So sad,* I thought as I lay back down seeking the solace of sleep.

The next morning I went to him as I headed out for another day's march. "Zinh, Zinh." No answer. "Zinh. I go, now. I'll see you soon. You'll be fine." He moaned softly. If he tried to speak, I couldn't hear.

We left the poor devil all alone in what were surely his dying hours. I'm certain the communists ignored his moans and weak cries, ignored his pitiful state, and ignored his humanity. They left him lying there, alone, until he was gone and they were done with this burden.

Over the next days, my dysentery got worse, and I was asking to shit several times a day along the trail. Dzu's patience grew thin. Sometimes there were leaves, but often not. I would grimace and bleat a distressful groan, "Got to shit, now."

Dzu would command, "Shit here," and I would.

"Quickly. We go," he'd bark.

I'd pull my pants back up over the fresh mess moistening my filth-encrusted butt. We'd walk on.

At the end of one particularly tough day's march, we stopped in a fortified camp by a small river. It was impressive. We must have been near a road or a truck park. Dzu and I moved into a hut and stepped down into a deep, almost bunker-like, excavation in the floor. It was nicely dug with wood reinforced walls and plenty of space for the two of us.

Dzu looked hard at me and said, "No shit here."

I looked at him and concentrated hard. My forehead furrowed. My face tightened and turned crimson. "Got to shit. Got to shit, bad. Now!"

"You wait. No can shit here. Wait."

He scrambled out of the bunker-hut to find out where the camp latrine was. I couldn't wait. I squeezed my ass shut as tight as I could and groaned as pressure mounted. The torrent of diarrhea gushed from my asshole like a jet of warm liquid spewing from a fire hose.

Dzu returned, smelled my deed as he entered, and saw my miserable person, crouched in a ball of self-pity. He raved, shouted, and screamed, waving his arms all about as spittle spattered from his mouth.

"Come. Come," he ordered.

We crawled up the dirt steps and outside. He dragged me viciously as I stumbled down to the river. He pushed me in and yelled, "Clean self. You filth pig." He was still spitting as he screamed. Several uniformed NVA watched the spectacle in awe, pity, amusement, or bewilderment. Hard to tell.

It felt good to rinse my body and grungy flight suit. Dzu didn't let me eat that night. He said food caused my diarrhea, but we both knew that was simply my punishment. I was back on my ration of twice-a-day rice the next day as we kept marching north.

I had learned a bit of Vietnamese on the trail. I'd listen and match phrases to gestures as some would try to communicate with me. That's how I learned to point to my back and say it hurts, "đau lắm"; to ask to pee, "Xin đẹp bộ đội, cho đi đái"; or to take a crap, "Xin đẹp bô đội, xin đi cầu." One other expression I knew well was "mệt quá" (I'm pooped, winded, exhausted). Everyone used it as we'd press on toward the top of a tough hill.

I loved to smoke and relished whatever I could scrounge. I had gotten adept at rolling a cigarette with any bit of tobacco and scrap of paper I could beg. At the top of one particularly tedious hill, we came upon a group of soldiers taking a break, smoking a water pipe. I was intrigued.

The pipe was about a foot-and-a-half long piece of bamboo, one end gouged open, the other left closed. A hole, smaller than a dime, was cut into the wall of the bamboo near the closed end, and a whittled wooden pipe bowl was inserted into the hole. The bamboo was partially filled with water, with special pipe tobacco pressed into the bowl. While the smoker held a lighted match on the tobacco, he inhaled the smoke deeply into his lungs. He sat, transfixed for a moment, emptying his lungs in a long, slow exhale.

One soldier looked at me and smiled. "Hãy dê anh ta cô gang." I read his expressions and gestures and, not needing a translation, nodded my head. He handed the pipe to me with a fresh measure of tobacco added to the bowl. I pressed the open end of the bamboo tube to my lips and inhaled deeply at the same time someone held a lighted match just over the bowl. Water gurgled in the tube as my lungs inflated with smoke. My head spun. I never knew if it was something strange in the tobacco or simply the sudden large amount of smoke filling my lungs. The sensation was one of a very short-lived euphoria. I liked it.

I learned how to ask for cigarette or pipe tobacco, "Xin phép bộ đội, cho tôi thuốc lá," or "cho tôi thuôc lào," or for a light, "cho tôi lửa." I smoked whenever I was able, though that wasn't often.

I noticed the trail twisted more down than up. We still pushed up monster hillsides that made my thighs burn and my lungs heave, puffing air like a blacksmith's bellows. But we were descending, coming out of the highest mountains to markedly lower terrain.

One day, we moved down a long open sloping hillside covered in ten-foot-high elephant grass. As we descended, I saw we were coming into a wide valley. I jerked to a stop. *What the fuck?*

The trail passed the rim of a large bomb crater. I hadn't seen a bomb crater since crossing into Cambodia a few days after my capture. There wasn't a single bomb crater anywhere along the trail we'd traveled all these weeks, until now.

The trail flattened, and bomb craters appeared more frequently and in clusters. Scampering down the steep bank of a river, Dzu hustled me along. At the bottom, we got into a boat, and the oarsman propelled us across quickly. As rapidly as my wrecked body allowed, we scurried up the far bank and crossed a major dirt road that showed frequent repairs. Scores of bomb craters ran along both sides.

I recognized exactly where we were. I was standing on Highway 9, somewhere just inside Laos. To the east was the Vietnam border and the old Special Forces border camp at Lang Vei, lost in a bloody battle back in the 1968 Tet Offensive. A bit farther east from Lang Vei was Khe Sanh, where U.S. Marines had withstood a communist siege at the same time.

After acknowledging this milestone of my journey, I strode barefoot across the dirt surface of Highway 9 continuing, ever onward, ever northward, ever forward to my goal of Hanoi. I was about a third of the way there.

In the days that followed, the ground rose, slowly at first, then more steeply, bringing us back into mountains. We crossed a small river, balancing across a log bridge. To the right, I could see high karst formations towering above a steep valley descending to the east. I knew we were on the upper reaches of the Ben Hai, the river that flows to the ocean through the center of the DMZ, the demilitarized zone between the two Vietnams. I had flown Mohawks here. We were probably within forty or fifty miles of the sea. I wondered, *Could I make it that far without food? Any chance of finding friendlies along the coast? How the hell could I escape, anyway?* I turned. Dzu was close behind me, his AK-47 at the ready, the sling over his neck to support the weight.

A few miles farther, Dzu became engaged in conversation with a couple of fellows. I was ahead of them, tagging behind a larger group. Those in front of me sped up, opening a gap. Dzu, focused on whatever story was being told, fell further behind. I rounded a sharp curve and found myself alone on the trail. Those in front were out of view. I turned and saw nobody behind. I reacted instantly and without thinking. *Go! Move out.* I headed up the hillside to my right, my mind racing. *Get away from the trail. Head up the hill. Bear to the right. Find the valley. Get to the coast.*

I tried to run. That didn't go too well. My best effort was more like a three-legged race, or a three-legged hobble, only I was by myself. The hillside was fairly open under scattered large trees. I was able to move well, though I made a lot of noise crashing through what undergrowth there was.

I couldn't have gone more than a couple of hundred yards when I heard shouting below. I turned to see a small group of soldiers running up the hill. From among them, Dzu shouted. I couldn't understand anything. His screaming was pure raging anger growing to an ever-higher crescendo of fury.

You dumb fuck. What now, smart shit?

I had stopped. They saw me. I desperately renewed my hobble up the hill, but they gained on me fast. Amazingly, no one shot me. They must have thought I was going to be an easy catch. I stopped again and collapsed to the ground in exhaustion and fear.

I'm dead. It's all over.

Dzu hovered over me, his AK muzzle shifting from the center of my face to the middle of my chest. He shrieked, "You! You! Why, you . . . ?" His face burned red, his eyes wild in rage. Spit sprayed as he screamed at me.

This is it. His finger's on the trigger. He's gonna kill me.

"I missed the trail! I got lost!"

He didn't shoot. He pointed his rifle away. In a sullen voice he commanded, "Get up. You do very bad. You have big problem now." He was shaking, enraged. He motioned down the hill and said, "Go."

I guess the big problem was the big trouble I was already in, being a POW trying to survive this trek up the Ho Chi Minh Trail. Dzu treated me with more disdain than usual for the rest of that day and several days following. The other soldiers obviously talked of my misadventure among themselves, but nothing more was ever done to me. I never heard about the incident again.

That night we slept in bed-sized hollows scooped out of a strange rock formation along a dry creek bed. It was as if I had my own Mesa Verde bed-sized cliff dwelling for a shelter that night. The next day we spent climbing most of the way up a long, high mountain trail. Near the top, we came to a large camp. Rows of single-story barracks sat in lines stretching up the steep slope. Soldiers occupied some of the buildings, though most were empty. Dzu took me into a vacant structure.

"Put bed, here."

He left two soldiers with me and disappeared. Other NVA, seemingly people of some authority in the camp, came by to see me. They looked at me and talked among themselves. Some were officers.

One, in very broken English, asked me about my condition. He looked at the bottom of my feet, seemed concerned, shook his head, and left. He came back with a pair of the NVA sneaker-style canvas shoes and threw them on the floor by my hammock. They were too small. No Vietnamese had feet the size of mine.

He said something. A soldier took a knife and cut off the front top of the shoe over the toes. I was able to get them on with my toes sticking out the front. They smiled. Someone laughed. Comical, but it felt good having something on my feet again after so many weeks of marching barefoot.

Rice came later that afternoon. Once again, I forced down as much as I could. I shook with a chill as I slept that night. Dzu didn't return till morning.

"Get up. You move."

I packed my stuff, put on my new shoes, pulled on the crappy bag that served as my sorry rucksack, and headed out for another day's march. We went only about a hundred feet, stopped, and entered another barracks. It was like the one I'd just left. Half a dozen older men wearing uniforms of the army of South Vietnam were inside. They looked like they'd been through hell. Even so, they appeared better than me, not as sick, dirty, or wretched.

Who are these guys? I asked myself.

Dzu said, "You stay." He left.

They stood there looking at me with empathy in their eyes. They saw a wasted, wounded, diseased wreck dressed in a tattered, stained, foul-smelling flight suit, sporting months of beard and uncut hair matted into a dirty, greasy mess. One of them stepped forward and put out his hand. In good English he said, "Hello, I am Nghiem Ke. Lieutenant colonel, engineer officer, 22nd Division."

"Nice to meet you. I am Bill Reeder, Captain Bill Reeder, U.S. Army helicopter pilot."

"You with us, now." He looked me over. "We go tonight on trucks into North Vietnam over Ban Raving Pass." He paused a few seconds and then introduced the others as each shook my hand. "This is Colonel Binh, division chief of staff. Lieutenant Colonel Trịnh Triển, artillery officer. Lieutenant Tri, surgeon." He went on to introduce the rest of the group, then added, "We all from 22nd Division. Capture near Tan Canh."

My God. The whole 22nd ARVN Division headquarters staff. They survived that horrendous battle in April that I supported. But no commander. What happened to him?

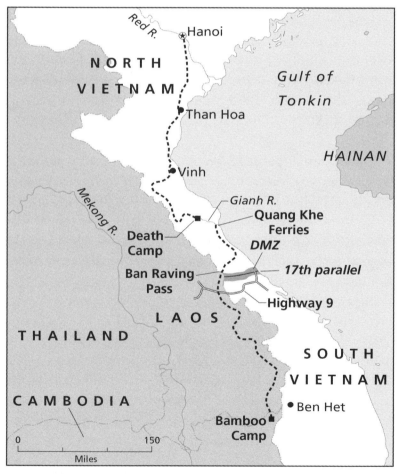

Map 4. The journey northward

CHAPTER 11

Into the North

Nearby, antiaircraft artillery fired two shots. The shells burst in the air. The NVA soldiers in the camp dashed about shouting, "Bê năm hai! Bê năm hai!"

"What's up?" I asked.

My new friends looked at each other with concern. All except Colonel Binh. He sat stoically on the edge of his hammock, unaffected by the commotion.

Nghiem Ke said, "B-52."

Above us, the mountain erupted with explosions as hundreds of bombs dropped from a flight of the big American aircraft. The ground trembled beneath us. The strike was close but it was farther up the mountainside and off to the right. We were fine.

Word came that we would not go that night. The strike had blown up the road and destroyed several trucks. I thought it would be several days, if not weeks, before the road could be fixed and trucks repositioned. I wondered, *How long are we going to be stuck here now?*

The next night, a North Vietnamese officer ordered us to pack up and leave. We hiked in the moonlight about half a mile above the camp to a road where trucks waited. Our group climbed into one, our guards clambering in behind us. NVA soldiers from the camp filled the other trucks. Off we went. *I'm riding, not walking. Good God, hallelujah,* I thought.

The trucks were Soviet-made stake-bed style. A wood frame built out over the top of the cab provided a platform to attach foliage for camouflage. The drivers fixed fresh tree branches to the staked sides, adding to the illusion of a traveling bush and hopefully deceiving American aircraft once the truck stopped.

Even in the darkness, I could see that the trucks were rolling wrecks, dented, rusted, and missing parts. The front bumper on ours was hanging half off. The left front fender looked more like a piece of metal art than a truck part.

We drove down a narrow, foliage-covered side lane, which hit the main road in about a mile. We turned left into a world of churned earth, bludgeoned by bombs. Huge craters gouged the soil, evidence of the pounding this place had taken again and again and again. We looked anxiously toward the sky, our ears straining for the sound of American fighters or bombers that might blast us to oblivion.

The trucks followed a path just wide enough for their wheels, snaking through the rubble. Workers had finished their rough repairs hours, maybe minutes, before. The vehicles strained up and down through partly filled craters and over mounds of debris.

After moving through a devastated saddle high on the ridge, we plunged down the steep east slope of the mountain. The road cut across the bombed face of one precipice like a saber scar slashed into the cheek of a warrior. Freshly packed dirt caved away under the weight of our wheels, inches from the edge. I expected one of the trucks to roll off, smashing down onto the rocks below, lost in the dark chasm.

My joy over sitting in a truck quickly left me, as the trip was as uncomfortable as it was scary. The jolting ride riveted me with pain. Every bump was agony to my broken back, and the road was made of bumps. The truck had no shock absorbers and no discernible springs. I slammed, slammed, slammed onto the hard metal bed, in misery through the night.

We finally stopped and got out. We assembled in a long line and marched away from the road on a gently rising trail into what seemed a broad flat valley. The moon had gone, leaving us in sticky black darkness.

I walked painfully, dull, tired, unable to see the wild pressing around us, not knowing how far we had to go.

Looking up into the night sky, the brilliance of so many stars in the blackness lifted my spirits. I hadn't had a chance to see many stars over the past weeks through the dense jungle. I'd never known much about stars, anyway. Now I was fascinated by an impressive group of stars.[1] *Looks like a backwards Q. Hello friend.* We hiked more than an hour before coming to a camp deep in the jungle, where we spent the rest of the night and the next day, mostly sleeping.

Late in the afternoon, one of the guards barked, "Hãy sẵn sàng để đi."

Colonel Binh translated, "Get ready. We go."

We packed our shit and stood there waiting. I must have seemed anxious. Nghiem Ke came over and said, "Everything be OK."

I looked at him and smiled. "I know."

He reassured me. "We are special prisoners," he said. "We have good guards. I think yours not so good, but ours OK. They try to take care for us. Get us to Hanoi. Leader is officer, major."

"You speak very good English."

"Thank you. I study in U.S. I am engineer officer. Have American engineer friends."

He looked around and then he whispered. "I have gold Cross pen. Very expensive. Worth much." He held his shirt so I could see the small bulge in the lining. "I sew here before I get capture. When we get to Hanoi, I trade for something. You see."

We started down the trail at dusk, arriving at the road after dark. Trucks waited, hidden to the side under the trees. Our group and guards got into the same truck again. Other NVA soldiers filled the remaining vehicles. Down the road we rumbled and jostled and bounced. Pain tortured me once more as the bumps slammed my back. Riding in trucks was no fun. Worse yet, I felt god-awful heartburn attacking in waves of sour acid rising from my stomach. My face was scrunching to push back the discomfort even as I winced from the pain shooting through my back.

The sudden light from a flare floating in the night sky turned me from my misery. *Oh shit!* I thought. *Night Owls.*

One of our Mohawk missions had been flying radar along the coast of North Vietnam looking for indications of moving targets, convoys of trucks. We'd relay our targets to F-4 Phantom jets from the night fighting unit out of Ubon, Thailand, the 497th Tactical Fighter Squadron, the Night Owls. My truckmates looked at each other, bewildered. "Air strike!" I shouted.

Under the flares, the convoy trucks jerked off the road in different directions, scattering across a broad open area. Our truck stopped beside a mound not much higher than itself. There we sat, our camouflaging foliage looking pitiful. I knew what was coming next.

The first F-4 screamed down from altitude, and bombs exploded nearby. NVA antiaircraft fire responded. The next F-4 screeched toward us. More bombs. More antiaircraft. I began repeating, *The Lord is my Shepherd, I shall not want. . . . Yea though I walk through the valley of the shadow of death, I will fear no evil, for thou art with me . . . for thou art with me. Good God!*

The earth shook. Our truck banged about as if in an earthquake. Soldiers yelled from other trucks as some were hit. The world shuddered in explosions and flames. Then it was done.

An eerie quiet settled upon us except for distant screams of the wounded. The pitch darkness returned, save a few smoldering fires and the burning hulks of the truck in front of ours and the one behind. Close. *Too fucking close.* I thanked God and counted my blessings. We pulled around the wreckage in front of us, drove back up onto the road, and went rumbling and bumping and bouncing along once more.

It was still dark when the guards ordered us off the trucks. We tramped down a narrow lane as the vehicles drove farther along the main road to some concealed truck park, their refuge for the day. It would be a while before I'd see trucks again. I did not miss them.

We stumbled down the lane in the predawn darkness. Dogs barked in the small villages we passed through. No one was awake. As the sun rose, I saw we were traveling among rice paddies, our path the top of a raised berm, water-filled rice fields on either side. I sensed we were near the coast. Having grown up close to the beach—in Hawaii and Southern California—I knew the smells, the sense of being by the ocean. I felt that now.

The rising sun confirmed our northerly course. I walked and I walked, dealing with my pain. To relieve the hurt, I pressed my hands onto my hips, my elbows back and out. We continued past a few villages, drawing little attention at that early hour. Finally, we stopped at one. After chatting with sleepy-eyed officials, our guards took us into a large storage building on the edge of the settlement. Inside, we found crates along one wall to serve as beds, and we collapsed.

I woke to a sharp jab in my ribs, then another. I rolled to see a stick thrusting through the thatched wall. My friends were waking to the same. A growing number of kids were outside. They wanted to harass or maybe kill the unwanted visitors. The guards periodically chased them away. Their assault was little more than an annoyance, but it did force us to shift to the dirt floor in the middle of the building. We didn't get much rest with hostile shouts continuing sporadically all day.

Ke tried to draw me into conversation, maybe to lessen the effect of the hecklers. "They only children, but already hate us."

I said, "Don't know that I can blame them. We bomb the crap out of this part of North Vietnam. I'm sure they've all had family killed. What a miserable way to live."

He asked, "Do you have children?"

"Yes, a boy five years old and a daughter one year old. How about you? Do you have kids?"

"Yes, many. Have seven, four boys, three girls. My wife is Bé. All live near Saigon. I give money to my wife. If war go bad, they go United States. I make plan for them. I like U.S. very much. Have friend in Virginia, my advisor when I command engineer battalion." Ke, ten years my senior, struck me as outgoing, nice, and well-mannered. We were becoming friends.

We stayed the night, and the next morning we packed up and headed out of the village. Our guards kept the children and groups of angry adults at bay. We tramped up the southern part of North Vietnam, most days walking, sometimes riding in trucks at night. The logic seemed to be to walk through areas with the greatest threat of air strikes, staying on small lanes and away from the roads. Then sometimes we'd travel at night, riding in trucks where the danger was less. Passing one small city, Ke pointed to a sign that read, Dong Hoi. I knew where we were, still less than halfway to Hanoi.

At times we'd see American air strikes against some unknown target. *Truck park or fuel storage*, I'd think, watching the jets scream down their bombing runs. The bombs exploded as distant thuds. Just the screeching noise of the diving planes instilled terror nearly as great as the bombs themselves.

One night, after a long, painful truck ride, we came near the mouth of a large river. It was the Gianh, the location of the Quang Khe ferries, a target we'd bombed the living shit out of forever.[2] *Here we go again*, I thought. The truck pulled down a short, steep grade to the bank. We were astonished to be ordered aboard a shabby passenger boat and ushered below deck. Other NVA soldiers boarded with our guards, filling the boat's thirty-person capacity. The engine chugged and the boat got under way, headed upstream. Flares filled the sky and a series of air strikes thundered on targets downriver. We had boarded above the main ferry sites, which were blasted in frequent air raids just as they were this night. Our boat picked its way along tributaries and canals to avoid the most dangerous spots. We felt anxious until the chaos faded into distant rumbles far behind us. I fell asleep.

We motored through the night. At dawn we pushed ashore, climbed from the boat, walked across twenty yards of sandy beach up a trail to the top of a sharp bluff overlooking the river. After trudging a few miles from the river across a level, brush-covered landscape, we emerged into sugar cane fields. Past them, we entered a military compound, where a group of thirty or so ARVN prisoners squatted in an open area near the center. We joined them. I squatted with the others.

An NVA officer appeared before us. He launched into a long speech, which at times seemed to be reading the prisoners the riot act.

Ke, always looking out for me, said, "He camp commander. He telling camp rules and lot of propaganda. I tell you later."

The tirade lasted more than half an hour. Toward the end, I heard a word sounding like "fine" spoken about half a dozen times. The officer's harangue built to a crescendo in the last minutes. Then he walked away and disappeared.

Ke looked troubled. He turned to me and asked, "You know Captain Fine?"

"No."

You sure you no know Captain Fine. He American who die here some days ago."

"Was it Captain Finch? Was the name Finch?" I asked.

Ke assured me, "No, Fine. Captain Fine. You don't know him." Still, I worried. A spasm jerked my head and shoulders in a shudder.

The guards took us to a small hut with posts enough to tie our hammocks. They fastened the door shut and placed local militia guards outside. We settled in, getting comfortable and resting. The door opened. A guard came in and said something. A South Vietnamese prisoner entered behind him. Lieutenant Hung. *My God.* I knew. It was Wayne who had died in this camp, Capt. Wayne Finch. Wayne was dead. *My God.*

Hung stared as if at a ghost, astounded to see me alive. He cried. I sat slumped, devastated at the realization that Wayne Finch was dead, my friend Wayne who had helped me, cared for me, my friend Wayne who I owed so much. He was dead.

Shocked, disbelieving, I introduced Hung to the others. He told us how everyone thought I was dead, how the group suffered on the march north after they left me, how two tall American pilots joined them, how Wayne continued to get sicker, lost hope, and grew weak. Hung told us of the decision to leave them here when the group moved on, Wayne to regain his strength, Hung to look after him. Hung told the story slowly, mixing English and Vietnamese, the others whispering short bits of translation back and forth. "Captain Fince ask for Bible. Communists no have. He die while pray to Jesus."

I sat feeling like shit, feeling bad for Wayne, for his months of struggle coming to this miserable end. I fell into sadness, twisting it into melancholy self-pity, sinking to the lowest point I had known.

The door opened again with an order for Hung and me to come out. The NVA commander waited outside with a couple of soldiers. I thought, *Oh great. Here goes more indoctrination, maybe interrogation, even torture.* The officer escorted us up a hill to one edge of the camp. There, not far from a garden flourishing with fruits and vegetables, the NVA officer pointed to a recently disturbed patch of soil. The officer spoke, Hung translating. "He say this where Captain Fince bury. He say he do all he can for Fince. He give best food. He give meat and banana. But Fince die." Hung paused, listening to more. "He say they wrap in white cloth for bury. Treat body well. What he say true. I here with him. I see him bury here. He die six of September." I shook with a chill, feeling sickness coming on, not knowing if it was real or the dread of what fate might bring me.

Shortly after we returned to our hut, screams told us that some horror was taking place across the compound. Guards ordered us back out to the field at the center of the camp. The commander strutted to the front, his face set sternly. He began speaking, his tone filled with anger. Ke translated. "He say some prisoners take melon from garden. They be punished."

Six South Vietnamese prisoners stood before us, their arms pulled behind them, straining their backs and shoulder joints, locked in place with elbow irons, a cruel device that looked like a stout set of rigid hand-cuffs. I was reminded of my own ordeal after capture when they dislo-cated my shoulders. As the prisoners screamed, Hung explained, "They airborne. They take back Quang Tri city in South Vietnam. Big fight. Paratrooper drop from sky. Beat NVA. Win battle. Communist run from city. Take some prisoner. But NVA get defeat in their offense. They mad for that. Want to punish prisoner. Steal from garden not problem. It only a reason to punish some for good fight airborne make." Hung was a paratrooper. I sensed the pride and anguish he felt for his comrades.

We stayed in that dreadful camp for days. Ke worried about my gloom and the undeniable illness settling into me. I lay in my hammock look-ing, open-eyed, into nothingness. My mind wallowed in sadness and grief, my body slammed from chills to fever. Ke feared malaria. I dreaded whatever it was that had taken Wayne. Would we both meet the same fate in this nameless cesspool, wrapped in white sheets, dropped into the ground, lying under that dirt by the garden, together forever?

One of the local militia guards detailed to watch us was a curious fellow. A simple kind of man, slightly pudgy, he'd talk with my friends at length. Ke told me he asked questions about life in South Vietnam and about America. One evening, Ke was talking to him in earnest through one of the many gaps in the back wall. Ke fumbled with his shirt, sliding his gold Cross pen from its hiding place, passing it through the wall to the guard. Footsteps shuffled away. An hour later, the guard returned, forcing a cloth bag through the space in the wall.

Next morning, other surprises came in through the door. Ke had negotiated for us to be able to cook our own rice in our hut. We made a small fire pit in the center. Militiamen brought us two cooking pots, one large and one small, along with some wood, rice, and water, and we were soon boiling rice in the large pot and water in the smaller. Ke smilingly pulled one potato from the bag he'd got the night before and put it in the smaller pot. When it was done, he gave it to me. I tried breaking it into pieces and offering one to each of the others, but they wouldn't take any. It was my potato. Ke insisted that I eat it all.

Ke pulled another potato from the bag the next day, and another every day after that for the rest of the week. He had traded his precious pen, the one that was to gain him some special favor in Hanoi, for six potatoes. Those six potatoes gave me the strength to get through my illness and, more importantly, lift my spirits from the gloom that had possessed me. Ke had traded his prized possession for my life.

The day came for our departure, and I was anxious to leave. We rolled our hammocks and stuffed them into our packs along with all our worldly belongings: a small rice bowl, canteen, chopsticks I'd fashioned from twigs, and my T-shirt that had served as a precious rag for months. We climbed into a truck waiting just inside the main gate. Oddly, the camp commander and a group of NVA soldiers got in the same truck with us. Two empty fifty-five-gallon fuel drums took up a chunk of the space, which made this trip a tight fit of strange traveling companions.

Ke tapped my arm. "Look," he said. The curious militia guard who'd been so interested in learning about South Vietnam and America, who'd fetched my potatoes, stood there smiling like a kid with a new puppy.

He came close to the truck and I leaned against the staked side. "Good-bye," he said, grinning. His simple humanity made me smile and I said, "Good-bye."

Ke saw my astonishment. "He want to learn to say good-bye to you when you leave. I teach him. He good man." *Yes*, I thought. *No doubt he is. There are good men everywhere. It's the governments, the systems, the leaders that are bad. It's communism that sucks, not the people of North Vietnam. They're not so different from the South. Not so different from me.* Our truck rumbled off, a single vehicle headed down the road in the daylight. We mostly stood, the space was so tight. We stood and bounced. The two empty fuel barrels bounced.

"Chết tiệt đau quá! Chết tiệt! Chêt tiệt!" The camp commander squealed. One of the fifty-five-gallon drums had bounced high and come down on his big toe. The Ho Chi Minh sandals gave no protection. His toe was nearly severed, hanging grotesquely off to the side. He wailed the rest of the ride. *Due punishment*, I thought, but at the same time I felt for his suffering.

When we got off the truck at the end of the day, two NVA soldiers, one on each side, tried to help their commander walk. He took two steps and was done. Then one soldier tried to carry the commander on his back. His pitiful effort brought an angry reaction and a scream as the commander landed back on the ground. A good deal of commotion ensued. "Không!" (No!), the commander finally shouted, shaking his head. Then he motioned toward me. A soldier spoke to Colonel Binh. Binh talked to Ke. Ke turned to me and said, "Officer want you carry him. We think good idea. You big. He impress with American. You show him American better than *bộ đội*.[3] You try?"

"Oh God, Ke. I don't think I can. That'll be tough. I'm a mess." Ke looked disappointed, mostly for the pride of our small band. I saw his expression and thought, *What the heck.* I grudgingly said, "I'll try."

The soldiers lifted the officer onto my back. The commander of the camp where Wayne had died sat on me, piggyback-style, his bloody toe dangling by my right knee as I carried him. That he was small and light-weight didn't help the pain. My back and shoulders cried in protest. I struggled along the path for almost half a mile to a military camp set away from the road. I walked as tall as I could, showing American grit. I was the only one big enough to bear this injured communist pig. The effort, though, proved something to me. *I'm getting a lot better, stronger. If I can do this, I'm going to make it to Hanoi.*

Ke was sick that evening and the next morning too. We walked through another day to a village several miles distant. Colonel Binh said, "He have malaria. Sickness come. Sickness go." Ke could have used potatoes, or meat, or medicine, but he had traded his prized pen for me. Now he had nothing. Luckily, the malaria attack passed and he got better.

We left that village on trucks, moving further inland, into the foothills of the high mountains to the west. I figured there must be horrendous bombing closer to the coast. We drove from village to village, finding shelter in commandeered outbuildings. Ke told me, "This Ha Tinh Province, very poor part of Vietnam. Not much food. Hard life for people here. Don't know why we come this way by mountains. Off of our route."

In one small settlement, a guard grabbed Ke and me from the dilapidated shed we called home that afternoon. He led us through the village of scruffy dwellings, dirty, disheveled people, chickens and dogs everywhere, the sounds of snorting pigs in the distance. We came up behind a shack, where an elderly man sat hunched on a bench in the yard, his long, wispy white beard waving lightly in the quiet breeze, his eyes studying us as we approached.

Our guard spoke to the man, then looked to Ke for translation. "This Vu Dinh Huynh. He want to meet you." Thereafter, the old man spoke directly to me, pausing for Ke to repeat his words in English. "He say he know Americans. In World War Two, he fighter in Viet Minh with American advisors. They fight hard together against Japanese." The old man went on, his voice cracking with emotion. Ke kept translating, "He like Americans. He like you. He not understand why Americans and Vietnamese enemy now." The man put out his hand. I took it, and he gave me a long handshake. "He say he wish you always be his friend." Tears streamed down the old warrior's cheeks, soaking his thin beard. A sad smile curled the corners of his mouth. He stood, still grasping my hand, pulling me along into his shabby home. On one wall, near a simple Buddhist family shrine, hung a framed certificate of his long-ago military service. He stood beside it, erect, thumping his index-finger on his chest proudly proclaiming, "Viet Minh. Viet Minh." He shook my hand two more times and bid us farewell.[4]

The next day, our truck rumbled through the gate of a big military compound tucked into the foothills. The buildings were large, single-story structures in good repair and clean. The well-kept park-like grounds were hidden under the high canopy of giant trees. This was a major headquarters.

An army cadre met us, exchanged words with our guards, ordered us out, and escorted us into the most impressive of the buildings. Inside, the cadre took the South Vietnamese prisoners down a hallway to the right. I was pulled from the group and taken left into a small room off the main hallway where two soldiers sat, waiting. One looked to be an officer. I was worried. *What the fuck's up now?*

They both studied me. One asked, "How are you?"

"I've been pretty sick. Had an infected wound, dysentery, chills, and fevers—also lots of pain in my back and shoulders. But I feel better now."

The other, possibly a doctor or medic, spent several minutes examining me, my eyes, ears, mouth, teeth, ankle wound, back. I sensed concern as the two chatted back and forth. I had no idea what they talked about, but assumed it was me.

"You are going to Hanoi. There is still some distance. You will make it."

Damn right I will. What is this? A physical evaluation? A pep talk?

Staccato footsteps approached down the hall, and the door opened. I looked, closed my eyes, shook my head, and opened them again. Surely I was dreaming. There in front of me stood a female North Vietnamese officer, tall, beautiful, her dark hair pulled back, shiny black leather jackboots rising to just below her knees, her uniform impeccable. She looked me over for a few minutes, turned around, and left. The two NVA soldiers followed. The cadre who had brought me in took me back to the truck where my friends already waited. A strange encounter indeed.

As we climbed into the truck, a crowd of soldiers assembled to see the prisoners. Most stared silently, but a number shouted angrily. I didn't realize how heated things were until our guards started brandishing their weapons. The officer in charge of our guards shouted retorts to the most vocal in the crowd and yelled at the driver to get going. We accelerated out of the camp, roaring down the road for a distance before we slowed. Hours later, out of the hills, the truck stopped at a settlement, let us out, and sped away, dust clouds rising behind it. We settled into another night in a strange shed amidst hostile villagers.

The next morning, we walked from that village. Approaching another, we were met by local leaders on the road. Our guards followed them to a small, windowless adobe storage building alongside the road, short of the town. It was still morning, an unusually early day. We sat inside for hours. I had to piss, and I asked several times. The guard responded each time, "Chờ đợi!" (Wait!) Finally, he told me to piss inside. I looked at Ke questioningly when he translated the order. He repeated, "He say piss here." I did. Others joined me.

Only later did I understand. About midafternoon, our guards took us outside. They looked worried and assembled us in a defensive formation. I was in the middle, my South Vietnamese friends ringed around me, our guards forming an outer ring.

We had to move through the village. There was no other way. As we shuffled along the only street, throngs of angry villagers came at us, swinging and jabbing shovels and hoes and rakes. They poked and jabbed with whatever they had. Some threw rocks.

I felt bad for my friends, even some small compassion for the guards. Ke, Binh, and the other prisoners took the brunt of the assault. I was hit with a few rocks, but that was it. My friends were bruised and bloodied. After we left the village, we waited by a larger road. Just after dark, a truck came. We got on and drove only a few hours.

That night found us in a village a short walk off the roadway. The next morning, another agitated mob assaulted us on our hike back to the truck. They chased us, forcing us to hobble frantically toward the vehicle. The guards waved their weapons, but that didn't stop them. Several bursts of AK-47 fire over the mob kept them back long enough for us to load and drive off. *Amazing. They shot at their own people to protect us.* Ke, still breathing heavily, said, "We near Vinh city. No like us here. Much bombing close to here for long time. Many have sons in army. Many die in war. They hate us."

After a short ride into the countryside, the truck stopped and left us on the road. We walked and we walked and we walked some more. The road was obliterated, obviously an area at high risk for air strikes. We picked our way through bomb craters, which stretched for hundreds of yards to either side and far ahead of us. I saw scores of trucks and crates under the trees off to our left. I figured this must be a major transportation hub, maybe fuel storage, pipeline, or supply depot.

Two distant rounds of antiaircraft artillery fired into the air. *Oh shit!* The guards started screaming, "Bê năm hai! Bê năm hai!" *Oh shit. B-52s.*

We leapt into one large crater together, with prisoners and guards huddled close. The officer lay next to me, his pistol drawn, pointed close to my head. I don't know what he thought I would do, if we would try to take their weapons in the commotion, or what. He wasn't taking any chances.

The bombs dropped. Hundreds of bombs fell all around us, big bombs, nearly on top of us. I knew there was little chance of living through a B-52 strike, but by the grace of God, no bombs fell in our crater. The earth trembled, it shook, it ruptured and heaved. Waves of crushing pressure blasted through us, squeezing, hurting my head and ears. The suffocating pressure was painful, awful, frightening. It stopped. All was quiet. I was dead. I knew it.

I felt ringing in my ears, throbbing in my head. *I must be alive.* Next to me, the officer sat up and holstered his pistol. I looked around. Ke was moving. Others began sitting up, dazed but alive. No one could hear. No one spoke. We crawled out of our hole and started walking in the direction we'd been traveling. Our journey continued, one catastrophe closer to Hanoi. It would not be our last.

Two days later, we were back near the coast. We plodded along an attractive gravel road lined with tall, stately trees, widely spaced at even intervals, planted during French colonization. Green fields gave way to sand in the distance to our right, scattered dunes dancing toward the sea. Ominous dark clouds built in the sky, and a rising wind blew hard against us. For hours, its force mounted as we walked along. Debris flew across our path, pelting us with branches and pebbles mixed in sheets of rain as the gale turned to an angry thunderous roar. Our soaked bodies leaned into the wind, struggling forward against a full-blown typhoon. We pressed on.

A few days later, we came to a tidy village of smart-looking homes in a tropical setting surrounded by low hills. The war seemed far away except for the scarcity of men. Only children, women, and old men moved about the hamlet; there were no males of fighting age.

We walked toward a nice home down a well-tended walkway bounded by landscaped shrubs and gardens. After a polite conversation with the middle-aged matron of the house, our guards assigned sleeping spaces to each of us inside. Mine was the top of a large table, hard and uncomfortable, but pleasant at the same time. Though lying on that hard flat wood hurt me everywhere, it felt good to be in that lovely house.

I heard giggling outside. Two young women were sneaking peeks through a window and laughing at me sitting on the edge of my table. Our hostess spoke and Ke relayed in English, "They want meet you. To see American. OK with you?" What was I to say? "Sure." They entered, walked up beside me, laughed, fidgeted, and chatted nervously with each other. They were cute girls in their late teens or early twenties, clean, dressed neatly in the traditional manner, and smiling. My fellow prisoners were all agrin. I was embarrassed. "They say you very handsome." I couldn't believe it, but I answered, "Cám ơn" (Thank you).

After they left, I heard a squeal outside. Ke exclaimed, "Neighbor kill pig."

"What?" I asked.

"They kill pig. Maybe we eat." He got up and moved to a back window. "Here, look. You see."

Outside, in the yard next door, I saw a group of old men and boys circled around a tied hog, beating it with sticks and tree limbs. The more they hit the beast, the louder it snorted and screamed. We listened to unnerving pig shrieks until it died. It was bled, gutted, and butchered. The beating, I was told, made the meat more tender. That evening, we all got two small pieces of fatback with rice. I suspect our NVA guards got better. As gross as the fatback looked, it was the closest thing to meat I'd had since being captured. I chewed through the rubbery toughness with gusto, enjoying the flavor. I looked at Ke and asked a question I'd been wondering about.

"Ke, what happened at Tan Canh? What happened to the 22nd Division commander?"

Ke frowned and answered, "Very difficult. We get shelled for days before. Very heavy shelling. Ask for B-52 strike. No get. Enemy attack with tanks at dawn. Our antitank weapons don't work. Our tanks broken long time. They don't work. Enemy tanks roll right into us. American advisors leave. Some on helicopter. Colonel Dat, our division commander, he stay in bunker. He very afraid. He no come out. He coward. He die in bunker. Colonel Binh lead us. He good man, good leader. We escape to northeast. Get capture next day."

I awoke in the morning having to pee and needing to shit badly. "Bộ đội. Bộ đội. Cho đi đái. Xin tào lao." (Guard. Guard. Have to go pee. Got to crap.) A guard escorted me out back to an outhouse and stood by with his AK-47, watching me. A frog hopped around one corner of the outhouse, passing just in front of me. I stopped with a start, looking only long enough to think, *Cute fellow.* Then a poisonous king cobra slithered from around the same corner, rapidly gaining on his prey. I jumped back yelling, "Cobra, cobra." The guard buckled in laughter. The frog and snake disappeared in the tall grass. I went on into the shitter, squatted over the small hole in the floor, and did my business. Within two hours we were back on the road once more on our never-ending journey north.

Standing in the back of the truck as we drove slowly through a small town, some of my fellow prisoners began bantering with a group of townspeople beside the road. They'd talk a bit, laugh, talk some more, and laugh again.

"What's up?" I asked Ke.

"They make fun. Like in U.S. where South people talk different from North. Here, too, same thing. These North people. They make fun how we talk. We think they sound funny."

That evening, our hammocks strung in yet another village, Ke explained further. "I from the North. Did not leave until 1954. I can speak both ways. Today it funny for one side to hear other talk. Good chance to laugh."

"Yeah, good to laugh. It's always good to laugh. Humor is very important. I think we must have it to survive. Humor and faith."

"You have good spirit, Reedo. You always find good thing to see."

"Thanks Ke. Hey, why did you leave the North in 1954?"

"We very worry about communist. My father professor at university. He very worry. Many Catolic go South. We not Catolic; we Buddhist, but we afraid of communist. Not all family get out. My grand-brother, he stay in North."

"What's a grand-brother?" I asked.

"In Vietnamese family, oldest boy is very important position we call grand-brother. He now high rank officer in army headquarters in Hanoi. It strange. He fight for North. I fight for South."

A town meeting began in front of a community hut thirty yards from us. Crude log benches provided seating. A young firebrand exhorted the audience, then seemed to threaten some of them.

"Is this a church service, Ke?"

"No, no church here. This political meeting. They have every week. The man, he political officer in this town for Communist Party. He have message. He own the truth. He say much propaganda. He ask others to tell what they do wrong and how they do better in future. Also tell about other people in the town. Good and bad. People condemn bad actions and praise good. You no want to be bad person. Then you have plenty of problem. People don't like the communist. You see every day. Remember man at Captain Fince camp? But they must do like this. No choice."

"Wow, talk about mind control."

"Yes. Communist control everything. You see bicycle. All register to government. They own, not people. You hear radio sometime. All belong to government. All station belong to government. All news from government. Same thing newspaper. Same thing church if they have. All control by government."

"Ke, how much further do you think it is to Hanoi? We've come so far."

"Still almost one hundred mile more. We go slow. Not go far every day. Many problems for communist. Trouble with road, with bridge, with truck, with American air strike. Much problem to move everything even short distance. Maybe better after Thanh Hoa city. I think maybe we close."

The next morning we climbed on a spiffy new truck with nice paint, good tires, a smooth-running engine, springs, and shocks! Down the road we drove, coming to a highway unlike any I'd seen. It was paved. No craters. After several miles of the most comfortable riding I'd had, we came to a small city. Ke craned his neck, reading signs. His eyes lit up and he started shouting, "Thanh Hoa! Thanh Hoa! Sign say Hanoi only 150 kilometer." As we left the city, we accelerated, moving down the highway at a good clip, heading north.

We stopped in the dark at an isolated farmhouse on the side of a hill. It had been an exciting day, but disappointing at the same time. As much ground as we had been covering, we had built a hope that we'd reach Hanoi, my goal for so long. We hadn't. I was exhausted. After eating my evening rice, I fell fast asleep.

Just before sunrise, Colonel Binh shook me awake. The room was dimly gray in the faint predawn light. "What's up?"

He said, "You go. You go now."

Ke was up, rubbing the sleep from his eyes and straightening his uniform. I got up and packed my shit. Colonel Binh again said, "You go. Good luck." He and the others shook my hand, each wishing me well in broken English or Vietnamese.

Saying good-bye to each of them, I thought of the weeks we had spent together. Colonel Binh had been the rock that had held our group together, a well of strength that we drew from, a reasoned thinker guiding us with right decision after right decision. Triển, the artillery major, oldest of the bunch, always gracious, encouraging, kind. Tri, the young 22nd Division surgeon, so concerned about me and always haunted by helplessness because he could not give me medical care. Hung, gung-ho airborne lieutenant to whom, along with Xanh, I owed my life. He had helped drag me through the jungle when I was half dead, and he had helped Wayne through the final hours of his life. And Ke, my dear friend, translator of most of what was spoken to me by other Vietnamese, my confidant, mentor, comforter in my lowest moments, encourager, sacrificing so much when I needed him most. These guys had been my comrades, my family, my brothers. I'd never been closer to anybody in my life. I owed each of them so much that I had not repaid, could never repay. My heart sank, not knowing what was ahead for me, or what might be in store for them. Our paths separated here. We moved into an unknown future.

Ke followed me outside, where an army jeep waited. Two cleanly dressed NVA soldiers stood beside it. They spoke briefly to Ke. He turned to me, tears in his eyes. In the breaking dawn, a beautiful broad plain stretched out before us. The rising sun gleamed off the roofs of farms and villages merging, in the distance, with the expanse of a grand city. Ke waved his arm over the splendor.

"This the valley of the Red River. That Hanoi, capital of North."

He put out his hand and I took it. We held our grasp for a long time, looking at each other. Then he spoke. "You go Hanoi now. To place with other Americans. We go farther, to place for Vietnamese." Sadness welled inside me. I bit my bottom lip for fear of crying. Ke smiled a sad smile, and with his voice cracking, he bid a final farewell, "I never forget friendship between our two countries. I never forget friendship between you and me. Good-bye."

CHAPTER 12

In the Company of Heroes

I lay across the back seat of the jeep like a sack of smelly trash, blindfolded, hands tied behind my back, bouncing uncomfortably down the streets of Hanoi. The morning warmed with exotic smells and strange new sounds, a cacophony of people, bicycles, livestock, and birds. An occasional truck blasted its horn, forcing its way through the chaos around it.

The din quieted as we rolled into a courtyard behind high, thick walls. My escorts pulled me upright and removed my blindfold, and I sat in the jeep absorbing the world around me. Large shade trees, brick walkways and patios, and shrub-filled planters surrounded a French colonial mansion off to my left. In front of the jeep stretched a ten-foot-high makeshift wall framed in two by fours covered with large black sheets of tarpaper, bisecting the length of the courtyard, denying a view of what lay beyond, a flimsy screen that concealed but could not secure. The soldiers ordered me out of the jeep and took me through a rickety narrow wood and tarpaper gate into the inner courtyard.

I faced a long, single-story warehouse building of concrete walls and corrugated metal roofing with doors evenly spaced along its length. We turned right, walked past the end of the building into an open-air alcove. A concrete, water-filled trough stood in the center. Along the backside was a row of four small open-doored rooms. It looked like a dressing area for a public swimming pool. But there was no pool here.

Two guards approached. One handed me a bucket and a bar of soap. He told me, in broken English, to get water from the trough and go into one of the little rooms and wash. I did. I took off my sorry backpack, removed my toeless Soviet shoes and the rags that had once been my flight suit. I stood there naked, looking at my thin arms and my ribs sticking out. *Wonder how skinny I was back on the trail in Laos. Much healthier now than I was then. Still, I'm a mess.*

I poured water on my head, letting it stream over my long hair and beard. I washed months of dirt and grime from my body, scouring dried, caked filth from my ass and crotch. I scrubbed and scrubbed, then rinsed with the rest of the water. A guard handed me a small towel and clean clothes, a maroon and gray striped prison uniform, a long-sleeved shirt and pants. I also got a pair of Ho Chi Minh sandals, my very first. I was delighted. I felt clean and comfortable for the first time since I'd been shot down 154 days ago.

I sat on a small stool by the water trough. A guard wrapped a sheet around me and took scissors and an old-fashioned pair of hand-squeeze clippers to my shabby five-month growth of hair and beard. Once the beard was shorn, I was given a double-edged razor and soap and commanded to shave in front of a small mirror. I had not seen myself all these months. The mirror was poor and distorted, but still I thought how odd that person looked, how thin and haggard. *That guy's been through hell.* The shave was brutal, but in a few moments I was clean-shaven and my face felt strange and tingly.

A soldier brought a burlap sack and dropped it on the ground, while another dragged my flight suit and pack out of the bathing room using a couple of sticks. With an expression of disgust on his face, he manipulated the sticks to lift the rags into the sack. Another soldier opened the pack I'd hauled all that way from northern Cambodia and dumped the contents on the ground. He picked out my cup, rice bowl, and canteen. The other used the sticks to deposit the remaining stuff into the sack. My scroungy T-shirt I had prized so dearly went with the cup and bowl and was carried off. Everything else went into the sack to be trashed.

One guard marched me back the way I'd come, leading me along the front of the long warehouse building past a number of closed doorways. He stopped at one, opened the door, and ordered me in. The room was about twelve feet by ten feet with tall concrete walls and a concrete floor and ceiling. It had no windows. High on one wall was a small speaker box. A single light bulb glowed weakly in the center of the ceiling. On the floor, in one corner, a bamboo mat covered a rectangular board the size of a door, my bed. A folded blanket was on the mat along with a cup, spoon, toothbrush, and toothpaste. On the floor next to the wall sat two buckets. The guard gestured that one was to pee in, the other to shit in. Next to the buckets were several pieces of paper the consistency of coarse brown paper towels, my toilet paper. The door slammed shut.

I sat on my bed on the floor and took in the new world around me. Quiet, dim, lonely. *Solitary confinement. Not bad, actually. Wonder how long I'll be here?*

A small window at shoulder height in the door opened, and a shallow metal bowl was thrust through the opening. The bowl, dinged and rusty, was filled with bean sprouts; a four-inch piece of French bread lay across the top. I took it. I delighted in the most pleasurable meal I'd had. No rice! Bean sprouts and French bread! *My God.*

Odd clicking sounds came from the speaker box high on the wall, then music, the Carpenters singing "We've Only Just Begun." It all came home to me. I'd left the prison camp in northern Cambodia on July 2. It was October 10. My trek had taken more than three months, three months in hell. At least six of the South Vietnamese prisoners were dead; Wayne was dead. I'd almost died a dozen times. All the pain. All the agony.

I sat there, overcome by emotion. Tears streamed down my cheeks. I finally knew I would survive. I had made it to Hanoi. I was clean. I was safe. My fight was done. Now all I had to do was wait. I would live. I would go home someday. My mind filled with thoughts of family, hope pounding strong in my heart. *Thank you, God.*

After the song ended, an American voice came over the speaker with a plea to stop the atrocities being waged by the United States against the Vietnamese people and to cooperate and support the good peoples of Vietnam in their struggle for freedom from American oppression. A well-spoken Vietnamese woman's voice followed. The woman highlighted the news, slamming the puppet government in Saigon. She said thousands of U.S. soldiers had been killed and hundreds of aircraft shot down. I knew the numbers to be preposterous exaggerations. "Utter bullshit," I said out loud, immediately checking my outburst and glancing around the cell in an involuntary reflex. I feared unseen eavesdroppers.

The door burst open. An angry-looking guard stepped in. "Come," he commanded. I got up and followed him to the big colonial house. Inside the grand entryway, the guard directed me into a room to the left. There sat half a dozen neatly dressed North Vietnamese in crisp, clean uniforms, rank insignia bright on their collars. They studied me. Their penetrating eyes briefly undercut my confidence. I looked steadily at each, in turn, reaching deep within myself for the courage I would need to deal with the interrogation I knew was coming.

"Please sit," said the most senior of the group. I took a chair at a small table. He sat on one side. A younger soldier sat directly across from me. The others occupied chairs away from the table. The older man, an officer of some rank I guessed, did nearly all the talking.

"Some tea? Cigarette?"

I took the cigarette, accepted a light, and sipped the warm tea.

"You are here under the care of the Vietnamese people. You will be well cared for as long as you follow camp rules. You must listen to the instructions of the *bộ đội*, be respectful, and do not make trouble." He bent forward, earnestly looking me over and then studying my eyes. "You know you are a criminal. You are not a prisoner of war. America does biocide, genocide, and ecocide against us. They kill pregnant women, babies, and old people. We could have trial of you for these crimes. You have no rights. We have the authority to do with you what we will. We have chosen to treat you well. So long as you follow rules, you will receive the humane and lenient treatment of the Vietnamese." *Well there's that old bullshit again*, I thought. *What's next?*

I heard another spiel on the two-thousand-year history of the Vietnamese people, a lesson on French colonialism and American neocolonialism. But no interrogation, only indoctrination. Then I got another cigarette and a strange proposition.

"The prisoners help with the camp radio broadcast. Perhaps you have heard them. We would like you to help as well. This will be very good for you." I sat, not believing what I was hearing. How could he ask an American army officer to do that? I responded without a pause, "No. I will not." I tensed. *Here comes the shit.* But no. Other than looks of disappointment, that was the end of it for today. "You think about it. Come to good decision." Back to my cell I went.

Solitary confinement served two purposes. It punished me for not cooperating and it segregated me from other prisoners who could fortify my will to resist. The unspoken understanding was that once I agreed to the demands of my captors, I would get out of solitary. *Not going to happen*, I promised myself. *Remember the Code of Conduct. Don't cave in to these bastards.*

I went through indoctrination sessions every other day for a couple of weeks. Besides the propaganda bullshit, pressure continued for me to help with the camp radio and to write or make verbal statements. I refused again and again and again.

As I'd sit alone in my cell, I would occasionally hear air raid sirens followed by air strikes around the city. Sometimes, though, I'd hear bombs explode first, then the swoosh of a plane screaming by, and finally the tardy wail of air raid sirens, the supersonic FB-111 doing its deed as no other could.

A few days into my indoctrination sessions, I learned that the United States had bombed the French diplomatic mission in Hanoi the day after I arrived. My captors claimed it was an intentional provocation. I saw it as an obvious and regrettable mistake. As always, the communists ensured we got all the bad news they could gather, factual or otherwise.

One day, my door opened and the skinniest human I had ever seen walked in, wearing maroon and gray striped prison garb, ashen, speaking softly. "I'm Anton. Frank Anton. I'm here to move you. Get your stuff together and come with me." *An American!*

My stuff consisted of a cup, toothbrush, toothpaste, a spoon, a blanket, and a bamboo mat. Frank rolled the bamboo mat as I grabbed my few things. *Christ, is this how bad it gets here? This guy looks like a skeleton. Is that what's going to become of me?* I followed him outside, down a few doors to the left, where a guard stood outside an open door. In we went. Frank set the mat down and left. The door shut behind him.

I stood in a cell about twelve feet wide and twenty-five feet long. Six bunks lined up to my right, head end against the wall. Two others lay lengthwise against the wall to my left. The bunks were three-by-six-foot pieces of wood resting on sawhorses of the same width. Each was covered with a bamboo mat, a blanket neatly folded at one end. Between the bunks on my left I saw two buckets, just like the ones in my solitary cell. A row of three small window slits, six by eighteen inches each, opened high at the top of the back wall.

Seven sets of eyes fixed on me. One approached and put out his hand. "I'm John Murphy, captain, Air Force. How you doin'?" *Americans. A room full of Americans. Oh, God, bless you.*

"Doing OK. Bill Reeder, Army captain, Cobra pilot."

A surprised voice came from across the room. "My God, we heard you were dead. We thought you must be Wayne Finch. Al and I marched north with his group. He got sick and needed a few days to rest before catching back up. When we heard a new prisoner was here, we thought it was Wayne. He told us you'd been left in the jungle. He was certain you'd died." The really tall guy who had been speaking walked over and shook my hand. I had to tilt my head back to take in his height. "Hi, I'm Bill Gauntt, Air Force. And that's Al Kroboth, Marine A-6 B-N, bombardier-navigator. We were with Wayne. Met up with him after we crossed into North Vietnam."

I broke the news. "Wayne's dead. Died in the camp several days after you guys left. I saw his grave. Lieutenant Hung was still there. He was with him when he died."

I glanced over my left shoulder at Al, who was sitting on his board, looking sickly and nursing a badly broken shoulder. Grotesque boils covered his back and arms. He nodded as best he could. "Sorry. I'm not well," he said. "Been throwing up everything I eat." Al looked old, thin, and drawn.

Next I met John Parsels, Bill Thomas, Bill Henderson, and Dave Mott. Eight of us lived together in this small cell, eight American prisoners, four of us named Bill. Bill Thomas, a thirty-six-year-old Marine Corps intelligence officer, was "Old Bill." Bill Henderson, a twenty-four-year-old Air

Force OV-10 pilot shot down a month before me, was "Young Bill." He'd gone down while trying to help rescue an RB-66 crewmember, call sign Bat 21 Bravo.[1] Bill Gauntt, a six-foot-five-inch F-4 reconnaissance pilot, was "Big Bill." I had just arrived, so I was "New Bill."

I soon heard all their tales of being shot down, captured, and marching north. All but one had been captured within the past year. That one was John Parsels. He'd been a prisoner for more than two years. Only one of the others had been held longer than I had been.

We were all captains except 1st Lt. Al Kroboth and WO Bill Thomas. Three had crewmembers as fellow POWs. Parsels was copilot of a UH-1 Huey that had flown into a mountain in bad weather, killing the pilot. The gunner and crew chief survived and were being held elsewhere in the camp. Mott and Thomas had been flying together in an OV-10. The rest of us were the only member of our crews to be captured. We didn't know the fate of our other pilot. Most suspected theirs had been killed. I was sure that mine had been rescued.

As we talked, I asked about Frank Anton. "That guy that brought me in here, Anton? He looked like shit."

John Murphy answered. "Yeah. That's just the way he looks. Nickname is 'Bones.'"

Parsels picked up, "He has been through some shit, though. He's been a POW for almost five years. Half of his group died in jungle camps in South Vietnam. Doc Kushner was with them. He's a flight surgeon in the cell next to us. Something like eight or ten guys died in his arms. He's a medical doctor, but was not allowed to do anything for the guys. He hurts bad over that."

Clearly I wasn't the only one who had had a rough time getting here. All the guys had suffered a lot, some far worse than I had. We were lucky to be alive, each and every one of us.

Parsels added, "Things aren't too bad here now. My last camp was the pits. And there was a lot of torture here until this summer, but now it's OK. This place is called Plantation Gardens. It's one of the nicer camps. Food isn't great, but keeps us alive. We get a couple of cigarettes most days. Little interrogation. Mostly propaganda sessions. No torture. They beat you if you violate the camp rules. I got punished for talking into the wall, communicating with the guys next door. Much better than things used to be, though. The rumors are that peace talks are making progress. Think there's a bombing halt. Haven't heard any strikes for a couple of days."

"Who's our senior officer?" I asked.

Dave Mott spoke. "John Murphy is for our room. You can address him as 'Captain Murphy, sir.'"

John interrupted. "You're so full of shit." We laughed. Dave kept talking.

"The SRO, that's senior ranking officer, for the camp is Colonel Ted Guy. He's in the shed up at the top of the camp. That's where they've segregated the senior officers and NCOs from the rest of us. He's an Air Force lieutenant colonel who must have been promoted to full bird by now. He went down over Laos in an F-4 in 1968. He's a good leader, a real hard ass. Runs a tight ship. Doesn't allow making any propaganda statements. No one can accept early release. We live by the Code of Conduct. He's taken a lot of beatings and torture for us. We call him the Hawk."

Al Kroboth jumped in immediately. "Yeah, and we're 'Hawk's Heroes.' Just like 'Hogan's Heroes' on the TV show, only we don't have as much fun." He had a shit-eating grin on his face. He also looked like crap.

"What happened to you?" I asked.

"Our A-6 got blown out of the sky near Khe Sanh. We were in a steep dive. Airplane went out of control. My shoulder hit the upper console as I ejected. Can't remember much. I think Len, my pilot, was killed. Don't know that he ever got out of the airplane." Al sat there shirtless, his arm sticking up in the air, covered in some shabby plaster cast material and bound up with splints and bandages. He looked bizarre.

Big Bill, Bill Gauntt, spoke again. "Al was a basketball player at the Citadel. He tied Lew Alcindor out at UCLA, Kareem Abdul-Jabbar, for the most rebounds his senior year. Heck of a ballplayer."

"Yeah," Al chimed in. "And I was drafted to play professional ball, but delayed that until after my time in the Marine Corps." Looking at his shoulder, he lamented, "That's not going to happen now." I felt really bad for the guy.

That afternoon, we had bean sprouts and a small piece of French bread. That had been my diet in solitary for a couple of weeks, bean sprouts and French bread, twice a day, every day. The joy of the sprouts was wearing off. The bread sometimes had tiny rocks, small bits of wood, and other assorted junk in it. Still, it tasted good.

Evening passed with more talk. I couldn't get enough conversation. Regrettably, I had no news for them. Bill Gauntt, the most recent shoot-down on August 13, was the source of the most current happenings in the world outside. As it grew late, the guys strung pieces of twine above the beds the length of the cell. Folded with our blanket was a mosquito net along with another prison uniform, a pair of maroon and gray striped shorts and a short-sleeved shirt. We attached the nets to the twine and *voilà*, we had protective cocoons over our beds. Everybody took turns using the shit cans and brushing their teeth. A loud gong sounded in the courtyard. "Time to go to sleep."

Morning began with another gong. We got up and tended to personal housekeeping, putzing around taking down mosquito nets and folding whatever clothing we weren't wearing. We did a lot of busy work to take up as much time as we could. After finishing our chores, we waited for the morning meal, more bean sprouts and bread.

Al was only eating the bread. He'd vomit the bean sprouts and often much of the bread. He wasn't doing well, and I tried saying something cute to lift his spirits. He gave me a look like, *I hear you, man. This ain't working, but don't give up.* I didn't. I kept up with my absurd sense of humor, and Al started to crack bad jokes of his own, almost as bad as mine. It started a bond that built into a close friendship. He got slowly better with each day that passed. Al Kroboth became the best friend I had as a POW.

A gong in the afternoon announced the start of the daily rest period. The guards demanded quiet. Another gong marked its end. Gong to wake up. Gong to rest. Gong to stop resting. Gong to go to sleep at night. That was the routine. A couple times a week, we'd get to go to the area with the water trough and take a bath. Once every couple of weeks, we'd get to have a painful shave with rusty Czechoslovakian blades. Once a month, one of the prisoners would be the barber and give haircuts under the close supervision of a guard.

Every other day, they would allow us outside for a while, sometimes with the guys from the cell next door. The enlisted guys got out at separate times from us. The senior guys got out in their own area and never mixed with us.

Sometimes I could hear a lot of noise from the other side of a wall separating our row of cells from those on the farther end of our building. I could see the top of a basketball hoop. An occasional volleyball arched high over an out-of-sight net.

"What's up with that?" I asked.

"That's the Peace Committee," came the answer.

"What's the Peace Committee?"

"Eight guys who collaborate with the enemy. They've been ordered to stop, but they won't. They study communism, do propaganda, make radio broadcasts, even rat on other Americans. For that, they get packages, get to write letters, and can go outside whenever they want and play games. We call them the ducks because of the way they follow the guards around and do their bidding."

"They'll rot in hell." I said.

"That they will."

The collaborators were a small but significant minority among us. There were 107 prisoners at Plantation Gardens, and except for the eight in the Peace Committee, all were patriotic, loyal Americans who resisted enemy interrogation, propaganda, and pressure to sign statements and make radio broadcasts. We resisted with everything we had.

All of us had been captured in South Vietnam or Laos. Most of us were listed as missing in action. No one knew that any of us were being held in Hanoi. It would have been difficult for the communists to explain how prisoners of the supposed guerrilla movement in South Vietnam were being held in the capital city of the North. For that reason, we were kept separate from the prisoners taken inside North Vietnam.

John Parsels explained that we had some real heroes among us. "We've got three Special Forces guys captured at Lang Vei in February 1968, Staff Sergeant Dennis Thompson, Sergeant First Class Harvey Brande, and Spec 4 Bill McMurray.[2] Thompson was soaked in blood, standing knee deep in bodies at the height of the battle. He was calling in air strikes and fighting hand to hand when he was knocked unconscious. He woke as a prisoner of war. A few days later, he was joined by Brande, whose leg was badly wounded."

"Less than a week later, the two of them escaped. Thompson's an animal, a real bad-ass. There's no one tougher than him. They escaped and made it all the way back to Lang Vei, hoping the camp was back with friendlies. Thompson carried Brande most of the way because his leg worsened and he couldn't walk. When it became clear they'd have to continue on to Khe Sanh, Brande, being the senior sergeant, ordered Thompson to go on alone. Thompson disobeyed the order. He kept carrying Brande until exhaustion slowed them to a crawl. They were overtaken and recaptured. Tortured and starved for months after that, they both almost died many times. Tough guys."

A few days later, the guards let us outside with those from the cell next door. I met Doc Kushner and the others. One of them introduced himself as a fellow Cobra pilot, another captain, Jerry Chirichigno. Jerry shared that he was from Peru, South America. He had been the kicker on the University of Alabama football team under coach Bear Bryant and had played with quarterback Joe Namath in the 1964 Orange Bowl, winning the national championship. He'd served a Vietnam tour in Special Forces, gone to flight school, and come back flying Cobras with B Troop, 7/17th Cavalry, the same unit as Wayne, but more than a year before. As we talked, Jerry got into the story of his shoot-down.

"I was captured in November 1969. On the 2nd, we were a flight of four, two Loach observation helicopters and two Cobra guns. I was commanding the mission from the front seat of the lead Cobra flown by Mr. Peterson. We found a lot of enemy near the Cambodian border, about eight miles southwest of Duc Lap. You know where that is?"

"Not really," I admitted.

"It's on the southern end of the Central Highlands, below Ban Me Thout."

"OK. Got it."

"One of the Loaches took hits and started leaking fuel. I told him to land and the other would pick them up. He landed in a clearing on top of a hill. The second Loach came in and got them. But when he took off he got blasted. The helicopter came apart in the air, crashed, and rolled down the hill. We immediately began firing at the enemy along the tree line. As we made our first pass I saw someone coming out of the helicopter wreck on the ground with his clothes on fire. It was Warrant Officer George Grega, the pilot of the first Loach. As we started to make our second pass, shooting at the enemy to protect the downed helicopter crews, we got shot down. We came into the hill sideways. The rotor blades beat the ground and snapped us over onto our back. Hell of a crash. I climbed out of the aircraft. My pilot, Mike Peterson, got out too. I was hurt bad, shot in both my hands and my leg." Jerry showed me noticeable scars and a missing finger.

"We had three aircraft shot down within minutes of each other. The enemy moved in more troops and antiaircraft weapons. We became bait to draw other aircraft in for the kill. Even so, taking lots of fire, a Huey got in to rescue Lieutenant Curran, the observer on the second Loach. Intense fire drove him off the landing zone before anyone else could get on. Another Huey tried to reach us, but he got hosed badly and was forced to break off his approach. He was about ten feet above us. No one else could get close. It was a death trap for helicopters.

"Jim Nowicki. That's Jim sitting over there." Jerry pointed at another prisoner from his room, and I nodded. "Jim was the pilot of the second Loach. He and Sergeant Shepard, the observer from the first, had moved away from the crash with Lieutenant Curran. They thought George Grega was dead. But later, George staggered over to Peterson and me, behind our crashed Cobra after we got shot down. He was still alive, but in really bad shape. He was just about naked, his flight suit burned off him. He looked awful, moaning pitifully. There was nothing we could do. That bothered me. I felt horrible.

"After a couple of hours, Peterson took off to find a more secure area to try to signal a helicopter to get some help. I was hurt so bad, I couldn't go with him. George died a little after Peterson left. Jets dropped napalm and bombs all over the area that afternoon and night. I lay in a ditch near the Cobra while everything around me exploded and burned.

"The next day, despite a lot of pain, I was able to get up and walk. I stumbled in the direction of a Special Forces camp I knew of. Don't know if could've made it or not, but I was going to try. I didn't get far before I was captured.

"They marched me for the rest of the day to a military camp. Within a few days, they brought in Peterson, then Nowicki and Shepard. Only Curran had gotten rescued. Grega was dead. The rest of us ended up as POWs. They tied us together with ropes around our necks and marched us across the border, into Cambodia.

"We lived in cages with our feet in wooden stocks for eight months. We were joined by Roger Miller." Jerry looked around. "That's Roger there. He was captured five months after us. He went through some crap too. He was a brand-new WO1 copilot with only two weeks in country. A couple of Hueys shot down, others shot up, several guys killed. Roger got his thumb shot off. So he joined us and then Nowicki, Miller, and I marched for over a month to North Vietnam. We rode trucks the rest of the way to Hanoi. Finally got here to the Plantation."

"What about Peterson and Shepard?" I asked.

Jerry answered, "They got early release from the jungle camp. Went home." He didn't say what they'd done to get the communists to let them go. I didn't ask.

It was eerily quiet without the sound of air strikes every few days. I'd sit on my bunk and watch the geckos crawl up the walls. They'd magically move, upside down, across the ceiling, looking for bugs to eat. Sometimes, if there were no bugs, they'd eat each other. It made me think. *Always big ones eating little ones. The message is the big and strong devour the small and weak. Circumstance makes us weak, but our country is strong. Don't forget it. Our country is strong.*

We all wondered what was going on with no air strikes. One day, a guard smiled and said, "Much talk with U.S. and Le Duc Tho. Almost peace. Maybe you go home soon."[3] Treatment improved for a few days. The guards had a ping-pong table along the fence, outside our cell. They began playing with gusto, laughing and having a good time. Then it soured. Guards became sullen, scowling, and short-tempered. We suspected the peace talks weren't going well.

Bill Henderson had a big grin on his face when we came in from the courtyard one afternoon. In his hand, he held a ping-pong ball.

"Where'd you get it?"

"Wedged between two bricks by the ping-pong table."

"There'll be hell to pay if they find out you've got it."

"Yeah, OK."

Al's eyes lit up. He raised his bony six-foot-five frame from his bunk, picked up the small wicker trash basket we'd use for sweepings off the floor, and stuck a piece of its unraveling wicker into a crack high on the wall above the shit cans, suspending it there. "There's our basket. The game is Horse." The afternoon gong sounded for rest time. Young Bill took the first shot, followed by the rest of us. That series of shots was pretty easy. The difficulty of the shots grew and some began missing.

The idea of the game of Horse is to use the exact same technique as the guy making the first basket. If you miss, you are assigned one of the letters of the word "horse," in sequence. When everyone has tried the shot, another guy is given the ball. He shoots, setting the pattern for the next series of shots. Any player missing five shots and getting all five letters of the word, H-O-R-S-E, is out of the game. The last man standing wins.

It was quiet time, but we were having none of it, and the game got raucous. Al's turn came up. In his frustration, he pulled the cast material, splints, and bandages off his arm so he could shoot better. He set up the next shot with some goofy footwork, stepping into a big arching hook shot. I came next with what I thought was a beautiful replication of his approach and shot. The ping-pong ball went right in but my hand brushed the basket and knocked it off the wall. "What a shot. I made it."

Al protested, "No way. No way! You missed it. You can't get credit for a shot if you knock the basket down." We exploded in shouts for and against that shot. The ping-pong ball rolled out of the basket and came to rest in the middle of the floor.

The small window on the door flew open and an AK-47 rifle barrel thrust in, the red-faced glare of a guard behind it. "No talk! No yell! Must be quiet. No noise." We froze. We had violated the camp rules. The ping-pong ball was right in the middle of the floor, and he had to have seen it. We were in deep shit. The rifle barrel withdrew and the window cover slammed shut. He was gone. We looked at each other, struggling to keep our snickering as quiet as we could. We feared for our lives if the guard came back, but we couldn't help ourselves. We relished in the silly delight of the moment.

Al positioned his bad left arm as if taking an oath, rewrapping the bandages as best he could. It was a more hideous contraption than before. As he clumsily picked up the pieces of cast material scattered on the floor around his bed, I asked, "What are you going to tell them?"

"That their crummy cast broke," he answered.

Al sat down on his bed and groaned, looked at me, and smiled.

The routine went on in Plantation Gardens. Twice-a-day meals of bean sprouts gave way to pumpkin soup, a welcome change. Like the bean sprouts, we got it for both meals, day after day after day. The treatment worsened, though it was nothing like what prisoners had suffered earlier in the war. We were, after all, Hawk's Heroes, whiling away our time in possibly the most decent prison in Hanoi. All we had to do was stay out of trouble and remain healthy.

One day, they let us out with the enlisted men, which only happened a few times. The enlisted guys were amazing, good soldiers, resisting the enemy at every turn, standing firmer than some of the higher-ranking prisoners. I gained a great deal of respect for these young, proud American soldiers. They were hard-core, following orders, not only accepting the leadership above them, but also seeking to strengthen its authority and effectiveness in any way they could. They covertly passed messages throughout the camp at great risk to themselves.

Some of these guys proved to be interesting characters. One of the most interesting was a young specialist-four named Marty Frank. I'd seen Marty scouring the courtyard for cigarette butts. He'd empty the few remaining strands of nicotine-soaked tobacco into a nasty-looking pouch of paper, eventually rolling that recycled tobacco into disgusting-looking, second-time-around cigarettes.

"How you doin', sir?" he said to me.

"I'm fine, Marty. How are you?"

"Doin' good. You got any tobacco, any extra cigarettes?"

"No, Marty. I've adopted Big Al's philosophy, 'If you got 'em, smoke 'em.' I know some guys save what they can to trade or smoke tomorrow if we don't get any. But I like Al's approach, 'If you got 'em, smoke 'em.' That's what I do. Wish I had some to give you, but I don't."

"That's OK, sir. I got plenty. You want one of mine?" He held out a nasty-looking thing in his hand.

"No thanks," I answered. "How'd you end up here?"

"I'm from New Jersey. I split up with my wife and joined the Army in 1966. After training, I was sent to Vietnam, assigned to B Company, 1st of the 12th Infantry Battalion, 4th Infantry Division near Pleiku. Our company got overrun in July 1967. We'd been fighting all morning, lots of NVA, heavy mortar fire. We ran outta ammo. Company commander got killed, platoon leader got killed. Cordine McMurray, there—" Marty pointed to another prisoner on the other side of the courtyard. "He was our platoon sergeant. He said we should fight to the death. That was pretty hard with no ammo. We swung our guns, fought with our hands. Everything.

"Everybody was getting killed all around me, shot or blown up by mortars. I don't think anybody got away. I got shot and couldn't move. We laid there, a bunch of bodies, the wounded and the dead. The enemy came and poked at us. They dragged me and Cordine, and Perricone and Newell, those guys over there. They dragged us away. We watched them shooting the other wounded guys in the head. They murdered them. I think our whole company was wiped out. I know our platoon was. I think everybody got killed but us four. Later, Nate Henry, the company radio operator, that's him there, joined us as a prisoner.

"We were all hurt bad. They barely got us to a VC jungle hospital alive. We got some treatment, recovered a little, then marched for days to a jungle prison camp. There were two other POWs there who had been caught before us, Joe DeLong and Mr. Sooter.

"After a few months, we had a chance to escape. They left only one guard on us. He put down his rifle and wasn't paying attention. We jumped him, beat him unconscious, and left the camp. We got recaptured before we got over the first hill. They shot DeLong, killed him. They took the rest of us back to camp. Said they were going to give us a trial and kill us too. Never came to anything, but they sure watched us closer after that.

"We stayed in that camp for a couple of years, then we marched all the way to the DMZ, then rode trucks the rest of the way to near Hanoi. We went through hell and a bunch of prison camps over the last five years to get here."

"God, Marty. You guys have been through some shit." He didn't answer. He looked away and changed the focus of the conversation.

Marty asked, "See those two guys over there? The one on crutches and the other guy next to him?"

I saw a young prisoner leaning into a pair of crudely crafted crutches. A skinny redhead stood next to him.

"Yeah." I said.

Marty continued, "Bill Baird, on the crutches there, got hisself blown up and it did something to his spine and legs. He's mostly paralyzed from the waist down. Then the VC shot him in the head after he was blowed up. You'll see he can barely walk, even on the crutches, and he carries a bottle around with him all the time to piss into because he can't control himself. He wasn't captured until 1968, but he's in real bad shape.

"That guy there next to him. That's Gail Kerns. He got hurt real bad too. Gail was captured in 1969. He was shot in the head. When you look at him, you'll see a big soft spot on the side of his head. His skull was blown away and the skin grew over the big hole. He's almost died a bunch of times. The NVA never did nothin' for him. If you see that soft spot start to pulse, he's goin' into a fit. It happens to him a lot."

"OK."

Marty concluded, "Its real sad, but they're both great guys."

After three weeks, pumpkin soup gave way to boiled kohlrabi, a turnip-like vegetable. A few weeks of that crap made me hate it forever. I couldn't believe I was craving rice. How I'd hated it at first. The slowly rotating mundane diet became part of the routine that settled in, getting us through the days while hope and faith buoyed our spirits, faith in God, faith in my family always being there for me, faith that my country would never abandon me. I imagined the 101st Airborne parachuting down on Hanoi to get us out if the peace talks failed.

We also tried to keep humor going in our cell, with Al and me the central culprits, telling disgustingly bad jokes back and forth. Al was getting a lot better. His nausea was subsiding and his boils healing. Some of the guys exercised to fight the deterioration of their bodies. I couldn't even lie on my back, let alone try doing sit-ups. What I could do was get into position to try pushups. I'd tried once in the jungle and failed. I couldn't raise myself off the ground. Now I was able to push all the way up once and halfway through a second. Pretty sad for a guy who could do a hundred pushups before. I kept at for weeks it until I was able to do several as part of my daily routine.

I felt funky one day. Just lousy. In the midmorning I got a chill that turned into shivering, then violent shaking. I suspected malaria, but this was worse than anything I'd had before. My cellmates covered me with blankets as I shook uncontrollably. In the afternoon, the chill gave way to a fever, building slowly at first, then mounting rapidly until I became delirious and fell unconscious.

My cellmates yelled through the wall for advice from Doc Kushner. He told them to find whatever pieces of rags or clothing they might have and soak them in water and cover my body with the wet material in an attempt to cool my core temperature. They did. Doc Kushner raised hell with the camp authorities, demanding that I be treated for malaria. After three days of shaking chills and spiking fevers, I was finally given quinine. But only long enough for the symptoms to subside. I would have other attacks in Hanoi, but I got quinine right away for each of those. Doc Kushner had made his point.

I had no idea how close to death I had come. Later I would learn that I had three kinds of malaria: vivax, malariae, and falciparum, the last being the most deadly form of malaria on earth. Doc Kushner had saved my life.

On December 18, 1972, after many weeks of quiet, we got bombed like none of us had ever been bombed before. Air raid sirens wailed, barrages of SAMs fired, and bombs poured down. American B-52s had arrived in force over Hanoi. Bombs fell close, and Plantation Gardens shook.

We lay on our bunks, hoping our bombers knew where our camp was. Still, we fell back into a mindset we'd all developed in captivity: What will be will be. No sense worrying about something you have absolutely no control over.

Big Bill Gauntt stood on his toes on his bunk at the back wall and peered through the little windows high up on the wall to give us a running account of the raids. The Vietnamese, who couldn't pronounce "Gauntt," called him Ga, and we started calling him, "Ga, the on-scene reporter." Our spirits were buoyed. We didn't know what had happened to the peace talks, but we were glad the United States was putting the full weight of our military might against the North.

The next morning, the guards were clearly rattled. Some dug holes in the courtyard for shelter. Radar-deflecting chaff, dispensed by the American aircraft, lay around the camp like Christmas tinsel. Still they let us outside for our scheduled bath. Repercussion, a guard so named because of his violent outbursts and threats against prisoners, stood against the wall as we milled around the water trough. He spoke some English. Old Bill Thomas walked over to him and said, "You think those air strikes were bad?"

"What?" the guard asked.

"You think those air strikes were bad last night?" Bill said again.

"Yes, bad bombing."

"Well you ain't seen nothing yet. Wait till they drop the A-bomb on your fucking ass."

I gasped, then smiled. Old Bill. Proud Marine. He'd been a pretty quiet guy, but not anymore. We all glowed inside over the bombing. It was a huge morale boost.

The bombings went on, night after night, not with impunity. B-52s got shot down, their ghastly giant carcasses burning, falling. We wondered sadly about the fate of the crews. We lost aircraft, yet they kept coming. We quietly cheered them on.[4]

After a few days of this, the guards brought us picks and shovels. They ordered us to dig a long trench down the middle of each cell. We had to break through the concrete floor first. We dug like champs and within the day had a pit big enough for all eight of us to get into. Whenever the B-52 strikes came, we sat in our hole.

Christmas was coming. Our thoughts turned to the season and more than ever to our families. We chanced a few carols, singing quietly at first. There was no reaction from the guards, so we turned it up over the next days. After one time through the Twelve Days of Christmas, we rewrote the lyrics under Al's leadership to incorporate B-52s, aircraft each of us had flown, slams against Ho Chi Minh, and other tidbits from our prison life experience. Camp authorities never had a clue.

We awoke Christmas morning to see preparations taking place in the courtyard for a special meal. That afternoon we went out to fill our bowls with pieces of chicken (they said it was turkey), fatback, vegetables, and the old standby French bread. We also got something akin to a small brownie, half a bottle of beer apiece, and a pack of North Vietnamese factory-made cigarettes. We took our feast to our cells and relished it. The brownie was extraordinary. When I was done, I eyed Al sitting there. His brownie was still by his side.

"Are you going to eat that brownie?"

"Yeah, why?"

"I'll buy you a steak dinner when we get home if you'll give it to me." He tossed it over. I devoured it.

Christmas ended and the bombings kept up. On the evening of December 27, right in the middle of a B-52 strike, the order came to "roll mats." John Parsels said that meant we were moving. I rolled my blanket, mosquito net, and other prison uniform inside my bamboo mat, grabbed my cup, toothbrush, toothpaste, and spoon, and waited. They directed us into the courtyard to a line of army trucks. There was a lot of chatter among the prisoners.

"Where we going?"

"Probably out into the country to get away from the bombing."

I looked into the night sky. A B-52, just hit, was burning, falling slowly at first, like a swaying leaf, then plummeting to earth. I put my rolled mat onto the bed of the truck and climbed in. We drove out of Plantation Gardens onto the streets of Hanoi.

CHAPTER 13

Five-Star Resort

I gripped my rolled bamboo mat and slid off the back of the truck, hitting the ground hard. Pain shot up my injured spine. I stood in the darkness on a street beside a high stone wall. Enormous. The words "Maison Centrale" were etched in large letters on the arch above the doors. A little window slid open, allowing a beam of light to stream out.

Prisoners I'd never seen milled around in the street, the senior officers, the senior sergeants, and those captured in Laos. John Parsels pointed to Colonel Guy and called out some of the others. One exclaimed, "The Hilton. We're back at the Hilton."

Interesting. We'd set out thinking we were headed into the country to get away from the bombing. We'd traveled a zigzag route through the city for over an hour, only to end up less than a mile from where we had started. This was the infamous Hoa Lò, the formidable prison built by the French in the nineteenth century, known to Americans as the Hanoi Hilton.

The big doors creaked open ominously. We entered into the belly of the dragon that had held us in its talons until now. I was intimidated by the size, design, and reputation of the place. This was the Hilton, the infamous Hanoi Hilton, the principal fortress holding American prisoners of war for years and years and years.

Inside, we took a right turn. Someone protested as the guards separated the prisoners captured in Laos, taking them away in a different direction. I never saw the Peace Committee. I suspected they, too, had been moved. We walked to an isolated section and were divided between two large cells in one corner of the prison complex.

Colonel Guy, our senior officer, chanced a few words, "You guys know where you are? They call this section of the Hilton 'Little Vegas.'"

Staying at Little Vegas, inside the Hanoi Hilton. Bizarre.

Colonel Guy and the senior officers and sergeants went into the cell to the left. The rest of us funneled into the one to the right. Twenty-seven prisoners in their cell, thirty-six in ours. A single light bulb hung from the center of the ceiling at the end of a long cord. It dimly illuminated the big cell, giving us a view of our new home.

The stucco walls rose twelve feet, increasing to eighteen along the center peak that ran the length of the cell. Three large windows sat six feet off the floor along both the long walls, each window measuring six feet wide by four feet high, topped with a row of arched windows, vertical metal bars firmly fixed outside.

If we stood on our beds, we could look out the front windows onto a small courtyard with a tree in the center. Out the back windows we could see the massive exterior stone wall a few feet away, tall, thick, capped with broken shards of glass. Three strands of bare, high-voltage electrical wires ran above that. Strategically positioned lights illuminated the wall and the narrow concrete walkway between it and our cell. Guard towers rose at intervals along the top of the wall.

The beds were familiar except the heads rested on a six-inch lip running the length of both side walls. Pieces of taut cord ran above the head and foot of the beds so we could tie our mosquito nets in the evening.

A narrow hallway led off one end of our cell. It passed several solitary confinement cells, now empty, on its way to a latrine and the bathing area just beyond. That was the very corner of the Little Vegas quadrant of the Hanoi Hilton.

My bunk was between Al Kroboth and Cordine McMurray. Cordine turned out to be as much of a wit as Al and me. He would start talking about how much he missed his family. Al would jump in, saying Cordine's wife had probably run off with another guy and spent all his money. Cordine would moan woefully and cry, "No, not my money. Not all my money from all this time in jail." Their routine drew other prisoners who'd listen to their antics and burst with laughter.

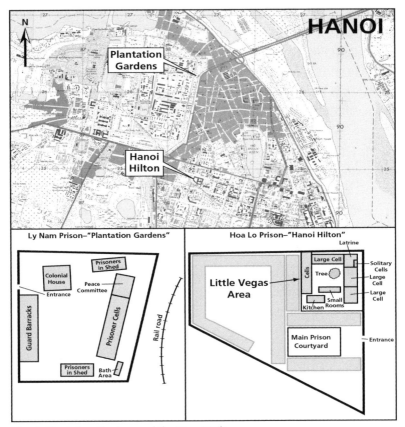

Map 5. Plantation Gardens and the Hanoi Hilton

The other survivors of Cordine's rifle platoon were all in our cell as well. The most vocal was Marty Frank. Puffing on one of his reused-tobacco cigarettes, he'd go on about what he was going to do when he got out of this mess. "I'm going to find some property in the country in New Jersey, and I'm going to raise deers."

"That's deer, Marty," someone would always correct.

"Yeah, like I says, I'm goin' to raise deers's. There's lots of money in deers's and other wild game. An untapped market."

"OK, Marty."

Marty was always smoking. He'd gather any speck of tobacco left in anyone's discarded butts and use it to make his scroungy-looking cigarettes. Resourceful guy.

I met lots of new people in our big cell. It was good to be with so many Americans. Even in the midst of the B-52 strikes, or maybe because of them, our mood was upbeat. Two days later, on December 29th, they stopped. No more bombs. That was it for the Christmas bombing.

A guy named Steve Leopold told me he was captured near Ben Het.

"I was captured near Ben Het, too." I said. We shared a connection to that same spot on the ground in South Vietnam. He said he was captured on May 9, 1968, exactly four years to the day before I went down.

I told him, "I was flying a Cobra when I was shot down. Captured three days later, a few miles from the camp."

"Well," Steve said, "I was XO of a Special Forces A-Team at Ben Het. Was with Sergeant Mike McCain leading a hundred-man force of Montagnards on a combat mission to secure a hilltop four kilometers west of Ben Het. The hill was just above the old French fort where the road went from Vietnam into Laos. Our task was to block enemy use of the road and keep them off the hill. They'd been launching rockets into our camp from there.

"Sergeant Mac had been in country for four tours of duty. This was his fifth. He loved Vietnam. Loved what we were doing. That night, he set up the Montagnards in a circle of defensive positions. He was concerned because our guys were armed with old World War II weapons. That's all the Vietnamese would let the Montagnards have. He and I settled into a fortified hooch near the top of the hill.

"Next morning, all hell broke loose. At least two companies of NVA hit us, swarming through our perimeter. Mac and I couldn't get out of the hooch before an NVA soldier rolled two grenades inside. Mac took the brunt of the explosion and died instantly. I was blown out of the hooch and lost consciousness. When I came to, I felt shrapnel in the back of my right leg and saw the barrels of AK-47s pointing at my head.

"They moved me into Laos, then swung down into Cambodia, a couple of miles away. I hobbled some, but they mostly carried me. I was kept in a bamboo cage in a jungle camp. I was sick a lot. Had malaria and God knows what else. Moved north after a year and a half, first to Camp D-1, a god-awful place, and then to Plantation Gardens."

Steve and I became friends. I found we had another thing in common. Both of us had degrees in political science. Mine was from the University of Nebraska at Omaha on an Army bootstrap program. His was from Stanford, where he graduated magna cum laude and Phi Beta Kappa. Though he'd been accepted into graduate school at both Harvard and Columbia University, he'd elected to serve in the Green Berets instead.

Sometimes guys shared movies they'd seen. We called it "Tell a movie." Whoever was sharing would stand and recount one of his favorite films. The goal was to describe the movie in such detail that listeners could close their eyes and see it.

There were no stocks or leg irons at the Hanoi Hilton or Plantation Gardens. We could roam the inside of the cell at will. How different life had become. This was heaven compared to the days in the bamboo cage or struggling to get here. All I had to do was stay healthy and endure the days or weeks or months of imprisonment that remained until I was released and home again, free. That was really the worst of it all, not being free. Freedom is precious beyond belief if you've never lost it. I yearned for it from the day I was captured.

My trials were not unique. Most of the guys in the cell had suffered as much as I had, many far worse. Five of my cellmates were the survivors of the crew operating an armed forces radio and TV station in South Vietnam. They were the last guys you would expect to find in a POW camp.

They had been assigned to Detachment 5 of AFVN (American Forces Vietnam Network) at the network's station in Hue, the old imperial capital of Vietnam. The city bore the brunt of some of the worst fighting of the 1968 Tet Offensive. I got to know one of them, Don Gouin, pretty well. Don had been the chief engineer for the TV part of the station. At forty-three, he was older than most of the POWs, and he looked even older because of years of mistreatment. The enemy had also taken his dentures. All he had were his gums.

One day, I asked him. "Don, what happened in Hue? How were you guys captured?"

"It was a mess," he said. "Hue had been a great place to be. The old walled citadel. The throne of all the emperors of Vietnam. Lots of culture. Beautiful architecture. And the work at the TV station was great.

"Our crew was me; John Anderson, our senior NCO; Marine Lieutenant Dibernardo, our brand-new commander; and Harry Ettmueller.

Harry was a Spec 5, another engineer, a great guy, really gung-ho. We all came to the Plantation together. We're all here now."

"What happened in Hue?" I asked.

"Yeah," Don continued. "Well, four other guys had just arrived a few days earlier to add radio broadcast capability to our TV station. The program director was John Deering, a Marine corporal. He had three young broadcasters with him, Marine Sergeant Tom Young, and Steve Stroub and John Bagwell, both Army specialists. They hadn't even got the radio station up and running yet when Tet started.

"We went from quiet one minute to VC and NVA running all over the city the next. We hunkered down in our house, unnoticed for a time. We had Mr. Courtney Niles there with us. He was a civilian. NBC engineer. Lived in our place with us. He'd been in the Army.

"Started taking mortar rounds and sniper fire. When the NVA finally attacked, we fought back. We fought hard for five days. Mr. Niles fought too, just like the soldier he used to be. He killed a slew of NVA. He was a good shot. We pushed back a lot of attacks by hordes of bad guys. That last night was the worst. They hit us with a lot of guys. Shot Tom Young bad. He got hit a bunch of times and died right away. Poor kid.

"Next day they used rocket-propelled grenades to blow holes in our walls and set the house on fire. We kept fighting though, till we ran out of ammo. Then, with the house coming down on us, we escaped and ran for our lives. We ran like hell through a rice paddy trying to get to the MACV compound. Ran like hell. Mr. Niles got shot dead coming out of the house.

"We were all gettin' shot and shredded by grenades. Every one of us got hit, but we kept on running. John Anderson got shot in the chest and fell. The enemy closed in around us, and we were captured. All except John Bagwell. I never saw what happened to him. Right after they captured us, they shot Steve Stroub in the head. Executed him, just like that. He'd been wounded by grenades and shot in the leg while we were running. Looked bad. Broken bone sticking out. But they didn't even try to help him. Just shot him dead right there. Bastards.[1]

"They tied us and marched us off. Even badly wounded John Anderson had to march. They'd have killed us for sure if we hadn't kept on walking. It was hard for all of us, but especially John, marching every day with that bullet in his chest. Even so, he tried to escape three times. The first time he didn't get far before he passed out from his wounds. The second time he wandered right into a group of NVA soldiers. The third time, he got away good. But we were in North Vietnam. Soon, he was recaptured by local militia. They drug him through a village where he was nearly beaten to death by women swinging bamboo clubs. Next time I saw him he was swollen and bloody. Looked awful.

"We marched for weeks to a holding camp north of the city of Vinh. It was tough. I don't know how we made it. We called the camp Bao Cao because that's how we had to address the guards. We had to bow and say 'Bao Cao' whenever we talked to any of them. It was some demeaning expression asking for permission to speak. We stayed there for a couple of months and then moved through a series of camps around Hanoi before coming to the Plantation in 1970. And now we're all here at the Hilton, together."

He paused, then added, "They treated us like shit before we got to Plantation. The camp called D-1 was horrible. Kept worse than animals there. Starved, beaten, tortured. Some guys spent months in solitary. One guard, 'Cheese,' was sadistically cruel. John Anderson almost died. John Deering too."

Our diet shifted to cabbage soup, which was pretty good, at least for a while. Same routine. Cabbage soup and a piece of foul French bread twice a day for weeks on end. Incessant propaganda broadcasts continued from the speakers in our cell. Time passed.

One evening guards summoned us into the little courtyard. The prisoners from the next cell joined us. We sat on the ground in front of a portable movie screen. An old 16-mm movie projector teetered atop a small rickety table, with a long, worn extension cord running off down a dark passageway.

Someone said, "Look at that jackass there." The guy operating the projector was having fits getting the film loop set right so the film would project without jerking incessantly on the screen.

"Quiet. No talk!" barked a guard.

The film was of Jane Fonda visiting North Vietnam. We saw an American cavorting among the enemy leadership, supporting their cause. Scenes appeared of her climbing into the gunner's seat on an NVA antiaircraft gun, wearing a clean white blouse, smiling broadly, laughing, donning a North Vietnamese army helmet, with live ammunition at her feet that would later shoot down American planes. In the film, she sent a message to American servicemen, calling us war criminals. She said we were following the orders of other war criminals that were like the leaders of Germany and Japan in World War II who were executed for their crimes.

I was stunned. We didn't dare speak out loud, but we had plenty to say to each other when we got back inside our cell.

Days later they showed us some news clippings from American newspapers and magazines. They all had news of war protests. One was of former U.S. attorney general Ramsey Clark demanding that the Americans stop bombing North Vietnamese dikes. He had been attorney general under President Johnson during the buildup of American forces in Vietnam. Now he was making statements from Hanoi that it was inhumane to bomb dikes and that we should never do it again. A photo showed him standing beside a dike with a single bomb crater. I knew we did not have an air campaign to destroy the dikes. This was an errant bomb.

The war protesters at home never bothered me. In fact, I took pride in fighting communism in this far corner of the earth so Americans could have the right to protest in the streets. It was a sacred honor to defend the right of other Americans to disagree with me or anything within our American system of government.

———————

Damn rats ran all over our cell every night. I hated rats from my days in that first prison camp in the jungle, and I still had nightmares about them chewing my feet and gnawing my ankle wound while my legs were in the stocks. We didn't have rats at the Plantation, but they were all over the place here in the Hilton, running across the floor at night. Once in a while, a rat would get under a mosquito net up onto a bed, and I would wake to someone thrashing and yelling, "Get off of me, you fucking rat!" If rats appeared earlier in the evening, while the light was still on, which they often did, we'd throw our Ho Chi Minh sandals at them, hard. We got pretty good at killing rats and got a good number of them.

I'd dream often of being home with my family, hiking and backpacking with my kids, playing catch, just talking. Sometimes I'd have nightmares about my shoot-down, capture, and struggles, but not too often. A few times I dreamed I was in a phone booth, inserting a dime, and calling my high school friend, Bob deKorne. "Bob. I'm in Vietnam. I got captured. I'm a prisoner of war. Call Amy and my folks. Tell them I'm alive."

One dream I had again and again. I'd be walking down the sidewalk in the small town of Montrose, California, where I lived for much of my youth. I would spot a bakery on the other side of the street. I'd cross and look at the baked goods in the window. My gaze would rest on chocolate éclairs. My mouth watered. I moved toward the door. A sign read, "Closed. Will return at 1:00 PM."

I'd walk around town, and when I would come back at precisely 1:00, the store was no longer a bakery. It was a hardware store. Shovels, hoes, rakes, and pipe wrenches sat in the window where the éclairs had been. I'm not sure what the message was, but that dream haunted me.

Life was no longer about fighting to stay alive. It was about enduring the time in prison until I would see freedom again. It was easier, but still agonizing, waiting for the war to end. *Could it be years?* Some of these guys had been prisoners more than five years, waiting, praying, hoping all that time. How much longer would they have to wait? How much longer would I?

One evening, I lay on my bunk and imagined myself looking down on us squeezed inside the Hanoi Hilton, miserable, none of us knowing when we might get out, when we might go home. That image turned to verses in my mind.

What is that moan from the prison,
   From ghostly souls in the prison,
That ghastly forgotten terrible sound
   Echoing out to the sea?
Doomed broken men locked behind bars,
   Plagued with filth and festering scars,
All of them crying in strained weak voices,
   Dear God, please let me be free.

CHAPTER 14

A Season

To everything there is a season.
—Ecclesiastes 3:1

A guard sat on a stool in the small courtyard outside our cell listening to a radio playing typical North Vietnamese martial music mixed with dialogue. It was weird. I'd never heard a radio playing in camp before, not at Plantation, not here. At least I'd never heard a radio other than the tightly controlled propaganda blasts that spewed from the hard-wired squawk boxes in our cells. The guard's radio interrupted my sleep a number of times. When the morning gong signaled us to get up, the cell was abuzz with excitement.

Dave Mott passed along pieces of conversation he was hearing from the far end of the cell. "War's over. Anzaldua heard it on the radio last night."

"Is he sure?" I asked. We walked toward Anzaldua's bunk at the other end of the room.

"We'll find out. Think so. Pretty sure, at least. Anzaldua speaks Vietnamese. He was a translator."

We joined the rest of our cellmates pressed close to Jose Anzaldua, a tall Marine corporal captured a couple of years before. He quietly related what he'd gathered from the broadcasts. "The guard had the radio up loud enough I could hear what they were saying. It sounded like a peace agreement was signed and the war's ended."

Al Kroboth stepped his six-foot-five-inch frame up onto one of the bunks and, peering out the window at the guards now on duty outside, he shouted, "Hey! War's over. War's over!"

It wasn't long before the cell door opened and a small group of guards entered, none too happy. One asked, "What you yell at soldiers?" Al smiled and answered, "I told them the war is over. We heard it over the radio last night."

"Who hear on radio?"

"Anzaldua. You know he speaks Vietnamese. The guard had a radio outside last night. It was loud enough for us to hear. Anzaldua heard the war is finished."

The guard spoke, glaring at Jose. "He speak Vietnamese like a baby. He no understand well. He wrong. Not true." The guards stormed out of the cell, locking the iron door.

That afternoon, we were taken into the courtyard with our fellow Plantation Gardens prisoners from the cell next door. Film crews stood behind a couple of big old funky cameras set up on tripods. We stood in rows, as instructed, waiting for whatever might come. An order passed through the ranks, "Hawk says if it's good news, no reaction. No smiles, no shouting. Nothing for propaganda."

Duck, the camp commander, took a position in front of us. Holding a piece of paper, his focus moved from the cameras to us. He began awkwardly reading the English words. "The parties participating in the Paris conference on Vietnam, with a view to ending the war and restoring peace in Vietnam on the basis of respect for the Vietnamese people's fundamental national rights and the South Vietnamese people's right to self-determination, and to contributing to the consolidation of peace in Asia and the world, have agreed on the following provisions and undertake to respect and to implement them."

Duck looked up. "The peace agreement is signed. You all go home." He waited for us to cheer. Nothing. He looked apologetically at the film director, then back to us with a hint of a scowl. "I give summary of main points. Article 1: The United States and all other countries respect the independence, sovereignty, unity, and territorial integrity of Vietnam as recognized by the 1954 Geneva Agreements on Vietnam.

"Article 2: A cease-fire shall be observed throughout South Vietnam as of 2400 hours G.M.T., Greenwich Mean Time, on January 27, 1973."

He looked up and added on his own, "That is today. It is past the time here. The war is over." Still no reaction from us. He looked back at the paper and continued reading. "Article 3: The parties undertake to maintain the cease-fire and to ensure a lasting and stable peace.

"Article 4: The United States will not continue its military involvement or intervene in the internal affairs of South Vietnam.

"Article 5: Within sixty days of the signing of this agreement, there will be a total withdrawal from South Vietnam of troops, military advisors, and military personnel, including technical military personnel and military personnel associated with the pacification program, armaments, munitions, and war material of the United States and those of the other foreign countries.

"Article 6: The dismantlement of all military bases in South Vietnam of the United States and of the other foreign countries shall be completed within sixty days of the signing of this agreement.

"Article 7: From the enforcement of the cease-fire to the formation of the new government, the two South Vietnamese parties shall not accept the introduction of troops, military advisors, and military personnel including technical military personnel, armaments, munitions, and war material into South Vietnam.

"Article 8: The return of captured military personnel and foreign civilians of the parties shall be carried out simultaneously with and completed not later than the same day as the troop withdrawal mentioned in Article 5, within sixty days. The parties shall exchange complete lists of the above-mentioned captured military personnel and foreign civilians on the day of the signing of this agreement."

As he kept reading the remaining highlights, all faded into a dull drone. I'd heard what was most important to me. *The war's over. We're going home within sixty days. I made it. Thank you, God!* We went back to our cells.

That night, fireworks lit the skies over Hanoi. We heard them and could see a bit of their brilliance through our barred windows. A large

North Vietnamese flag was raised atop a high radio tower next to the prison. It was upside down. We pointed it out, haranguing the guards who tried their best to ignore us, but their embarrassment was clear. Later, the flag was lowered and raised again, right side up.

From that day, the guards treated us differently, as our custodians, no longer our captors. Some tried to be friendly, but that didn't go real well. We despised everything they stood for. The food improved dramatically, though. We got plenty of better quality bread and daily fruit, often bananas. They gave us cans of spam-like meat along with a small stove to heat it with. We got tea instead of hot water.

Books appeared. We got Russian novels printed in English. Others were selections from the Time Reading Program. I buried my head in books and read all I could. I really enjoyed *Three Men in a Boat (To Say Nothing of the Dog)*.

I hadn't realized how much I yearned to read, to gain knowledge. I loved my country, and I knew something of its story, having minored in history in college. But I wanted to know more. I wanted more facts at hand to rebut the propaganda garbage the communists threw at us each day.

I wished I'd paid more attention in school. Too many history classes had been so awfully boring. Teachers read from stilted notes, or even from the text itself, while my mind daydreamed about adventures and thoughts of the girls I might ask out that weekend. There must be a better way to teach. It had to be possible to make history interesting, even fascinating. A desire took hold within me to someday become a history teacher, a really good one, enthralling students with a captivating dynamism, teaching them and igniting their own thirst for knowledge.

Chessboards and checkers showed up in the rooms. Playing cards too. We got plenty of cigarettes. A water pipe appeared with the appropriate *thuô c lào* pipe tobacco. The communists made a concerted effort to improve our treatment in every way. I suppose they hoped it would translate into stories of how well we'd been treated by our benevolent captors. That wasn't going to happen.

Many of us got a package from home after the war ended. Mine was the first and only during captivity. No letter, just the package that had been inspected, with a number of items probably removed. I got goodies, a T-shirt, and a pack of cigarettes. I shared everything except the shirt, which became a prized possession.

Camera crews came around a lot, documenting our humane and lenient treatment. We recognized the propaganda value but could not resist enjoying the new amenities and relaxed atmosphere over those last weeks.

In the midst of the improved treatment and our anticipation of pending release, Steve Leopold took sick with what Doc Kushner thought was hepatitis. Steve's skin took an odd yellow tone, and his eyes were also yellow. He lay on his bunk looking miserable. He was feverish and puked when he tried to eat. His pee was dark reddish-brown. He'd moan in pain each time he walked to the piss can, so someone moved one of the cans over by him. He was in a bad way. We all said, "Hang in there, Steve. The war's over. We're going home real soon. You gotta get better."

One evening, guards escorted us to the large open courtyard inside the main entrance of the prison complex. Steve was too ill to move. He lay on his bunk, a strange ashen-yellow color, looking like death.

In the courtyard, we joined the entire population of the Hanoi Hilton, the rest of the prisoners from the South and Laos, and all the prisoners who had been captured in the North and kept segregated from us. We sat together facing a stage.

A last group of prisoners filed in. Someone close to me recognized a few of them, "That's Colonel Purcell, and Don Rander. Must have been brought in from an outlying camp." Another voice nearby exclaimed, "And there's Captain Thompson, Jim Thompson. Can't believe he's still alive. I saw him have a heart attack years ago while trying to climb into the back of a truck. They carried him away. I thought he was dead." He was a white-haired wisp of a man, bent over, shuffling slowly, looked aimlessly ahead. He sat with obvious difficulty. He looked seventy, maybe eighty.

Lights came up on the stage and a show, so strange in this setting, began. The performance was by a military troupe whose purpose in life had been to entertain NVA soldiers. Performers dressed in army uniforms put on patriotic communist songs and dances. The highlight of the evening was a renowned North Vietnamese female singer named Trường Vi. She too wore an army uniform.

Back in our cell after the show, the buzz was about Jim Thompson and the new group of prisoners we'd seen. Dick Ziegler, another Army chopper pilot, brought me up to speed. "I was with Jim Thompson at camp Bao Cao in 1968. He's the longest-held POW. Been here longer than anyone. Longer than Alvarez.[1] Jim looked horrible even then, and that was more than four years ago. His eyes were dark and sunken in his head. His cheekbones stuck out. He was emaciated, just a skeleton with dried up skin hanging on it. He looked like death, like a living ghost. Scared the shit out of me. I can't believe he's still alive."

The next day, guards came and took Steve Leopold out of our cell. He looked terrible. We had no doubt he was being taken away to die.

A few days later, the newly arrived old-timers we'd seen at the show were put in a cell next to ours. They were let out with us each day, and we became friends. The new group included a handful of military guys captured in and around Hue, along with a number of civilian prisoners ranging from a Voice of America employee to a Foreign Service officer, a CIA agent, a fire chief, a construction worker, and a USAID agricultural advisor. They had been brought to the Hilton from outlying camps as soon as the Paris Peace Accords had been signed on January 27th. After being kept segregated for several days and gaining weight on an improved diet, they were moved in next to us.

In addition to that group of new arrivals in the cell next door, two others joined us. They were put in smaller rooms along one side of our Little Vegas courtyard. The two, Monika Schwinn and Bernhard Diehl, were West German nurses who'd been captured in 1969 while on a picnic outing near Da Nang with three other German nurses. They had been doing humanitarian hospital work with the Knights of Malta, treating anyone regardless of what side they were on in the war. The five captured Germans were held and treated in the same miserable manner as the American prisoners they were confined with over the years. They suffered the same forced marches, barbaric prison camps, and starvation diets. Before their four-year ordeal was over, three would die. Only

Monika and Bernhard survived. Monika showed up at the Hilton with a pet cat, which disappeared. We all became sleuths in search of Monika's beloved *Méo*, but the poor cat was never seen again.

After the new group joined us, we'd hear god-awful shrieks in the middle of the night. I thought it might be Ted Gostas, an intelligence officer captured at Hue in 1968. He'd been hung from ropes, denied water, severely beaten for extended periods, bashed in the head with an AK-47, and kicked in the stomach in an effort to gain valuable intelligence that he never revealed. Gostas was now a physical wreck who'd been driven to the precipice of insanity, sometimes dangling dangerously over its edge. But it wasn't Ted who was screaming in the night. It was Jim Thompson.

Jim kept to himself. He was hard to get to know, but in time he began to open up to me and share things about himself. He was only thirty-nine years old and, God, he looked like hell. He'd been through more shit, for a longer time, than any other American soldier in history.

He was a lonely man in spite of the reverence everyone held for him. We developed a special relationship, though. I was in awe of him, maybe even a bit more than the others were, and it showed. I told him we were the Alpha and the Omega of Army POWs. No other Army prisoners in the camp had been captured after me. Air Force pilots, yes. At least one Marine, yes. Navy guys, yes. Army, no. After a while, Jim began to open up to me and share things about himself.

I said, "So you're the Alpha and I'm the Omega. I was shot down in a Cobra last year. You got captured nine years ago. What happened?"

Jim stared straight ahead for a long time, his jaw set as he focused on distant memories. Finally, he started speaking, haltingly at first, then with more ease. He talked and talked and talked, like he'd been just waiting for the chance. I listened in fascination.

"It was so long ago. So much time. The twenty-fourth of March, 1964. I was flying in the back seat of an L-19 spotter plane out of Khe Sanh. I commanded Detachment A-728, the eleven-man Special Forces team there. We were training a couple hundred indigenous Montagnards as CIDG, Civilian Irregular Defense Group forces. Our mission was to get them to fight the VC and protect their own villages. We were on temporary duty from the 7th Special Forces Group at Fort Bragg, North Carolina. It was only to be a six-month tour. Hell, I didn't even know where Vietnam was when I got my orders.

"Captain Whitesides was flying. He was Air Force. We saw a new bridge we'd never seen before. Decided to go down for a closer look. Whitesides rocked onto the left wing and let the plane roll just about onto its back. The nose dropped towards earth and the airplane dove steeply downward. Just above the tops of the trees, he pulled back on the stick, leveling the wings, making the plane skim low over the jungle. I looked for the area we'd seen. We came over the river, and just to our right I could see it, a well-built footbridge, made of logs and freshly cut planks.

"'There it is,' I yelled. I marked the location with a grease pencil on the acetate cover of my map. Whitesides pulled up, in a climbing right turn, for a better view as he increased power and urged the plane back to altitude.

"Just then, bursts of green tracers arched into the sky. They were off to one side, but moving closer, like a stream from the nozzle of a hose that's being moved to bring the water to a spot. Other weapons started shooting. Whitesides slammed the stick left, then right, making the plane dodge, trying to avoid the sting of the bullets. Rounds raked the fuselage and ripped into the cockpit. The engine sputtered, coughed, and quit. Everything went quiet. We were on fire. We glided, powerless, sliding downward in a whisper, crashing through the trees. Wings ripped. The fuselage tore with a screeching, scratching noise. Branches and limbs clawed our sides until we smashed into the jungle floor. A loud crash is all I remember."

He paused before continuing.

"Don't know how long I was unconscious or how I got out of the wreck. I figure the VC pulled me out. At some point I began to come in and out of consciousness. I remember feeling drained and soaked. Dried blood, dirt, and grime crusted my face. Pain shot through my body. I was caked in filth, felt trickles of fresh blood mixing with sweat and dirt on my face. I knew I was hurt bad. But I was alive, barely.

"I woke later in a hammock, the ends tied to a long pole. Two VC fighters, one in the front and one in the back, carried me along a steep jungle path. They lost their footing and slipped a bunch of times. It jarred me painfully. I grimaced. Smells were strange. Colors all blended dark, and shapes fuzzy. Sounds were dulled and muffled. My bearers fell. I hit the ground with a thud. I lay there for a few moments. The bearers rearranged themselves and prepared to hoist me again. Then they settled back onto their haunches.

"I felt a man by my side. I heard a rattle of voices I couldn't begin to understand. I knew I was in bad shape. I thought the guy beside me was tending my wounds. He lifted my right hand and was tugging at the ruby birthstone ring my mother had given me. I'd worn it since I was fifteen. The guy was pulling hard. Then he pulled a knife from his belt and began to saw. I jerked my arm back hard. Surprised myself with the strength I had. I took the ring off and handed it over. My first trial as a prisoner of war was done. The guys hoisted the hammock again and off we went into the night.

"I thought of my wife, Alyce, and my kids. I kept drifting in and out of consciousness. Alyce was pregnant. I wondered how they'd deal with this, if they'd even know I was alive or presume me dead. I love Alyce, missed her, have missed her every day, all these years. My kids too. I worry about them all. How they're getting along without me.

"I thought about my parents, too, my home, my youth. I grew up in a small town in the sticks of New Jersey. I'd been a scrawny kid with red hair and freckles. You see my ears. They're big and stick out. I always got teased. I learned to live with it, but it still bothered me. My father was a drunk. He was loud and abusive. He beat me and my mother. His life was a failure. He drove a commuter bus for a while, but got hurt on some drunken escapade and couldn't drive anymore, so they made him just wash and clean the buses. That's all he did, wash and clean the buses.

"He saw his own failure in me. I always disappointed him. He'd beat me for it. My older brother, Sammy, though, he was dad's favorite. Sammy was strong and athletic. He was what my father wanted to be, and tried to act like. Instead, everyone thought Dad was just filled with pompous bullshit.

"I guess I was a momma's boy. I never did sports. I was on the yearbook staff and in the school choir. I liked church a lot. I hated my brother.

Hated my father worse. Still do. I guess that's what drove me to do what I did in the Army. Wanted to prove myself. After I got drafted I went to OCS, then airborne and Ranger School. Found my home in Special Forces and made captain in six years. I love being a Green Beret. That's what I am. Special Forces."

He stopped, pride in his face, until I finally broke the silence and asked, "What happened after you got captured? What did they do with you?"

"I was in a bad way but a little better as each day went by. I was being carried from village to village, maybe avoiding forces in pursuit. They used that same crude hammock from that first day. The guys hauling it grunted. They also hollered what I took to be obscene protests over their task of having to carry me.

"After a few weeks, I was able to sit up and then to stand. Began to walk slowly. I pushed myself hard to get strong so I could escape. Get away while I could still get back to Khe Sanh. My chance came. I was being kept in a lean-to on the edge of a village. My guard was in the river, bathing. I got up with difficulty. I walked slowly down the path that ran into the jungle. I felt good as I moved toward freedom. It only lasted for about fifty feet. As soon as I rounded the first turn on the trail, I ran into a tribesman coming the other way. Scared the shit out of me. I reacted without thinking. I smiled, turned sideways, took a step off the trail, and began pissing. The man grinned, waited for me to finish, and escorted me back to the lean-to. My first escape attempt was over. I was crushed, but it could have been worse. I gave thanks that, apparently, I was the only one who knew I was trying to escape. Nothing was ever said beyond a reminder that I was to ask permission before going to relieve myself.

"I was being treated OK by the guerrillas who held me. It was tough, but there was little harassment, no interrogation, no indoctrination, and no physical abuse. I had shelter and food, rice and a bit of vegetable every day, a scrap of meat on occasion. I got medical attention, my wounds were cleaned. A few of the people around me even seemed to show concern. My next escape attempt changed all that.

"A few weeks later, in another village, I was being kept in a hut raised on stilts about ten feet off the ground. You got into the hut by climbing a ladder that was removed except when meals were brought or when I asked to go piss or take a crap. My guards camped just below the hut in a small shelter. At night they would build a fire. At least one would stay awake to guard me.

"One night I woke up, having to pee badly. I leaned out the doorway to bark my request. The fire was out. Everyone was asleep. I looked at the ten-foot drop, wondering if my hitting the ground would make enough noise to wake anyone. I saw the bright moon and felt the soft breeze. My heart was pounding. Then I did it. I rolled off, hung from the edge of the flooring by my fingers, and dropped the last two feet to the ground. I made a soft thud. A few leaves and small branches crunched under my bare feet. I froze, turning my head slowly to look back over my shoulder. The guards slept.

"I rose from my crouch. I stole away on bare tiptoes until I was well past the edge of the village. Then I moved quickly down a jungle trail. Remembering my previous experience, I left the trail and headed up a steep hill toward what I thought was the east. The rest of the night I went up the hill and then down the back side, using the moon and stars for direction when I caught glimpses through the jungle. The hill became a mountain. I struggled to make progress. It was goddamned difficult. I didn't believe the bad guys had tracking dogs. I didn't think they could follow my trail in this terrain. Still, I wanted to put as much space between me and the village as rapidly as I could.

"When the sun came up, it got hot. The jungle turned into a fucking sauna as the morning wore on. I was soaked with sweat and really thirsty. I struggled down a long hillside toward a river. I quickened my pace. Just shy of the river, I came to a stream. I fell to my knees and pressed my face into the water, overwhelmed with thirst.

"I crept the rest of the way to the river bank. Waterways this size were the major highways in this part of Vietnam. I didn't want to come this far only to be discovered now. I crawled under a bush, watching the river till dusk.

"I saw nothing, no activity at all. As the sun set, I slipped down the bank and into the water. I made my way downstream by walking in the shallows and floating short stretches where I had to. I planned to work my way along the river at night and hide and sleep during the day. A beautiful, nearly full, moon shone on me. I was free and on my way to find friendly villagers, or my Special Forces detachment at Khe Sanh, or a South Vietnamese military unit near the coast. I knew the area well. I knew where to go. I'd done it!

"I saw a bridge ahead. People were on the bridge. I sensed enemy. I thought I saw weapons. I scrambled toward the water's edge, falling, swimming, thrashing, dragging myself frantically toward the bank.

"The riverbank came alive with people. Men with weapons stepped from the bush, shouting and pointing at me. Some lit torches. Among them were a small number of uniformed Viet Cong main force guerrillas. Most of the others were the same brand of local tribal fighters I had known during my weeks of captivity. I turned, looking to flee. All I saw were enemy above me and on the opposite bank. I looked up at the bridge. It was lined with enemy. They had lighted torches. Their weapons were pointing at me. My heart sank. As I moved out of the water, men slid down the steep bank to grab me. My short-lived freedom was gone. I was a prisoner again.

"A guy in uniform stepped forward, barking orders. Others dragged me up the bank, through some foliage, setting me on my feet on the narrow trail. My torn-up feet hurt. The barefoot cross-country trek had taken its toll. I stumbled. Angry soldiers shoved me onto a major path at the bridge. I shook off the hold of those who had recaptured me. They glared. The uniformed Viet Cong cadre barked again. Off we set down the path. I walked unmolested, but hobbled badly in pain.

"In a couple of hours we were back at the village from where I'd escaped the previous night. I had traveled all night and most of the next day to get to the river and down to the bridge. We had moved from the bridge back to the village along a fairly level path in a few hours. We'd circled around the steep terrain I'd spent so much time clambering over.

"I was thrown into a storage shed with bags of rice stacked along one side. The guards shoved me through the doorway and onto the floor. They grabbed my arms and jerked me back to my feet, turning me around to face the door.

"Just behind them came the uniformed Viet Cong who had taken charge at the river. He glared at me for a few seconds, rocked his arm back, and smashed his fist into my face. The blow slammed my head back and to the side. A gush of blood splattered. I cursed to myself.

"I slowly brought my head back to center. He smashed my face again. And then again. I just glared back at the communist bastard for a long moment. He turned and left, wiping his hand with a cloth as he exited. His two accomplices dropped me to the floor and followed.

"The conversation outside was angry. Several men came in, tied cords around my thumbs, and lifted me off the ground. They held me up while another guy passed the loose end of the cords over the rafters, pulled and tied them tightly to a post. The guys holding me let go, my thumb joints popped. I hung there twisting in pain. Sometime later, I passed out. Thank God, you pass out when the pain gets bad enough."

I could relate. "I know," I said. "Thank God."

He continued, "I have no idea how long I hung in that shed. I'd wake for a time, mutter profanities through the pain. It hurt from my thumbs through my wrists and arms, across my shoulders and down my back. Then I'd pass out again. At some point hours or days later, I was cut down. I collapsed in a heap on the floor. The cord was removed from my thumbs. I was left alone until the next morning when a guard arrived with rice and water. I stayed in that shed for weeks, allowed outside only to relieve myself. I was watched closely by two armed guards constantly day and night. Another pair relieved them at irregular times. Hours of wondering what would happen next turned into days of solitude. Then I was moved again.

"That trip took some doing. I was in wretched shape by then. I'd lost a lot of weight and was suffering frequent malaria attacks. I wanted to do well, to show the enemy that I was a strong American, but I was weak. The trek to the new camp was tough. It took nearly two weeks. I guess the camp was just across the border inside Laos. It was newly constructed and clearly intended for prisoners. There was a bamboo fence around the exterior, one small hut in the center, and several buildings for VC cadre around it. A jungle prison camp had been built for one person, me.

"I was put into the hut, six feet by six feet and maybe five feet high, made of bamboo with palm leaves covering the roof. The door was shut and secured from the outside. I collapsed. I was about dead. I'd become a sliver of what I had been. A sense of dread clouded my mind. I still fought to survive, and resist those assholes, but I could feel despair pulling me down.

"The VC put me through interrogations and indoctrinations for weeks. They beat me with bamboo sticks. They starved me. I was half crazy when they finally got me to sign a propaganda statement. I hated myself for that. Never felt so defeated in my life. Then they left me alone.

"I sat alone, all by myself in my hut. Lonely day passed lonely day. Weeks washed into months which dissolved into years. My guards settled into a pattern of passive neglect. I got small servings of rice, sometimes some manioc, on rare occasion a piece of pig fatback or a tiny three-inch fish. I was wasting away, physically and mentally."

I asked, "How long did you stay in that camp?"

"Maybe three years. Maybe closer to four. My mind wandered. I lost track of big chunks of time, days at a time. Sometimes I didn't know where I was. I'd shake my head, look around, and wonder where I'd been. Hours would pass daydreaming or building things in my mind. I built a whole town in my head, including a church. I'd walk all around and go inside the buildings, praying in the church.

"I was sick. Awful malaria attacks. No exercise. Lousy food. Little of it. No real nutrition. I was in a bad way. Many times I thought I was dying.

"One day, a guard told me I was going north. My food improved tremendously, and they started letting me outside to walk around inside the camp. It was tough to even take a few steps at first, but after a while I started to get stronger.

"One morning, about half a dozen soldiers stood in front of my hut in clean uniforms, sporting pith helmets with the helmet badge of a gold star set on a solid red background. These were regular North Vietnamese Army soldiers, not Viet Cong. They seemed delighted to be taking me north, back to their homeland. They bound my wrists together and tied me to a guard in front of me and one behind. We set out marching. It was tough as hell. After weeks, we got to a camp inside North Vietnam. Finally, I came to another that came to be called Bao Cao.

"As soon as I got there, they put me in a small bamboo cage, two feet by two feet by five feet. I barely fit. I was chained with shackles around my wrists and ankles. I was kept like that for months, let out only to relieve myself or for interrogation. I was fed rice and gruel inside the cage. They wanted me to sign another statement. I would not. They cut my meager rations and beatings became a routine.

"It got cold and damp as the months stretched into winter. My physical condition got worse. Eventually, I couldn't eat even the small bits of food I was given. Only when they saw I was dying did they bring me out of the cage and put me into a cell. I got some medical attention. I was given adequate food. The interrogation and beatings stopped. I didn't die.

"More months went by. I sat in that cell, alone, waiting for the war to end. The NVA moved other American prisoners into the camp, but I was kept away from them. One day I was moved to another camp with two other Americans, Ben Purcell and Ted Gostas. It was the summer of 1968. I had not been with another American for over four years.

"Once in the new camp, I was put back in solitary confinement. That lasted many more months before I was finally put in a cell with other Americans: Lew Meyer, Chuck Willis, and Larry Stark—all captured in Hue during Tet of '68. Food was better there, and I started exercising.

"After a while, they separated us into two cells. My cellmate was Lew Meyer. The idea of escape began to brew in our heads. As we thought out plans, we started exercising more and getting ourselves ready. Before we had a chance, we were moved to another prison, the Rockpile. There were twelve civilian prisoners and one enlisted Marine. We were put in larger cells with more prisoners in each. Lew and I finalized our escape plans. All we needed was the right opportunity. That came on the first of October, 1971.

"We were in the courtyard of the camp. The only guard present at the time left for a few minutes. We saw the chance. Some of the guys helped us move a table next to the wall and placed a chair on top. Lew and I climbed over, dropping fifteen feet into bushes on the other side. Speed Adkins came with us. We moved away quickly.

"Lew and I separated from Speed. He was recaptured fairly soon. The soldiers used tracking dogs. It wasn't long before they caught us. They were shooting and shouting as they closed in. It's a wonder we weren't killed.

"They punished the whole group, but us especially. Life stayed miserable for a long time after that. No torture, though. That was weird."

Jim finished, "In late 1972, our treatment and food improved. Then on January 27th, a guard told us the peace agreement had been signed. On the 28th they gave us a big meal and then brought us here."

I looked into his eyes and saw a troubled soul. He'd survived captivity for nearly nine years, longer than any other American soldier in history. It had taken a lot from him. "My God, Jim. That's incredible." He smiled weakly and looked down.

Prisoner releases began a few days later. The North Vietnamese first sent home groups of pilots captured in the North, those kept away from us throughout our captivity, even now at the end.

We knew something was up when we saw uniformed officers from Canada, Poland, Hungary, and Indonesia walking across our small courtyard with high-ranking North Vietnamese officials. Word spread through the Hilton that these were members of the ICCS (International Commission of Control and Supervision), the body required by the peace accords to oversee our release. We waited our turn to go home.

CHAPTER 15

Homeward Bound

The heavy metal door of our cell opened. A guard entered, leading Steve Leopold. *He's alive!* He was no longer yellow! *Back from the dead. Unbelievable.* Steve grinned and said in his understated way, "I'm OK. Be going home with you guys." We smiled, relieved he was all right, knowing we'd all be headed home soon.

"One thing," Steve added. "There's a guy. They're holding him in a room near where they were keeping me. His name is Kientzler, Navy pilot. Says he was shot down on the last day of the war. Says they're claiming he violated the peace accords and they're not going to release him."

Next thing I knew, Big Al Kroboth was up at the window yelling at one of the guards outside, demanding that Kientzler be brought to our cell and released along with the rest of us. Others picked up on the call. We challenged the prison authorities with the same demand every time we saw them over the next days. How bold we'd become now that the war was over. The guys next door threatened a hunger strike if this hidden prisoner was not acknowledged. The camp authorities ignored us.

Groups of prisoners who had been captured in the North had been going home since February 12, but no one from our group had. Finally, on March 5, thirty-four of our guys rolled their sleeping mats, assembled in the courtyard, and left. They were "prisoners of the Provisional Revolutionary Government of South Vietnam," the Viet Cong. The Americans captured in the North were prisoners of the Democratic Republic of Vietnam, the government of North Vietnam. It was a weird political game.

Steve Leopold was on that first flight of our guys, as was Dennis Thompson. Cordine McMurray and the other 4th Infantry Division soldiers captured in 1967 were in the group, as were the radio/TV crew and some of the other folks taken in Hue in 1968. The two German nurses went as well. Surprisingly, Jim Thompson did not. The longest-held was not going home in our first release group. *How amazing and cruel*, I thought. Jim was shattered.

It felt odd. All these guys were flying to freedom while the rest of us remained locked in our cells. It was, however, only a matter of time. We continued to eat better than we ever had, drink tea, play cards, sing, and talk about how it would be once we got out of there. As we enjoyed a North Vietnamese cigarette one afternoon, Al Kroboth and I made a pact. After we were released we'd each buy a carton of Marlboros. Then we'd quit smoking once they were gone.

Other groups of prisoners were released over the following weeks. On March 16th, a second departure of our guys included the members of the Peace Committee. Rumor was that some of them wanted to remain with their communist hosts and had asked not to be released, but the request was denied. They had to return to the United States.

There was a lot of ill will among the prisoners toward the PCs. Colonel Guy issued a direct order that no one would touch any of them after our return. We were to let him handle the situation. He promised to bring formal court-martial charges against them. He was on the same flight and would make that happen. Jim Thompson finally got out too.

Those of us who remained in our Little Vegas corner of the Hilton were consolidated into one large cell. The time for release was coming soon. We were joined by another prisoner, Lt. Cdr. Phillip Allen Kientzler, the last American shot down in the Vietnam War, the last POW. What a surprise! Our protests, along with pressure from our government, had succeeded. Al Kientzler was coming home with us. All was good, or so it seemed.

We were told that we'd be released on March 24th. We knew we were the last of the prisoners of the Viet Cong. I'd been captured by regular uniformed NVA soldiers, moved to North Vietnam, and held in their capital city. I'd never been with Viet Cong guerrillas and had never seen one in all my time as a prisoner. Yet those of us captured inside South Vietnam, even if by North Vietnamese forces, were prisoners of the Viet Cong government in the South. A bizarre political charade. We knew the North ran the guerrilla war in South Vietnam. As the day for our release approached, our excitement grew.

The camp authorities asked if we'd like to bring anything back as a souvenir. All of us said we'd like to have our maroon and gray striped clothing and Ho Chi Minh sandals. Was there anything else? "Water pipe," I said. I'd enjoyed that pipe tobacco on those few occasions and would like to try it again in the States. Others asked for some small thing or another. We knew we'd never see what we asked for, but we asked anyway.

On Saturday morning, March 24th, we woke excitedly to our breakfast bowl of bean sprouts and bread along with mystery meat, a small banana, and tea. After we ate, we rolled up our sleeping mats, as the other groups had done. We sat on the edge of our bunks, waiting to begin the process of checking out of the Hanoi Hilton and going home. We waited, and we waited. Nothing happened.

As the morning wore on, we asked, "When," and were told to wait. We asked again, and the response once more was "just wait." Midday came and midday went. We bored into the afternoon. Still nothing. The time for the afternoon meal was well past. We should have been gone hours before. Just before dusk, a guard came into the cell and told us to assemble in the courtyard.

The prison commander, the Duck, came before us to make an announcement. He looked angry and disappointed at the same time. "You not go home today. The warmonger, Nixon, has done about face. War not over. War go on. You will not go home. You never go home. Go back to your room."

I thought, *My God.* We hung our heads and walked back into the cell, unrolled our mats and sat or lay down on our beds. No one spoke a word. Eventually, I fell into a fitful sleep, wondering what fate held in store.

The next morning we were back in our normal prison routine, a few sick jokes from me and Al, our morning ration of bean sprouts and bread, cleaning up, and doing a bit of exercise. There wasn't much talking. The most optimistic words were "something will happen." The guards kept their distance and left us inside the cell throughout the day. We asked nothing of them and they said nothing to us. The next day was the same.

Tuesday began no differently. Another day in the Hanoi Hilton, with morale crushed. There was something odd about the guards, though. They scurried around the camp. They were up to something, but what? The day dragged on. Early in the afternoon, a guard entered our cell and said, "All outside to shave."

"What's up? We going home?"

"No questions. Time to get clean up. You go outside, shave."

This must be it. Has to be it, I thought. But still we didn't know. We could only hope.

After shaving we were sent back to our cell. Only then did we hear the long-awaited command, "Get ready to go. You go home today. You must get ready."

We rolled our mats, stacked our few items in front of them on our bunks, and stood by, waiting again. Before long, we were taken to a room in another part of the prison, where we found piles of identical brand-new pants, shirts, jackets, socks, and shoes, our traveling clothes. We would be in uniformly identical civilian clothes. We were told to find what fit and take it back to our cell and change.

After donning our new duds, we looked at each other and smiled. We were going home. The joy of the moment filled me. Experience tempered my emotions, though. We'd begun the process, but we still had a way to go. A gnawing fear persisted. We knew a lot could still go wrong.

We were given small gym-style bags containing a new maroon and gray striped prison uniform, a pair of Ho Chi Minh sandals, and two packs of premium North Vietnamese cigarettes. We each got a souvenir too. Mine was a bamboo water pipe. Incredible! We formed up for forgettable words of farewell from Duck. When he finished, we walked out of the Hanoi Hilton, a few steps closer to freedom.

We got on an old dilapidated bus parked out front. The paint scheme was a mottled blend of bad camouflage and rust. Taking a seat by the window, I wiped the fogged glass with my sleeve so I could see out. We drove down the road in drizzling rain, leaving the Hilton ever-farther behind. They drove us past some of the more significant bomb damage around Hanoi. Key spots, such as the badly damaged Bach Mai Hospital, were pointed out. We knew the communists had ringed the hospital with military targets and SAM launching sites. Propaganda continued to the bitter end.

The bus drove across the Red River, through simple neighborhoods and areas of devastation, along small lanes running between ramshackle warehouses. We stopped. Our escorts got off the bus. They had an intense conversation with uniformed officials who had intercepted us in a staff car. The bus wound around a few blocks and stopped again. We got off and stood in a small parking area. None of the guards looked happy. *Oh shit. What's up?* I wondered. We all looked at each other. *What now!*

We milled around for half an hour, talking among ourselves and getting no information from the guards. The staff car returned, and we were soon back on the bus, afraid we were heading back to the Hilton. But when we came to a row of derelict hangars, we knew we must be on Hanoi's Gia Lam Airport, used by enemy MiG fighter jets throughout the war. The bus turned at a shabby hangar with a rickety control tower at its side.

I beheld one of the most wondrous sights I had ever seen. Before us was a big, shiny, beautiful C-141 medevac plane parked on the ramp. The American flag and a red cross were painted high on its tail. The words U.S. Air Force were printed boldly on the fuselage just behind the cockpit. I cannot describe the emotion that filled me.

We got off the bus and guards arranged us in rows. North Vietnamese soldiers, civilians, and reporters were all around. In front of us was a broad, ten-foot-high canvas canopy over a ceremonial area. In the middle was a table covered by a brilliant white cloth. High-level communist military and government officials sat behind. Next to them were uniformed members of the ICCS. Standing just beside them were a handful of Americans, some in flight suits, a couple in class-A uniforms. One, an Air Force brigadier general, stood in front of the others.

Beside the table, a North Vietnamese official read our names, one at a time. When my name was called, I stepped from the formation as had the others before me. I approached the Air Force general and saluted. He returned my salute and extended his hand to me. We both smiled broadly.

"Welcome back, Captain Reeder. Sergeant McClarin will escort you to the aircraft." He gestured toward the young man in a flight suit standing next to him.

During our walk to the airplane, my first words were, "Can you ask the pilot to see if he can find anything out about my front-seater, Lieutenant Tim Conry?"

"Yes sir. I'll ask him to radio after we're airborne."

"Thanks. He was in my front seat when I was shot down. Want to be sure he's OK."

The interior of the aircraft was set up with passenger seats, much like an airliner, but facing rearward. Soon the whole group was on board, and we taxied to the runway for takeoff. I was sitting by Al Kroboth and Dave Mott. The crew told us our first stop would be Clark Air Force Base in the Philippines, where we would spend a few days for medical evaluation and treatment before making the long flight home to the States.

I was happy yet anxious as the big jet rolled down the runway. Once airborne, we remained silent, absorbed in our thoughts. We seemed to be waiting for something, but none of us knew quite what it was until the pilot came onto the intercom. "Thought you would all like to know that we have just passed beyond SAM missile range."

We erupted in a spontaneous cheer. I was overwhelmed with joy. It was real. We were free. We were going home. Nothing could stop that now.

CHAPTER 16

Castles in the Sand

Before we landed at Clark, I asked a crewmember what the pilot had been able to find out about Tim. "Let me check, sir." He headed to the cockpit and was gone a good while. When he returned he said, "The pilot can't find anything out over the radio right now. You'll be able to get information once you get on the ground at Clark."

We landed after sunset. It was dark. As we taxied in, the crew warned us that there would be a lot of people there to welcome us. We had no idea. When the plane stopped and the left rear door opened, we could hear a roar of humanity outside. One of the crew asked, "Are you guys ready for this?"

When the first POW went out the door the crowd went crazy. They kept it up as we each made our way out of the aircraft and down the short ramp to the ground. What no one outside knew was that one of the flight nurses stood just inside the door, giving us each a kiss the instant before we exited. I loved it. I came out of the airplane smiling for my freedom, smiling for the kiss I'd just gotten, and smiling at the sight of a large American flag flying at the base of the ramp. Hundreds of people were assembled on the airfield in the dark of the night, all clapping and cheering for me. It was surreal. It was wonderful. It was an extraordinary moment!

For nearly a year, I had imagined the world as it would be when I gained my freedom. I had imagined time I'd spend with my family, especially my two kids, Spencer and Vicki. I had hoped Amy and I could work out the troubles that plagued our marriage. I imagined the food I would eat and the menu I had written in my mind for three meals a day for a full week. I had imagined activities and pursuits, studies and recreation, untold happiness once I survived my ordeal and was free once again. I imagined the home I would build in every detail of design and construction. I also imagined getting together with Tim, having a drink in an officer's club back in the States, sharing our tales of what happened that day we got shot down, how I was captured and he was rescued. I had created quite a wonderful world in my mind. Now was my moment. All those dreams could come true.

A bus took us to the hospital. We went through a quick medical screening before meeting our escort officers. To help deal with all the administrative requirements and medical appointments, to get any questions answered, to do whatever was needed to ensure our transition back into the world and ultimately our reunification with our families went as smoothly as possible, every returning POW was assigned an escort officer. Everyone except me. I had two. One was my official escort. The other was my brother Don.

Don was an Army specialist assigned to Okinawa. When it was learned that I was alive and on the list of POWs to be released, the Army sent Don to the Philippines to be there when I returned. No one knew which flight I would come out on, so Don spent several weeks at Clark Air Base waiting for me. It was a great thing the Army did. How fantastic to have my brother with me as soon as I regained my freedom.

I asked them both about Tim. They knew nothing, but they promised to find out first thing the next day. As soon as we got to our rooms, we changed into Army hospital pajamas. It felt good to get out of communist garb.

We went to the cafeteria, where we were allowed to eat whatever we wanted. They had tried to put the first groups on a bland diet and slowly reintroduce them to Western food. That resulted in near mutiny, so they abolished that stance and let us eat what we wanted and deal with the consequences later. I ate heaping portions of steak, lobster, prime rib, and an omelet, along with a number of side dishes, and a bowl of ice cream with chocolate sauce for dessert. I returned to my room holding my belly, and I didn't feel real well till the next day.

Later that evening, I had the opportunity to call home from a small private room. A phone sat on the table in front of me. I picked it up, and an operator placed the call. My wife, Amy, answered.

She said, "Hello."

I said, "Hi. It's Bill. I'm OK. Have you heard anything about Tim?"

"Oh. They didn't tell you?"

"No. What?"

"He didn't make it. He died."

"What? How can that be? We talked after we crashed. He had a radio. I saw the helicopters come in to get him. I was sure he was rescued."

"He died on the way to the hospital. The guys will tell you more. They've been great."

Only then did I remember to ask how she was doing, how she'd held up under all this, how the kids were, and my folks. I went to bed that night deeply saddened. The first of the sand castles I had built was washed away. Tim was dead.

I spent three days in the hospital at Clark, undergoing the most thorough medical exam imaginable. They tested everything. I had a badly broken back. An L1 spinal compression fracture had healed by itself as best it could. But the fracture impinged my spinal cord, leaving me with some nerve damage and numbness. I had three types of malaria, three varieties of intestinal parasites, tropical sprue (malabsorption syndrome), and a broken tooth, all needing attention. I showed the effects of malnutrition, dysentery, an ankle wound, and cellulitis (possibly gangrene), as well as evidence of previously dislocated shoulders, broken toes, lacerations, burns, and infected leech bites.

My cholesterol numbers were below the normal range, but that was nothing to worry about. They should come up once I had more time on a normal diet. The doctors began treatment for the malaria and parasites. One doctor told me, "You've got three types of malaria. One of them is quite deadly. You're lucky. But the malaria treatments we have now are 99 percent effective. You'll be fine." I would get an orthopedic follow-up for my back in the States.

Besides the medical workup, I got a haircut, manicure, and pedicure, all at the same time as I sat in the barber chair. A tailor measured me in every detail, and the next day I had a new uniform with rank, aviator wings, and medals. I felt so good to be back in the uniform of the country I loved so much.

The POWs were kept isolated from the public and the press for our own privacy, which was nice. Our schedule of medical appointments and administrative processing kept us occupied. Otherwise, we enjoyed our time together as free men. We had limitless American cigarettes. My stomach quickly recovered from that first feast, and I enjoyed every bite of food I had during those days at Clark.

On our second full day of freedom, the POWs were asked if we would be willing to visit children in an elementary school on the base. We all agreed. We were split among several classrooms, and we told the kids some things about our experiences in very simple terms. They listened closely. When we left, they gave us pictures they'd drawn and painted for us. That warmed out hearts.

After three days at Clark, we flew back to the States. On Friday, March 30th, we loaded on another C-141 cargo jet configured for medical evacuation. We were divided between two aircraft, one going to the West Coast and one going to the East. The smaller number of passengers meant we had airline-style seats like we'd had coming out of Hanoi, and a number of litters for anyone needing to lie flat. That provided welcome relief to my injured back. Sitting for any length of time was extremely painful.

We flew from the Philippines to Hickam Air Force Base in Honolulu, Hawaii, where we took a two-hour break to get off and stretch in the military passenger terminal while the plane was refueled. Thousands of people lined the parking apron next to the aircraft, separated from us by a short chain-link fence. As I made my way along the walkway next to the fence, an older woman gave me a look of such deep compassion that I paused and turned. She cradled my face in her hands and said simply,

"God bless you." I found out later that she had suffered herself, in a Nazi concentration camp in World War II.

Farther along, I noticed a guy back in the crowd jumping up and down, waving his arms and yelling. I looked again and smiled. He was my best friend from the year I spent in high school in Hawaii, Alan Kajikawa. *Unbelievable.* "Come inside!" I yelled as loud as I could. Alan and another friend, CWO Jim "Ziggy" Siegfried, a Pink Panther, were both there. They'd wangled their way into our room in the passenger terminal. It was great to see them. Alan had been such a good friend.

Ziggy was able to fill me in on some of the details surrounding my shoot-down and what happened to Tim. He told me Tim was spotted lying in a bomb crater a short distance from the aircraft. John Paul Vann, the civilian commanding that region of Vietnam, had refused to allow a rescue attempt because of the overwhelming enemy threat. The Pink Panthers, along with a Loach scout helo and some Cobra gunships from B Troop, 7/17th Cavalry, launched that evening anyway, saying they were simply conducting an "armed reconnaissance." The Loach pilot, Capt. Jim Stein, had landed and picked up Tim, still alive and aware that he'd been rescued. Ziggy then told me that when they arrived at the hospital at Pleiku, the doctor said Tim was dead. Jim Stein couldn't believe it. No one could believe Tim had been that close and didn't make it.

I began to dissect the mission, wishing I'd have done something differently. I was the air mission commander. I was in charge. My decisions brought about Tim's death. What could I have done differently?

"Stop," Ziggy said. "You did it the best way it could have been done. It was a mess in there. Nobody could have done any better."

"Thanks, Ziggy. That means a lot. But I'll always wonder if I could have done anything differently. I'll always wonder that." I still do.

The three POWs from Hawaii left us at Hickam, and the rest of us flew on to Travis Air Force Base, California. There, after another wonderful welcome-home greeting, we split up and were shuttled to the regional hospitals that would care for us. Four of us were bound for Fitzsimmons Army Medical Center in Denver, Colorado.

Our C-9 landed that evening at Buckley Air Force Base on the edge of town. I was the senior POW on the flight, so I had the opportunity to make a few comments to the press upon arrival. As soon as I finished, I was reunited with Amy and the kids. I had dreamed of this so long. This was what had kept me going when it would have been so easy to give up and die. I gave Amy a big kiss and hug, and then hugged my kids and hugged them and hugged them. Spencer had been four years old when I left for Vietnam. Vicki had been a newborn. Now Spence was nearly six and Vicki almost two. God, how I'd missed them.

Each family got into its own Army staff car and was driven to the hospital, with the escort officers following behind. These now included mine and Amy's along with my brother Don.

We were to spend two weeks in the hospital and then go out on ninety days of convalescent leave. This was to be time to enjoy with our families and readjust to a life that some had not known for years. After that, we'd either return to military duty or be discharged, likely with some amount of disability. I had decided to fight hard to stay on active duty in the Army and keep flying if I could.

In those two weeks at Fitzsimmons, the Army conducted intelligence debriefings. I talked with two intelligence officers for hours, sharing all I could remember. I told them all I could about missing Americans I knew anything about. I told them about being shown Specialist Ed Wong's ID card. I told them accounts I'd heard from other prisoners. I offered every detail I could about Wayne, the circumstances of his death, and where he was buried.

My medical checkout continued, including a psychiatric assessment. The psychiatrist offered follow-up sessions, which I politely declined. I was just fine. An orthopedic surgeon evaluated my spine and determined that though there were a number of issues and potential future problems, my back had healed itself. Though there was some pressure against my spinal cord, the decision on surgery would wait until I was returned to duty to see how I did under a normal routine. Spinal surgery carried risks, and we hoped I could function without it.

During the time at Fitzsimmons, we were given passes to do things with our families. I relished time with Amy and the kids. I ate Big Macs at every opportunity.

The rest of my family soon gathered in Denver. My brother Greg arrived. My father flew in from Alaska and my mother and stepfather from California. My parents had never been on good terms since their divorce, and the Army did a fine job of keeping them from ever crossing paths over those days. Well done!

My grandmother on my dad's side also flew out from California for a couple of days. During dinner at the nearby Buckley Air Force Base officer's club, she shared a story.

"I didn't know what to think about you until I had a dream one night. I saw a bus driving slowly down the road in the rain. The windows were fogged. As I watched, someone inside wiped the fog away from one of the windows so I could see them. It was you. I was looking at your face. From that moment, I knew you were alive. I never had a doubt."

My thoughts reeled. *Wow. I can't believe it.* I don't accept things so bizarre, but her story rocked me. I recalled getting on the bus in front of the Hanoi Hilton, wiping the fogged window with my sleeve so I could see out.

My grandmother, my six-year-old son Spence, and my youngest brother Don were the only ones in the family who believed I was still alive. Everyone else hoped but thought in their hearts that I was dead.

A uniformed Army officer and chaplain had told Amy and each of my parents that I'd been shot down in combat and was missing in action. The next day, Amy got a telegram stating:

THE SECRETARY OF THE ARMY REGRETS TO INFORM YOU THAT YOUR HUSBAND, CAPTAIN WILLIAM S. REEDER JR., BECAME MISSING IN ACTION IN VIETNAM ON 9 MAY 1972 AS A RESULT OF HOSTILE ACTION. HE WAS LEADING A FLIGHT OF ATTACK HELICOPTERS IN KONTUM PROVINCE, REPUBLIC OF VIETNAM, WHEN HIS AIRCRAFT WAS HIT BY ENEMY FIRE, CRASHED, AND EXPLODED ON IMPACT.

That did not sound good. When no word came as the months went by, everyone assumed I was dead. My name was never on a list of POWs until after the war was over, just before my release. I was simply an MIA, missing in action.

The day before I was supposed to depart Fitzsimmons on convalescent leave, I had a bad malaria attack. "Doc, I thought you told me the malaria treatment was 99 percent effective. What's up?"

The internist looked at me for a long moment, and then said, "You are the one percent. You have something we call tropical sprue, a malabsorption syndrome. It means your body does not absorb the nutrients from what you eat very well. That applies to medications too. You didn't absorb all the malaria medication you should have. We'll keep you here for another round of treatment and be sure you're OK before going out on leave."

"How long is that going to be?" I asked.

"Maybe two weeks. Shouldn't be any longer."

Great fucking fantastic shit, I thought. "Thanks," I said. I was stuck in the hospital for two more weeks.

Before the two weeks were up, an Army specialist from the hospital public affairs office came to my room and asked if I'd be willing to be the speaker for a group in town the next night. "No, I'm not interested. Thank you."

The next morning, the same young man came by my room again. "I wanted to check and see if you'd possibly reconsidered. You are the only POW left in the hospital. All the others are gone."

"Nope." I responded. "Have not changed my mind. Not interested. Thank you, anyway."

That afternoon, the hospital public affairs officer walked into my room and introduced himself. Before he could say anything more, I made a pre-emptive attack. "I told your guy yesterday and again this morning that I am not interested. I don't want to speak to any groups. I just want to get out of this goddamned hospital and be left alone to get back to my life."

He remained polite but asked me one more time. "I just wanted to ask you to please consider one last time. This group is the Bataan-Corregidor

Survivors Association and they really want one of the returned Vietnam POWs to talk to them at their gathering tonight. You are the only one still here."

I was blown away. "Wait a minute. These are the POWs who survived the Bataan Death March in World War II, and they want to hear about *me* after what they've been through?"

"That's right. They would very much appreciate you coming to their meeting tonight. They were really hoping . . ."

"Of course I'll talk to them. What do they want me to say?"

"Just talk about your experience. Tell them what happened to you. That's all they want. Just tell your story."

I did. They were most respectful and sincerely interested, and I, in turn, was in awe of their experiences during the Second World War. I'll never forget what those guys did for me that night. By giving me an opportunity I couldn't refuse, they made me come out of my shell and speak publicly about what I'd been through. They opened the door to what would become the greatest therapy possible to help me deal with all that had happened to me. Many of my friends who have not been able to talk about what happened to them have not readjusted well. Several still have major psychological issues haunting them.

A couple of days later, I got an invitation to speak to a high school assembly, which I accepted. In the weeks and months ahead, I'd be asked to talk to various groups, and I agreed to as many as I could. I strongly believe that the opportunity to share my experience has been one of the principal reasons I've been able to readjust and deal with life as well as I have—that coupled with my faith in God, love of family, and my inherently optimistic nature. The love of family would have a few bumps in the road though.

Amy had been a good wife during my captivity. She had held the family together while dealing with the stress of a husband missing in action. She'd raised the kids by herself. She was in touch with guys from my unit and active in POW causes including the National League of Families.[1] But Amy and I weren't getting along.

We'd had problems before I was a POW, and now they came to a head. Amy had grown into a strong and independent woman while I was gone;

her views sometimes were at loggerheads with mine. I had changed as well. I had created a world in my imagination that I'd come home to, a world that wasn't real, a fantasy I really didn't recognize as such at the time. When parts of my dream world crumbled, as they must, my disappointment and frustration grew.

I was impatient. Things had to happen right now. No waiting. Activities had to be planned in detail, and plans carried out with precision. I became a perfectionist, always critical, easily finding fault.

I would have occasional dreams where I'd be back in captivity or flying a mission that I knew would end with my capture. The prison walls in my dreams were real, absolutely real, until I woke in a shuddering sweat. The dreams didn't come often, but they were unnerving when they did.

I sometimes drank to excess. Most days I didn't drink at all, but drinking or not, I was always hard to get along with. My other escape? I immersed myself in my work. I'd always taken pride in being an Army officer. Now work was my salvation. Work and my children. I loved being with the kids, but Amy aggravated me more and more. I looked for chances to get away, to spend time with other people. After I'd been back a year, we separated, then divorced. Another set of dreams washed away. It was hard on me and much harder on her. It turned out to be hardest on Spencer and Vicki.

My troubles were not unique. The divorce rate among Vietnam POWs was twice the national average.[2] Out of our small group of eight cellmates at Plantation Gardens, Al Kroboth, Dave Mott, and I got divorces. There were also happy stories of couples that stayed together and thrived. One POW, Joe Rose, returned home to find his fiancée still waiting after five years. They were married at the Valley Forge Army Hospital chapel a few days after his return. But there were many others who faced difficult situations.

The saddest experience was Jim Thompson's, the longest-held of the POWs. Jim told me that his wife, Alyce, had taken up with another man a few months after his capture. She used Jim's missing in action status to claim that her husband was dead, despite evidence to the contrary. She told her four children their father had died and this new man was now their dad. But she continued to receive Jim's full military pay and allowances for all the years he was held captive. Alyce refused to let the Army release any information on Jim and would not allow his name to appear on the POW bracelets being worn around the country. That made Jim invisible to the world. The result was that Lt. Everett Alvarez (USN) was assumed to be the longest-held POW throughout the Vietnam War. He was not. Jim Thompson was captured four months before Alvarez.

For almost nine years, Jim imagined how wonderful his life would be once he was freed. He'd dreamed dreams that let him endure, that gave him the strength to survive captivity longer than any other American soldier had. Those dreams were demolished as soon as he returned to the world. He'd never recover from his disappointment. He was a shattered hero.

Jim and I were among the ten returned Army POWs selected to travel to Washington, D.C., to brief Gen. Creighton Abrams, the Army chief of staff, on our experience. We divided into groups to prepare presentations on several subjects. I was teamed with Jim for one of those presentations.

We found ourselves having the remarkable experience of briefing the entire Army staff with General Abrams presiding. The main point Jim and I made was that the biggest challenge faced by POWs was fear of the unknown, of not knowing what to expect. We said the Air Force and Navy did a far better job of preparing their personnel for dealing with the challenges of being POWs. The Air Force survival and resistance school at Fairchild Air Force Base in Washington State was legendary, and the Navy jungle and sea survival courses were noteworthy as well. We recommended that the Army look to the Air Force model, in particular, for a future Army training program. As a result of our briefing, the Army later established a SERE (survival, evasion, resistance, and escape) training program that now serves as a standard for our military forces.[3]

Jim and I became closer when we were teamed up for that briefing. He told me about the challenges he was facing at home, the troubles with his family, and the difficulties he was having in life. Jim was depressed and turned to alcohol. His career was in a shambles. Later he divorced, attempted suicide, and suffered a heart attack and finally a debilitating stroke. After the stroke, he walked with difficulty, could barely speak, could hardly read, and couldn't write. People often mistook him for being drunk. He told me, "I was a prisoner of war for nine years. Now I'm a prisoner inside my own body."[4]

I denied any psychological problems myself. I thought I was handling things pretty well. The opportunities to talk about my experiences, hiking and camping with my kids, my eternal optimism, a totally lame sense of humor, comfort in my Army working environment, all helped me cope mentally. My physical health was another matter.

I kept having malaria attacks for years. I went through the sure cure a few more times before I was finally free from the disease. My bowels were never quite right again. My back was the worst of my challenges. When I returned to active duty as a field artillery commander, I'd cry out in pain as we'd bounce along bumpy dirt roads in my Army jeep. It was unbearable.

I was scheduled for spinal surgery and entered Madigan Army Medical Center at Fort Lewis, Washington, on April 29, 1975. I watched Saigon fall to the North Vietnamese on April 30th from my hospital bed, a sad day indeed. All we had sacrificed, all those who had died in the effort to maintain South Vietnam's independence; it all seemed in vain as I watched NVA tanks roll through the gates of the Presidential Palace. What had it all been for? Had it been worth it?

On May 1st I underwent major back surgery, having my spine fused over three levels of vertebrae, with hardware installed to help stabilize the area. I spent two months on the orthopedic ward in a Circle Electric Bed. The bed allowed me to be rotated from front to back while I lay motionless. I had to use a portable urinal and defecate into a pot through a hole in the mattress. The nursing staff had to help me and clean me up. They also bathed me in bed at least once a day.

After I was placed in a plaster body cast running from my shoulders to my hips, I was allowed to move to a regular bed. I was only able to get out of bed many days later after intensive physical therapy. A few weeks later, I was released from the hospital on convalescent leave. I had to wear the plaster body cast for three months. That was no fun.

I married again after Amy and I divorced. Jean was an Army nurse, a kind, gentle woman, very caring and giving, well-respected for her role in the operating room. We hadn't dated long, but we were convinced we were in love and meant for each other. Jean tried hard. Once we got to really know each other, though, we came to find out that we were two very different people. And I was still not dealing well with disappointment. My fantasies of what life was supposed to be like continued to be washed away. Reality was harder than my dreams.

My solution, as always, was to channel my energies into my work, taking time only to spend with Spence and Vicki, the true joy of my life. My career was going great and I loved work. But my heart ached. I wasn't happy, and Jean knew it. I told her, "Life is too short for this." We divorced, knowing it just wasn't working.

I had lived through combat, survived a terrible crash, endured captivity, gutted out a death march up the Ho Chi Minh Trail, and suffered wounds, torture, and life-threatening disease. Since I'd come home, I felt I was dealing well with whatever demons those experiences had created, in spite of the growing string of disappointments as fantasy after fantasy crumbled in the face of reality. I was now a free man, the father of two wonderful children, successful in my career. Though medically unfit for flight duties by regulation, I'd been returned to flying status with a waiver from the surgeon general of the Army. I had it made. I had my faith in God. I had my kids. I had my optimism. I had hope. But something was missing.

CHAPTER 17

Hope

Hope springs eternal in the human breast.

—Alexander Pope

Fritz Trey, an officer I worked with (a tanker), grinned at me, "So you're looking for a place for your daughter to go horseback riding?" We had just completed a semiannual Army physical fitness test. We had done pushups and sit-ups and run two miles. I was assigned to the Army Personnel Command in Alexandria, Virginia. We took our PT test at Cameron Station, an Army support base in the area.

Amy had remarried another Army officer and was living at Fort Belvoir, not far away. Spencer was off to college at the University of Washington. Vicki, still in high school, was a horse-crazy teenager who wanted riding lessons.

I said, "Damn right."

Fritz asked, "Do you know Melanie? She has horses."

I said, "No."

"That's her, right over there. She works in our building."

I looked across the park and spied a lovely young woman in sweats. I pointed and asked, "Her?"

"That's right. That's Melanie. Captain Melanie Lineker. Come on, I'll introduce you."

Melanie was more than cute. She bubbled with enthusiasm. Her short blonde hair bounced as she gestured and talked about her horses. Her small farm was right on the Manassas Battlefield in the countryside just outside Washington, D.C. She was willing to take Vicki on as a student. *Of course,* I thought, *I'd love to bring my daughter by your place for riding lessons.*

My macho coworkers mocked me when I walked back to our group. "Hey, Bill. Bet you don't even know how to ride. Better learn. Goin' out to Melanie's, huh?" In fact, I had worked on cattle ranches and ridden a bit of college rodeo and did know how to ride, although it had been many years since I'd been on a horse. And then there was my broken back.

I began taking Vicki out on weekends for lessons. Sometimes her mom would deliver her and I'd pick her up. I began to get to know Melanie. She was a wonderful, genuine human being in addition to being beautiful, a rare combination. We got to know each other as the weekends went by, and we became friends. I told her I could ride, but it had been a while. One day, she asked if I'd like to go for a ride with her and Vicki.

She put me on a quarter horse named Nugget. We walked for a bit, then trotted, and finally broke into a canter. As we ran along the battlefield trails, we passed a scary looking portapotty. Melanie and Vicki were just ahead of me. Nugget shied, plopping me on the ground. I skidded along on my back while Nugget planted his feet and stopped. Amazingly, the reins were still in my hand. I remounted quickly and galloped to catch up, racing by my two companions. They never would have known what happened had they not seen the grass stains on the back of my shirt. My back ached for days, but I was on another horse again the next weekend.

Melanie and I rode together frequently after that. She was impressed with my riding. She didn't know that I was hanging on for dear life. One night we galloped our horses bareback down a dirt road with nothing to hold onto but a handful of mane.

"That was incredible," she said as we dismounted in front of her barn. The horses puffed with fatigue and excitement. She couldn't see my knees shaking in the dark, nor could she imagine my thoughts: *That was scary as shit. Can't believe I lived through it. This woman is crazy.* I said, "Yes, absolutely incredible."

The next time we rode, she led me up a small hill at a gallop. We came into an open space under a clump of trees at the top. Sunlight filtered through the leaves. It was magical. "This is my favorite place on earth," she said. Our horses turned, stepping close to each other so we were facing, her knee touching mine. I leaned over and kissed her. I was falling in love.

Melanie and I were married on September 5, 1987. With Melanie, I was able to put my career in perspective. I still worked hard, but work wasn't the central focus of my life. I have had the joy of being able to continue to fly, of commanding an aviation battalion and brigade. I was able to keep flying Cobras after the war. When the AH-64 Apache attack helicopter was developed, I was lucky enough to get an early transition and fly that marvelous machine for much of the rest of my career.

Our son, Chad, was born on July 20, 1991, his sister Chelsea on January 1, 1995. Just like their older siblings, they've been greeted each morning with, "Good morning. It's a beautiful day." I truly believe that every day God has given me on this earth since I came home from captivity is a beautiful day. It doesn't matter if it's raining or snowing, windy or calm, hot or cold, sunny or overcast. Every day is a gift. Every day is beautiful.

Our life was filled with a bliss that is still with us today. Of course we've had challenges. Yes, there have been arguments, but we've always stayed in love. We find joy in life and in each other. I have felt so at peace with myself and my world for the twenty-nine years we've been married. I am truly happy.

Spencer and Vicki are grown, each successful in their lives. Spencer and his lady, Joanne, have given me a grandson, William Muir, whom I adore. Vicki is happily settled with her husband, Roy, in Oakland, California. Chad is an Army lieutenant stationed in Alaska with his wife, Mary Kate. Chelsea is a college student at Central Washington University. I retired from the Army in 1995, Melanie in 2003, both colonels. We continue to work, but we spend as much time as possible together, enjoying the adventures we are able to weave into our life.

Still, I've wondered about the meaning of it all. Not a day passes that I don't think about Tim. Why did I live when he and others died? Am I also living my life for all three of us, not only for myself but for Tim and Wayne, who died so young? Why am I here? What is my purpose?

In 2006, I was attending the VHPA (Vietnam Helicopter Pilots Association) annual reunion in Washington, D.C., with my family. One of the events was a historical forum on the Battle of Kontum, that part of the 1972 communist Easter Offensive I participated in. A speaker at the forum was Mark Truhan, one of the two American advisors on the ground at the Ben Het border camp the day I was shot down. I had known he was going to speak, and I was excited to hear what he'd have to say. I knew who he was but had never met him.

Mark discussed his role in the battle as the two Vietnamese ranger battalions at Ben Het struggled against the assault of thousands of enemy soldiers and a dozen or so tanks from two NVA divisions. He talked about our Cobras providing gun support and then coming in to escort the critically needed ammunition resupply. He described the hornets' nest we stirred up and the intensity of the fire directed against us. He told of my radio call as I was hit and going down. He spoke of the crash and explosion, of seeing me struggling to get out of the aircraft, hanging with my head down outside the cockpit as the helicopter burned. He told of his experience of seeing a trucker burn to death years before, of putting his rifle sights on me to put me out of my misery but waiting for an instant before squeezing the trigger. He expressed his frustration as smoke obscured the wreckage and destroyed his shot, and his amazement that I was gone when it cleared.

He finished answering questions at the conclusion of his remarks. As the room emptied, he stepped over and we introduced ourselves with a hug. As we talked, he faced Melanie and said, "I just don't know what kept me from squeezing that trigger, what stopped me from shooting at that instant."

Melanie's eyes filled with tears as she turned and pointed to fourteen-year-old Chad and eleven-year-old Chelsea standing beside her. "That's why. That's why you didn't shoot." Mark's eyes welled, filling with tears that rolled down his cheeks. He cried. Melanie cried. I cried, as did Chad and Chelsea as we all embraced in a group hug. That's all the meaning I need. I don't need any more meaning in my life than that.

Epilogue

More than 2,500 Americans remained unaccounted for when I came home at the end of the U.S. involvement in the Vietnam War, with 1,350 missing in action and about 1,200 listed as killed in action but body not recovered. Many of those cases have been resolved over the years through the diligent efforts of JPAC, the Joint Personnel Accounting Command, based in Hawaii. No other nation in history has exerted a greater effort in determining the fate of its MIAs and recovering the remains of its war dead than has the United States of America. There is still much to be done, but I am confident that the United States continues to work as diligently as possible to resolve the status of the many Americans who remain missing.

Of all the U.S. Army personnel lost in Vietnam, only seventy-seven turned up at war's end as prisoners. Fourteen of those were Army aviators. Four of those were commissioned officers. I was very lucky, one of only four commissioned Army pilots to be returned at the end of the Vietnam War. I was also the last Army prisoner to be taken who survived. All Army prisoners captured after me died.

Everyone I was with as a prisoner was either released at the end of the war or died in captivity. I know of no one who was left behind save Robert Garwood, who returned years later to be court-martialed for collaborating with the enemy. The prisoners I was with at the end all came home. Some adjusted well; others faced a good deal of hardship and pain. All those who risk their life in combat pay a price. At the same time, they gain a special appreciation for the hard-fought liberties we enjoy. Of those who risked their lives in Vietnam, the few of us who became prisoners of war share a particularly precious joy of thanksgiving for our freedom, which for us for so long was only a dream.

And what has become of us today? Here's a rundown on some of those who shared this journey with me.

1972 COMMUNIST EASTER OFFENSIVE (BATTLE OF KONTUM):

Mike Sheuerman took me on my first combat mission with the Pink Panthers. Mike left the Army soon after Vietnam. I'm not sure how much an episode he had at Camp Holloway one night had to do with it. Mike had been drinking a bit much after a harrowing day of combat missions. He was crawling on the ground on his belly back to his hooch in the dark when Lieutenant Colonel Bagnal, the battalion commander, walked by. Mike, seeing shiny polished boots, rolled onto his back, saluted, and said, "Good evening, sir." Colonel Bagnal looked down and said, "Good evening, Lieutenant Sheuerman," a clear note of disgust in his voice. Regardless of the impact of that incident, or possibly others, Mike left the service, became hugely successful in the office furniture business in Dallas-Fort Worth, and married Melanie, a beautiful young woman. They have a son named Hunter, Mike's nickname in Vietnam. Mike is retired from business, enjoying life with frequent family vacations to their condo in Cabo San Lucas, Mexico. He is active in the Vietnam Helicopter Pilots Association (VHPA) and served as president for a term. He is the single person responsible for getting so many of us old Pink Panthers together each year at the annual VHPA reunions.

Forrest Snyder. Forrest always appeared more as a mild-mannered physicist than an attack helicopter pilot. As the Battle of Kontum continued to unfold after my shoot-down, Forrest was wounded in the legs while flying front seat on a mission with Jim "Ziggy" Siegfried. Ziggy was also hit in the legs, so they had a challenging flight home with a dicey landing, each trying to help the other on the controls. Forrest also left active duty shortly after Vietnam. Mitre Corporation hired him as an engineer with an office in the Pentagon. Forrest was hard at work in that office on September 11, 2001, and found himself not far from the point of impact of Flight 77. Forrest and his wife, Paula, are living in Northern Virginia, still deeply in love after more than forty-seven years together.

Dan Jones was with me on so many intense combat missions, including the horrendous fight at Firebase Charlie. Dan left active duty after the war and entered the Army Reserve. After getting his fixed-wing airplane rating, he became a commercial pilot flying out of Phoenix, Arizona, where he is still piloting corporate jets. He lives there with his wife, Carol, and son, Dan Jr. Dan was awarded the Silver Star, our nation's third-highest award for heroism, for his actions during the fight at Firebase Charlie. He also received two Distinguished Flying Crosses for other acts of courage in Vietnam.

John Duffy. Maj. John Joseph Duffy, the hero of the battle of Firebase Charlie, spent his career in Special Forces. He received the Distinguished Service Cross, America's second-highest award for heroism, for his actions during the fight at Charlie, an award that is being reviewed for possible upgrade to a Medal of Honor. He also received eight Purple Hearts for wounds received in action during his service in Vietnam. John retired from the Army after the war and made a small fortune founding an investment firm, which was later sold to Ameritrade. He now writes poetry and lives in a beautiful home near the central California coast with Mary, the love of his life.

Jim Stein, scout helicopter pilot extraordinaire. Jim was the guy I covered going into Polei Kleng. He's the one who courageously came in that night to rescue Tim from the jungle, only to have him die on the way to the hospital. Jim continued being the hero that he was. That's all he could be. That was him. Jim was shot down again and again, ten times in all. The last time, a bullet ripped into his right knee, costing him his leg.

Jim struggled to stay in the Army for a time, but eventually he was medically retired. He became active in paraskiing and spent time with the U.S. ski team. He worked as a business operations manager in the

San Francisco Bay area, where he now lives in retirement. He received two Silver Stars for heroism and four Distinguished Flying Crosses for his feats in Vietnam.

Mark Truhan left active duty and continued to serve in the Army Reserve while working for the State of Vermont. He remains amazed that he didn't squeeze the trigger in time to shoot me as I hung upside down on the side of my burning Cobra. Mark was called back to active duty and deployed to the war in Iraq some thirty-three years after the battle at Ben Het. He was possibly the oldest lieutenant colonel in that combat theater.

Steve Allen. A North Vietnamese machine gunner shot Steve in the chest with a .51-caliber machine gun bullet as he covered me when I was shot down. The doctors didn't believe he would live through the night, but he survived, losing his left lung and various other pieces and parts of his chest. He fought hard to recover and eventually returned to flight status in the National Guard, serving as a Cobra instructor pilot at Fort Indiantown Gap, Pennsylvania.

Bob Gamber, flying in Steve's front seat, landed their Cobra in enemy-held territory on a road a few miles from the Dak To airfield. Steve was transferred to a UH-1 Huey for transport the rest of the way to the hospital. Bob retired from the Army in 1988 as a lieutenant colonel. He worked for the Army and Air Force Exchange Service until retiring in 2007. He lives outside Wichita Falls, Texas.

FELLOW POWs

Al Kroboth, my best buddy in Hanoi. Al was a professional basketball prospect in college, but was never able to achieve that dream with the shoulder injury he sustained in his ejection. After his release, he was medically retired from the Marine Corps. He married again after a divorce. Following in his father's footsteps, he became the vice president for operations at the Rosedale & Rosehill Cemetery in Linden, New Jersey, and later president of the Cremation Association of North America.

Al and I promised each other we would smoke one carton of American cigarettes back in the United States, and then give up smoking. But Al didn't quit smoking when he got home, nor did I. We both did eventually kick the nasty habit, though. I had my last cigarette in 1978.

Dave Mott and **Bill Gauntt,** my other Plantation Gardens cellmates, finished their military flying careers and retired from the Air Force in the 1990s. **John Murphy** left the service in 1978 and entered the business world, advancing to vice president for operations of S-TEC, a general aviation autopilot and instrument manufacturer. **Bill Henderson** left the Air Force in 1975. **Bill Thomas** retired in his home state of Hawaii after our repatriation and is still enjoying each day in paradise with his wife Emilia. **John Parsels** retired from the Army as a major and became active in the POW/MIA cause, diligently working toward a full accounting of those still missing in action in Southeast Asia.

Ted Guy, our SRO (senior ranking officer), known as "Hawk," commanded our motley crew of "Hawk's Heroes." Colonel Guy pressed charges against the Peace Committee when we returned, as he'd promised. But both the military and political leadership in Washington decided there would be no charges brought against any of the POWs. Secretary of Defense Melvin Laird announced the fact publicly before our return.

Colonel Guy fought but failed. None of the Peace Committee were court-martialed. Colonel Guy's Air Force career was adversely affected, causing him to retire in 1975. He married Linda Bergquist several months after his release from captivity. They lived happily together until his death from leukemia on April 23, 1999, at the age of seventy.

Colonel Guy received the Air Force Cross (the Air Force equivalent of the Army's Distinguished Service Cross, our nation's second-highest award for heroism after the Medal of Honor), Silver Star, and Distinguished Flying Cross for his actions in combat and extraordinary service during captivity.

Dennis Thompson continued his Army career, becoming the first sergeant of B Company in the 2nd Ranger Battalion at Fort Lewis, Washington. Dennis was a great Green Beret and Army Ranger. After promotion to sergeant major, the highest enlisted rank in the Army, Dennis was reassigned to the post headquarters.

After retirement, Dennis found some solace for a time in working as a shipwright in Olympia, Washington. He is now fully retired, living happily with his lovely wife, Marina, though still deeply scarred by the terrors of combat and captivity. Dennis received two Silver Stars, our nation's third-highest award for heroism, for his actions in the battle at Lang Vei Special Forces Camp and for his harrowing escape attempt as a POW.

Harvey Brande also remained on active duty after the war. Upon retirement in 1975 as a master sergeant, he bought a country and western bar in San Antonio, Texas. Harvey's lack of business expertise and an incompetent bar manager doomed his dream to failure. He locked the doors and headed west, settling in the San Bernardino Mountains of California. The last address I had for him was c/o a bar in a small mountain town. Harvey also received two Silver Stars for his actions at Lang Vei and his escape with Dennis.

Luis G. "Jerry" Chirichigno was certain he'd been promoted to major during his five years as a POW. When he found out he hadn't, he left the service and went to work for the United States Agency for International Development (USAID), later moving to the U.S. State Department. He is retired in Florida. Jerry received the Distinguished Service Cross (America's second-highest award for heroism after the Medal of Honor) for his bravery during the battle that led to his capture.

Marty Frank. Like so many others, his marriage ended shortly after his return, but he later remarried. Marty did not pursue his Plantation Gardens dream of raising deer on a farm in New Jersey. Instead, he continued his Army career, retiring as a master sergeant in 1987. In retirement, he owned the Ebb Tide Lounge in San Antonio, Texas. He loved going to baseball games and spending time with family. Marty never shook his affinity for tobacco, though. He died of inoperable lung cancer in the VA hospital in San Antonio in 2008 at the young age of sixty-six. He received the Silver Star and Purple Heart for the action that led to his capture.

Bill Baird was truly a nice guy. In Hanoi, he hobbled on crudely fashioned crutches, piss jar in hand, suffering badly from the complications of the lack of medical treatment of his wounds and from the effects of brutal physical and psychological torture. He later received a Silver Star for his brave resistance. Bill battled greater physical disability than any other POW during his captivity. He relished his freedom on returning to America. He was medically discharged, struggling with his health every day of his life. Bill died on July 30, 2002. He was fifty-three years old.

Gail Kerns was the other badly wounded soldier with us in Hanoi. He had been shot in the temple and never received medical treatment for his wound. Gail walked only with extreme difficulty and had frequent violent seizures. Even so, on arriving at Andrews Air Force Base, Virginia, when he was released from captivity, he insisted on walking off the airplane by himself. Once down the ramp, Gail knelt and kissed the ground of America. Gail had successful surgery at Valley Forge Army Medical Center, Pennsylvania, implanting a plate into his head. That, along with medication, stopped his seizures and allowed him to have a normal life. He lives happily with his wife, Helen, in West Virginia.

Doc Kushner. Floyd Harold "Hal" Kushner saved my life in Hanoi by communicating the necessary actions to my cellmates during my horrific malaria attacks and by hounding the enemy until they gave me quinine tablets. Like so many of us, he was divorced after his return and later remarried.

Dr. Kushner always wanted to be an eye doctor, so he went through an Army residency to become an ophthalmologist. After military retirement, he went into private practice in Florida, where he lives with his wife, Gayle. Dr. Kushner received the Silver Star for his heroic actions in saving lives during captivity while suffering enemy beatings and other abuses in retaliation for his efforts.

Armed Forces Radio and Television Station crew in Hue. These were the last guys who would ever expect to be captured in war. They all served with pride, distinguishing themselves as POWs, resisting the enemy as well as or better than others. Some were extraordinarily hard-core.

Harry Ettmueller became an Army medic after the war, rising to the rank of sergeant first class before retiring near Austin, Texas. He received the Silver Star for his actions at Hue.

John Deering left the Marine Corps in 1973 to go into business for himself building custom cars in Tennessee. He received the Silver Star for heroism, as well. John died of a massive heart attack in 2007. He was sixty-four years old.

John Anderson retired from the Army as a master sergeant shortly after his return. He continued his career as a civilian employee with Armed Forces Radio and Television Service. John received two Silver Stars for his heroism at Hue and as a prisoner of war. John died of a heart attack in 1988 at the age of fifty-seven and is buried in Arlington National Cemetery.

Don Gouin, one of the older POWs, was forty-six years old when he was released. He also retired from the Army as a master sergeant. Don was a man of faith and a family man. After returning home, he said, "While being held captive all those years I came to learn what was truly the most important in life, the people you love." Don received a Silver Star for his heroism. In 2009, he passed away in Lima, Ohio, at the age of eighty.

Jim Thompson, the longest-held POW in American history, survived nine years in captivity only to see his marriage destroyed, his family alienated, and his career stalled. Jim became an alcoholic and attempted suicide before a stroke left him totally disabled, forcing him to retire from the Army he loved. His son was convicted of murder and sent to prison.

Jim and I were close for many years and saw each other frequently. We sailed and flew together and enjoyed each other's company. I helped him write his retirement speech, which had to be read by another friend at his ceremony in the office of the Secretary of the Army because Jim was unable. Jim moved to Key West, Florida, where I visited him a few times.

He said he liked it there, but he became more detached and our friendship cooled. My overseas Army assignment to Panama made it difficult to stay in touch. When I returned to the United States years later, we never rekindled the friendship we once had.

On July 21, 2002, on my way to Sunday services in the Memorial Chapel at Fort Leavenworth, Kansas, I heard a radio announcement that Jim had died several days before. I got to church, sat down, and cried. Jim was sixty-nine.

He had received the Distinguished Service Medal, the nation's highest award for military service, and the Silver Star for his heroism in Vietnam. I had submitted Jim for the Medal of Honor for all he had endured, for all he had sacrificed, for his bravery far above and beyond the call of duty. My submission was denied. Other efforts to push the award forward politically also failed, even on the occasion of his death.

Steve Leopold never had another attack of hepatitis. He left active duty upon his return from Vietnam and spent a year backpacking around the world. After that, he joined the Army Reserve, completing a full career and attaining the rank of colonel. As a Reserve officer, he served in the 12th Special Forces Group and later commanded a battalion and a brigade in the 85th Division. In his civilian career, he ran for the Wisconsin state legislature in 1976 and won, serving four terms in office. Steve later attended law school and became a practicing attorney. He received the Silver Star for heroism for his actions while a POW.

Nguyen Xanh, who helped me so much along the way North, saved my life when I collapsed on the trail and saved it again when I tumbled into the rapids crossing a log over a river. Xanh was sent to a prison camp near the Chinese border especially for South Vietnamese POWs. He suffered under terrible conditions there until being exchanged at the same time the American POWs were released. He returned to the South and continued to serve in the Republic of Vietnam Air Force.

Xanh was unable to escape when Saigon fell in 1975. The communists captured him a second time and interred him for the next six years. The camp was called a re-education camp, but it was a brutal prison compound deep in the jungle about thirty miles east of Pleiku. It was almost identical to the bamboo prison camp we had endured together in those terrible days in 1972. Xanh lived in agony all those years. When he was finally released at the end of 1981, he escaped from Vietnam in a small boat with his two teenage brothers. He left his wife, Nga, and seven-year-old daughter behind, not wanting to risk their lives in his perilous journey. In spite of confrontations with pirates and rough seas, the brothers made their way to Malaysia and ultimately found refuge in America. Xanh worked hard and put his brothers through school, the older brother becoming a Boeing engineer and the other an ordained Catholic priest. After nearly ten years, he finally reunited with his wife and seventeen-year-old daughter in the United States.

I had searched for Xanh ever since my return. I'd asked Vietnamese friends and scoured the Internet. Every shred of information told me he was probably dead, but I didn't give up.

Finally, in 2008 I found a website for South Vietnamese Skyraider pilots and sent a note to the webmaster. Sure enough, he wrote back saying Xanh was in the United States, that he'd send my contact information to him. We met in Southern California shortly afterwards in an emotional reunion of two old friends. We've remained very close ever since.

Nghiem Ke saved my life with the trade of his gold Cross pen for six potatoes. I looked for Ke after the war, but I had no luck until the Red Cross contacted me in 1982 saying a Vietnamese was trying to make contact. His name was Nghiem Ke. He lived in Cordova, near Easton, Maryland. I flew out and we got together that weekend.

Ke had escaped from Vietnam with his wife, Bé, mother-in-law, and eight children. He also brought along three brothers and two of their wives. Their journey was an incredible one. When Saigon fell in 1975, he and his seventeen-year-old eldest son, Dung, commandeered a good-sized ship in the Saigon harbor along with the rest of his family and about three hundred friends and tagalongs. There was no crew. Ke drew on his engineering experience and a manual found on board to get the engines running and the ship under way. Ke and Dung were heading out at high tide, not knowing anything about tides, the height of the boat, or clearance under bridges. The first bridge they passed under tore the top off the boat's bridge. Undeterred, they found their way to the U.S. Seventh Fleet offshore, where they were rescued, ending up in the United States after staying in a series of refugee camps.

Ke, along with Bé and the older kids, worked picking crops on the Eastern Shore of Maryland for a few years, saving their money. Ke eventually found better-paying work repairing machinery in an agricultural processing plant. In 1979, once they'd saved a small amount, Ke bought an old van and headed west with his family, against my good advice.

Ke knew what he was doing. He settled in San Jose, California. With his savings and the help of the local Vietnamese community there, he found a house and bought a liquor store. Business boomed, allowing him to live comfortably and get all his children through college, married, and successfully engaged in business. His son, Dung, added the new first name, Jeff, when he was naturalized. He earned a degree in industrial engineering and worked for years in computer technology before opening a successful Asian restaurant with his wife in Parker, Colorado. Ke and I have been dear friends all these years.

Me. I'm fine. I've survived whatever lingering effects my ordeal has had on me. I found love and happiness with my family and achieved success in my Army career.

Over the years, I'd often talked about how beautiful Vietnam was, how someday I'd love to return for a visit. That always seemed like a nice, distant dream until Christmas morning in 2000, when I found two round-trip airline tickets to Saigon under the tree.

Spencer wanted a father-son trip to allow me to revisit old memories while letting him experience this place that was so central to what his father had become. We saw all we could in two weeks. It was a good experience and provided a degree of closure, particularly our visit to what remained of the old Hanoi Hilton. Most of the prison was torn down and what was left had been turned into a museum to show how the Vietnamese had suffered under French rule. My old cell-room was a featured stop. It was almost exactly the same as I'd left it. I peered into the big space, memories rushing back as I stared at museum manikins sitting on their sleeping boards just as we had done. It was me, Al, and all the guys, sitting there waiting for it all to end.

Spencer and I walked down the hallway where there were small solitary confinement cells along one side, each secured with a heavy iron door. Spencer asked me to go into one so he could take a picture. I refused. He insisted. Finally I agreed to go in for a brief moment for just one quick photo.

I went in and sat down on the concrete bed. Spence snapped a picture. A grin came across his face as he grabbed the big metal door with his right hand and swung it shut. I bolted from the bed, slamming into the door hard enough to smash it back into him as I exited. Not a funny trick to play on your father.

That night, we dined at a fine restaurant little more than a block away owned by an American expatriate and his Vietnamese wife. We ate roasted venison covered with a wine sauce complemented with a glass of fine red Bordeaux. What a turnaround! Here I sat, a free man enjoying Hanoi's finest, only a short walk from the prison that held me all those years ago.

A year or so earlier, an Army officer whose name I've forgotten, but to whom I'll always be grateful, gave me a brick he'd gotten while assigned in Hanoi as a member of the Joint Personnel Accounting Command, JPAC. The brick was from a part of the Hanoi Hilton being torn down to make way for a new building complex. It was imprinted with the word Hanoi clearly visible in its center. I took the brick home and placed it in the center of the mantel over my fireplace, where it has remained, in every home I've moved to ever since. Wherever I live, it sits on my mantel as a reminder that I own a brick from the place that once owned me. Another nice turnaround.

The visit to Vietnam ended and we flew out via Singapore, where we spent a night before our flight home. That evening, we went to the iconic, radiantly white Raffles Hotel. We took a table in an open corridor on the second floor. I ordered a Singapore sling. After the waiter, dressed smartly in a colonial-era white shirt and trousers, brought our drinks, I made a toast to Wayne in memory of my sick Singapore sling joke cracked during our trek north along the Ho Chi Minh Trail. Poor Wayne. Then another toast, to Tim. I thought of him that night, like I have every day and every night, and will for the rest of my life.

Eight Steps for Survival in a POW Camp

1. EAT. Sounds simple, doesn't it? But, when you've got to force down nothing but plain, boiled rice day after day, month after month, eating becomes a difficult chore. Some found death easier.

2. PRACTICE PERSONAL HYGIENE. When you are sick and starving it is hard to motivate yourself to keep your body and your surroundings clean. Do the best you can with what you have. Filth leads to disease, and disease leads to death.

3. EXERCISE. Set up a daily exercise period. Do something. Even if you are in stocks and chains you can at least flex a few muscles and do some deep breathing.

4. DO NOT GIVE UP THE FIGHT TO STAY ALIVE. No matter how sick you are, how serious your wounds, or how hopeless the situation there is always a chance you can make it. Take that chance and, with your deepest courage, fight for it.

5. ESTABLISH COMMUNICATIONS WITH OTHER PRISONERS. Use your initiative and imagination to make contact with others and then develop a chain of command.

6. FOLLOW THE CODE OF CONDUCT. You must know the Code before you find yourself in a prison camp. Then you should adhere to the articles as strictly as possible.

7. KEEP THE FAITH. Faith in your family, your religion, and your country may be all that keeps you alive and sane. Hang in there; you are not forgotten.

8. MAINTAIN A SENSE OF HUMOR. This is difficult, but both possible and necessary. A bit of humor helps keep away fits of total depression, and remember, depression can kill.

Capt. William S. Reeder Jr. First published in *The Field Artillery Journal*, November–December 1974. Still used in the Army Survival, Evasion, Resistance, and Escape (SERE) training course at Fort Rucker, Alabama.

Notes

Chapter 2. Pink Panthers

1. Montagnard comes from the word used during the French colonial period to describe the tribal peoples of the mountainous regions of central Vietnam. The people who became Montagnards are thought to have originally inhabited the coastal regions in prehistoric times but were pushed further inland and eventually up into the mountain-shrouded Central Highlands by the migration of ethnic Vietnamese populations from the north. They struggle to retain their indigenous culture and forest economy in tribal villages scattered across the Central Highlands. Their long-standing animosity against ethnic Vietnamese was exploited by the United States in gaining their zealous support to American Special Forces operations against the Vietnamese communists.

2. The Military Assistance Command Vietnam–Studies and Observations Group (MACV-SOG) executed its covert missions from three field headquarters. Command and Control Central (CCC) operated from Forward Operating Base II (FOB II) outside Kontum in the central part of South Vietnam. Command and Control North (CCN) was situated in Da Nang; Command and Control South (CCS) in Ban Me Thout. In 1971, these headquarters were re-designated Task Force Advisory Elements (TFAE). See John L. Plaster, *SOG: The Secret Wars of America's Commandos in Vietnam* (New York: Penguin, 2010) for a detailed account of SOG's cross-border operations.

Chapter 3. Easter Offensive

1. Some say the 1968 Tet Offensive was the largest enemy campaign of the war. This is not so. The 1972 Easter Offensive was much larger in scope and scale.

Thomas P. McKenna notes in his book *Kontum: The Battle to Save South Vietnam* (Lexington: University Press of Kentucky, 2011):

> Unlike the Communist attacks during Tet 1968, an uprising in which the lightly armed VC led the charge, for the Easter Offensive of early 1972 the North Vietnamese had 15 combat divisions, including 2 VC divisions manned mainly by North Vietnamese. They would leave only one division in North Vietnam to defend the North and to serve as a reserve. The other 14 divisions would be committed outside the country. Two were already in Laos and Cambodia, and the other 12 divisions totaling 150,000 men were available to attack South Vietnam. This would be the largest military offensive and across-the-border invasion anywhere in the world since the fall of 1950, when the Communist Chinese People's Liberation Army attacked across the Yalu River into South Korea. (p. 60)

See also John G. Heslin's website, The Battle of Kontum, http://www.the battleofkontum.com.

2. Amazingly, all but Larry Woods survived the crash. After the B-40 rocket-propelled grenade blew the helicopter from the sky, Larry was hit by small arms fire and was killed. The other crewmembers got out of the burning wreckage and all but one were rescued by a ground team from Firebase Charlie. Sadly, one was missed and left at the crash site. The door gunner, Specialist Edward Wong, was never seen again and is still listed as missing in action.

3. The 219th Reconnaissance Airplane Company, "Headhunters," had officially ceased operations and gone home, but a few of their aircraft remained at Camp Holloway and were being used to train Vietnamese pilots to take over their mission. On this day, Capt. Ed Smith of the 219th, call sign "Headhunter 26," was paired with a Vietnamese pilot for the conduct of this special mission.

4. Earlier, my sister platoon, the second, had also engaged the enemy around Firebase Charlie. Bob Gamber, John Mayes, Ron Lewis, and Dave Mesa dueled against some of the same weapons we encountered. That mission ended on the hospital pad at Pleiku after Ron Lewis took a bullet in his leg. The battle at Firebase Charlie is remembered in the book *Mua He Lua Do*, or *The Red Flames of Summer*, by Nam Nhat Phan, and in Tran Thanh's song, "Nguoi o lai Charlie," or "The Ones Who Stayed at Charlie," still sung in the Vietnamese community today. The American advisor at Charlie, John Duffy, has put together an extensive collection of poetry related to the battle on his website, http://epoetryworld.com.

Chapter 4. Ben Het

1. The Hawk's Claw TOW system was truly extraordinary at the time. Its existence was classified SECRET but became less sensitive in the years that followed. It developed into the Army standard tube-launched, optically tracked, wire-guided (TOW) missile system that was mounted in later models of the Cobra. It proliferated across the United States Army and Marine Corps in various aircraft and vehicle configurations.

2. Spectre was an AC-130, a modified U.S. Air Force "Hercules" cargo airplane. This four-engine turboprop workhorse, built by Lockheed, sported 20-mm Vulcan 6-barrel Gatling gun cannons and larger 40-mm Bofors cannons. Some also had a 105-mm howitzer. A sophisticated fire-control system gave Spectre pinpoint accuracy.

Chapter 10. The Road

1. Ho Chi Minh sandals are rubber sandals made from old tire treads cut to the shape of the human foot. They are held on with a variety of criss-crossing black rubber straps. The NVA wore socks with them, or not, depending on weather and the toughness of their feet.

2. Karst formations are large protrusions of rock resulting from limestone erosion over millions of years. They thrust from the jungle floor in Laos and parts of Vietnam. Some are bigger than football fields rising vertically several hundred feet above the surrounding landscape. In some areas there are clusters of karst formations grouped together or running in long, impressive lines.

Chapter 11. Into the North

1. I only found out after I got home that this was Orion. I saw it frequently at night over the weeks ahead.

2. The Quang Khe ferries carried personnel, equipment, and supplies across the major water obstacle en route to the DMZ border with South Vietnam, sixty miles to the south. The river is half a mile wide at its mouth, where rail and truck cargo had to be transferred to the other side. Two principal ferries labored at the task throughout the war. Antiaircraft cannons and SAMs (surface-to-air missiles) saturated the area to protect the ferries and the Quang Khe naval base. Because of its importance, this was one of the first targets hit on the opening day of the Vietnam War on August 5, 1964. It was hit again, repeatedly and hard, for the rest of the war at the cost of scores of U.S. and South Vietnamese aircraft.

3. *Bộ đội* is the Vietnamese word for guards. Our North Vietnamese captors insisted we address them as *bộ đội*. Because it seemed to reinforce a form of superior-inferior relationship, I avoided the term as much as I could.

4. The Viet Minh, or Vietnam Independence League, was established in 1941 to seek independence from France and to resist Japanese occupation during World War II. The Viet Minh was an avowed communist organization, but it fought for Vietnamese independence. Indeed, the United States supported the Viet Minh during World War II and assisted their efforts by parachuting in a group from the OSS (Office of Strategic Services), the forerunner of the CIA. The OSS group was codenamed Team Deer. After the war, the Viet Minh fought viciously against the French, achieving independence in the form of two Vietnams in 1954. The Viet Minh then disbanded, supplying the nucleus of the NVA (North Vietnamese Army) and the VC (Viet Cong) guerrilla forces in South Vietnam.

Chapter 12. In the Company of Heroes

1. Bat 21 was the "largest search-and-rescue operation ever mounted for one man during the Vietnam War." See Stanley L. Busboom, *Bat 21: A Case Study* (Carlisle, Pa.: U.S. Army War College, 1990), and Dwight J. Zimmerman and John D. Gresham, *Beyond Hell and Back* (New York: St Martin's Press, 2007), for details. The event is also the subject of the bestselling book and popular Hollywood movie *Bat 21*. Five more aircraft, including Bill Henderson's OV-10, were shot down before Lieutenant Colonel Hambleton, Bat 21 Bravo, was rescued. During the rescue operation, eleven Americans were killed and two captured, Henderson and Army Specialist Jose Astorga. Astorga, the door gunner on a UH-1 Huey helicopter, was the only survivor of his crew. Both his pilots and the crew chief were killed. I'd later meet Jose, who was also held in our camp.

2. The fight at Lang Vei Special Forces camp was one of the bloodiest in U.S. Special Forces history. Twenty-four American Green Berets defended the small outpost on the Laotian border along with 463 Vietnamese and Montagnard fighters and 350 Laotian soldiers who had fled across the border after suffering a brutal and demoralizing defeat by the NVA in Laos. As part of the Tet Offensive, the North Vietnamese Army had surrounded the much larger Marine base at Khe Sanh, nearby. Just after midnight on February 7, 1968, over a thousand NVA launched massive waves of tank and infantry attacks against Lang Vei. No relief was possible. The brave force fought fiercely, killing more than six hundred of the enemy. Most of the Vietnamese, Montagnard, and Laotian forces were killed or captured. Of the two dozen American Special Forces, nearly half were killed or captured. One received the Medal of Honor, one the Distinguished Service Cross, nineteen

received Silver Stars, and three received Bronze Stars for the valor they showed at Lang Vei. For a full account of the battle, see William R. Phillips, *Night of the Silver Stars: The Battle of Lang Vei* (Annapolis, Md.: Naval Institute Press, 1997).

3. U.S. national security advisor Henry Kissinger and North Vietnam politburo member Le Duc Tho conducted secret peace talks in Paris beginning in February 1970. Those talks were long and laborious, but they made significant progress after the NVA's costly failure to achieve the objectives of their 1972 Easter Offensive. On October 26, 1972, Kissinger announced to the press, "Peace is at hand." As it turned out, that proclamation was wrong.

4. The peace talks had indeed broken down, and the North Vietnamese had refused to set a date for their resumption. In response, Nixon ordered massive B-52 strikes of Hanoi and Haiphong harbor. They were the beginning of the U.S. Linebacker II operation that became known as the Christmas Bombings of 1972, a campaign that lasted from December 18th through the 29th. More than two hundred B-52s and two thousand tactical aircraft were involved in the raids. Twelve B-52s were shot down and nine damaged. Forty-three crewmembers were killed in action and forty-nine captured as prisoners of war.

Chapter 13. Five-Star Resort

1. The fight for Hue was the largest battle of the 1968 communist Tet Offensive. The TV/radio crew of AFVN Detachment 5 was but one scene within the horrendous upheaval that unfolded around them. Ten North Vietnamese Army and Viet Cong battalions entered and quickly took the city. Two U.S. Army and three U.S. Marine Corps battalions and eleven Army of South Vietnam battalions responded as reinforcements and engaged in a twenty-eight-day battle that ultimately ejected the dug-in enemy forces from the city. During the fighting, 453 South Vietnamese soldiers were killed and more than 2,000 wounded, while 216 Americans were killed and 1,500 wounded. The North Vietnamese and Viet Cong lost more than 8,000 killed and untold wounded. During the four-week communist occupation, 5,000 to 6,000 civilians and captured military personnel were executed and buried in mass graves in and around the city. Many were bound and tortured, some buried alive. Many Western civilians, including Americans and Germans, were killed. Besides the AFVN Detachment 5 personnel, two other U.S. military personnel and eleven American and two Philippine civilians working for America were also captured in the battle of Hue. John Bagwell, the missing soldier from the AFVN station in Hue, evaded capture, hid in a Catholic church for several hours, and found his way to safety with American forces the next day.

Chapter 14. A Season

1. Lieutenant Everett Alvarez Jr. was a U.S. Navy pilot who was shot down over North Vietnam on August 5, 1964. During the war he gained notoriety as America's longest-held POW. He was not. Jim Thompson was shot down and captured in South Vietnam on March 16, more than four months earlier.

Chapter 16. Castles in the Sand

1. The National League of Families of American Prisoners and Missing in Southeast Asia was formed by a group of POW and MIA wives in 1967. The purpose was to make the American people aware of the plight of the prisoners and keep the issue at the forefront of the American consciousness. The familiar POW/MIA flag was first designed as the league's symbol.

2. POW divorce statistics are found in various sources, including "Behavior: POW Divorce Surge," *Time*, June 9, 1975. See any of the several works by Edna J. Hunter to better understand the psychological effects of being a prisoner of war and its effects on families. For an excellent treatment of coping with PTSD (posttraumatic stress disorder), see Patience Mason's *Recovering from the War* (High Springs, Fla.: Patience Press, 1990).

3. Major James N. "Nick" Rowe, one of only a few American POWs to have escaped during the Vietnam War, was called back to active duty as a lieutenant colonel to design and develop the Army SERE course based on our experiences and his own.

4. For a full account of Jim Thompson's ordeal, see Tom Philpott's *Glory Denied: The Vietnam Saga of Jim Thompson, America's Longest Held POW* (New York: W. W. Norton, 2001).

Index

About the Author

Dr. William Reeder is a training and leader development consultant living in the Pacific Northwest. He spends parts of each year in the education of NATO Special Operations Forces (SOF) at the NATO SOF School at Chievres Air Base Belgium and the training of counterterrorism forces in Saudi Arabia. He was formerly an associate professor of social sciences and deputy director of the U.S. Army School of Advanced Military Studies at Fort Leavenworth, Kansas. He retired from the U.S. Army in 1995 as a colonel and subsequently earned a PhD. in history and anthropology from Kansas State University. His military service included assignments in field artillery, cavalry, aviation, and he has extensive combat experience.

William Reeder is a thirty-year Army veteran with two tours of duty in Vietnam, flying armed OV-1 Mohawk reconnaissance airplanes and AH-1 Cobra attack helicopters. He participated in deep reconnaissance and surveillance operations throughout Southeast Asia and supported the special operations of MACV-SOG (Military Assistance Command Vietnam Studies and Observations Group). He has in excess of three thousand hours of flight time including more than one thousand hours in combat. During his second combat tour, he was shot down and captured by the communist North Vietnamese, spending nearly a year as a prisoner of war.

Subsequent military assignments included various Army command and staff positions and a stint at the U.S. Air Force Academy. He commanded at all levels, platoon through brigade (including command of an AH-64 Apache attack helicopter squadron). His last assignment before retirement in 1995 was as the

Deputy Chief of Staff, de facto Chief of Staff, for the United States Southern Command in Panama.

His military awards and decorations include the Silver Star, Valorous Unit Award, Defense Superior Service Medal, Legion of Merit, two Distinguished Flying Crosses, and three Bronze Star Medals, three Purple Hearts for wounds received in action, the POW Medal, Vietnamese Cross of Gallantry with Bronze Star, and numerous Air Medals (one with "V" device). In 1977 he was named Army Aviator of the Year and was inducted into the U.S. Army Aviation Hall of Fame in 2014. He was featured in the PBS documentary *The Helicopter Pilots of Vietnam*, as well as the "Attack Helicopters" episode of *Deadliest Tech* on the Military Channel. He has provided military commentary on CNN and the Discovery Channel.

Dr. Reeder is married to the former Melanie Lineker of Westminster, Maryland, who is also a retired Army colonel and works as the Deputy Director for Personnel (N-11) for the U.S. Navy Northwest Region, headquartered at Bangor Submarine Base, Washington. They have four children and one grandchild.